NATO IN THE BALKANS

Voices of Opposition

Ramsey Clark, Sean Gervasi,
Sara Flounders, Nadja Tesich,
Thomas Deichmann, and others

International Action Center
New York

Nato in the Balkans:
Voices of Opposition

© Copyright 1998

ISBN 0-9656916-2-4

International Action Center
39 West 14th Street, Suite 206
New York, NY 10011

Phone (212) 633-6646
Fax (212) 633-2889
email iacenter@iacenter.org

We want to make the ideas in this book available as widely as possible. Any properly attributed selection or part of a chapter within "fair-use" guidelines may be used without permission.

Opinions expressed by contributors to this book represent their personal views and are not necessarily those of the organizations involved.

Cover photos: Top left and center, USAF photos by Sr. Airman Ken Bergmann. Top right, USAF photo by SMSgt. Boyd Belcher. Bottom photo of M-109A3 155mm self-propelled howitzer as part of NATO force in Bosnia is a DoD photo by Staff Sgt. Jon E. Long, U.S. Army.

Library of Congress Cataloging-in-Publication Data

Nato in the Balkans : voices of opposition / Ramsey Clark . . . [et al.]
     p.   cm.
"This book began as a small pamphlet in October 1995 entitled Bosnia tragedy-- the unknown role of the U.S. government and Pentagon"--p. 1.
  Includes index.
  ISBN 0-9656916-2-4 (pb : alk. paper)
  1. Yugoslav War, 1991- 2. Yugoslavia--History--1992- 3. North Atlantic Treaty Organization. 4. United States--Foreign relations--1989- I. Clark, Ramsey, 1927- . II. International Action Center (New York, N.Y.) III. Bosnia tragedy-- the unknown role of the U.S. government and Pentagon.
DR1313.N38   1998
949.7103--dc21   97-42683
CIP

This book is dedicated to
Sean Gervasi, whose untimely
death in Belgrade in 1996 left
the solidarity movement bereft
of one of its finest and most
talented members. He spared
neither his time nor his health
in pursuit of the truth.

International Action Center

The International Action Center was initiated in 1991 by former U.S. Attorney General Ramsey Clark and other anti-war activists who had rallied hundreds of thousands of people in the United States to oppose the U.S./UN war against Iraq. It incorporates the struggle to end racism, sexism, homophobia, and poverty in the United States with opposition to U.S. militarism and domination around the world.

For the last five years the IAC has been a leader of the movement to unconditionally end U.S./UN sanctions against Iraq. It has published several books on the Gulf War and Iraq, including *War Crimes, The Fire This Time, The Children Are Dying,* and *Metal of Dishonor.*

The IAC has also mobilized opposition to the U.S. blockade of Cuba, delivered numerous medical shipments to both Cuba and Iraq, and actively opposed U.S. military involvement in Haiti, Somalia, Panama, and Bosnia.

The IAC is a volunteer activist organization. It relies on the donations and assistance of supporters around the country. To be part of a growing network, or to make a donation, request a speaker, or volunteer support, contact the IAC at:

39 West 14th St., Suite 206, New York, NY 10011
Tel: 212-633-6646; fax 212-633-2889
email: iacenter@iacenter.org
Web page: http://www.iacenter.org/

2489 Mission St., Room 28, San Francisco, CA 94110
Tel: 415-821-6545; fax 415-821-5782
email: npcsf@igc.org

TABLE OF CONTENTS

vi

ACKNOWLEDGMENTS

This book is a collective effort. As the International Action Center began work on providing an alternative to the daily war propaganda flooding the media, its probing efforts led to the development of research papers, articles, and speeches on what was happening in Bosnia. There began to emerge a rather diverse group of people who had opposed earlier U.S. invasions, sanctions, and wars. As subsequent events have shown, they saw more clearly than others where U.S. policy toward Yugoslavia was headed.

Long before NATO troops were stationed in Bosnia and the open-ended U.S. military occupation began, this small research group began to meet. It included at different times Sean Gervasi, Sara Flounders, Gary Wilson, Nadja Tesich, Lenora and Herb Foerstel, Barry Lituchy, and Heather Cottin. They began to exchange information and research. News clippings from international sources, U.S. foreign policy documents, old documents released under the Freedom of Information Act, and UN Security Council Resolutions were photocopied and shared. A clearer picture emerged of the competing Western interests in the region and their role in orchestrating the breakup of Yugoslavia. Many of these eye-opening documents are cited in this book.

Contact developed with individuals and newly formed groups in the U.S., Canada, and Europe. Sean Gervasi's work in Belgrade and New York was an invaluable link. Jean Toshi Marazzani-Visconti in Milan translated articles, arranged interviews, and contacted groups throughout Europe. The magazines *Balkans Infos* in Paris and *LM* in London, plus research by Thomas Deichmann in Germany, Michel Chossudovsky in Ontario, and Peter Brock in Washington, DC, enriched the information and analysis. Gary Wilson in New York, Richard Becker in San Francisco, and Peter Makara in Albany scanned the Internet for news sources, helping to post and circulate articles as well as information about protest activities.

Many forums, teach-ins, and protests were organized. The chapters of this book were a living part of this development. The materials were selected from articles and speeches of the past few years.

vii

The Peoples Video Network helped to produce videos based on these forums and activities.

Deirdre Griswold's years of editing experience were invaluable to this process. Her skill helped turn a stack of research papers, articles, and talks into a cohesive book. Paddy Colligan contributed to the editorial process and coordinated endless aspects of book production, along with proof reading, fact checking, indexing, and generally keeping us on course. Janet Mayes joined in proof reading, indexing, and spending hours of work on the IAC web page where parts of this and other IAC books are posted. Lal Roohk designed the cover and publicity for the book.

Frank Alexander, Kathy Durkin, Marie Jay, Vondora Jordan, Joyce Kanowitz, Kadouri Al Kaysi, Ed Lewinson, William Mason, Milt Neidenberg, Henri Nereaux, and Deirdre Sinnott performed numerous backup tasks at the International Action Center that helped keep this project going. Hillel Cohen's assistance on mailing lists made us better organized. Snezana Vitorovich, Nadja Tesich, and Heather Cottin were especially helpful in reaching out to other possible supporters.

This book would not have been possible without the encouragement and financial assistance of the many individuals whose names follow. We also want to give special thanks to one anonymous donor.

We are particularly grateful for the generous help of Alvin Dorfman, Phyllis Lucero, and Family and Friends in Memory of Steve Tesich, and for the continuing assistance of the People's Rights Fund. Their confidence in us helped begin work that has taken a year to complete.

Special thanks to Heather Cottin; Jean Toschi Marazzani-Visconti, *Balkans Infos*; Milka Stanisic; and Snezana Vitorovich.

Contributors: Association of Serbian Women; Jesse, Nori, and Nona Dorsky.

Donors: Ruth Dunlap Bartlett, Dr. Zagorka Bresich, C. de Maisoncelle, Pierre Djokic, Maria Djonovich, Gregory Elich, B. Ilic, Lila Kalinich, M.D., Helen Knezevich Malloy and Robert A. Malloy, Radoslav T. Mijanovich, Daniel Mudrinich, Tijana Nikov, Vincent Rozyczko, Mirjana Sasich, Ethel Shufro, Dr. Alex Srbich, Dr. Bojan Stricevic, Dr. Vera M. Stricevic, Dragan D. Vuckovic, Milo Yelesi-yevich.

Friends: Gayle Al-Maini, Edwin Badura, Estelle Badura, Bogdan Baishanski, S.D. Bosnitch, Billie Bubic, Kathie Cerra, Ph.D., Josif Djordjovich, Helen Gregory, Lazar Hristic, Dusan Isakovic, M.D., Dr. Radoslav Jovanovic, George Kolarovich, George Kolin, Mila Lazarevich-Nolan, Yovanka Malkovich, Bernard V. Malinowski, Nina Malinowski, Desanka T. Mamula, George Markham, Dobrosav Matiasevic, Dr. G. Milin, Nenad Milinkovic, Annette Milkovich, Minja Milojkovic, Alexandar Milosavljevic, James Mohn, John Philpot, Steven Prescop, Peter Radan, Alexandra Radojevic, Milos Raickovich, Negovan Rajic, Veljko J. Rasevic, Jan Reiner, John D. Savich, Dusan Stulic, Nikola Stulic, Dr. Vukan R. Vuchic, Sharleen Worsfold, Bozo Zdjelar, Nick Zunich.

Sara Flounders

AUTHORS

Richard Becker is a West Coast coordinator of the International Action Center. In February 1994 he traveled to Iraq with Ramsey Clark on an IAC fact-finding delegation. Becker co-produced the video "Blockade: The Silent War Against Iraq" and contributed to *The Children Are Dying*. He helped set up the International Commission of Inquiry on Economic Sanctions, London, 1995. He is a regular commentator on KPFK-FM's "Middle East in Focus" in Los Angeles.

Michel Chossudovsky is professor of economics, University of Ottawa. An earlier version of his contribution was presented at "The Other Face of the European Project, Alternative Forum to the European Summit," Madrid, 1995. His latest book, *The Globalization of Poverty: Impacts of IMF and World Bank Reforms* was published by Third World Network, Pinang, and Zed Books; it is available in the U.S. from St. Martin's Press.

Ramsey Clark, U.S. Attorney General in the Johnson administration, is an international lawyer and human rights advocate. He has opposed U.S. military interventions in Vietnam, Grenada, Panama, Nicaragua, Libya, Somalia, Iraq, the Balkans, and many other countries. Clark initiated the International Peace for Cuba Appeal. He is lead counsel for Leonard Peltier, prominent Native American political prisoner. He has authored or contributed to many books, including *Crime in America*; *The Children are Dying: the Impact of Sanctions on Iraq*; *The U.S. Invasion of Panama*; and *Metal of Dishonor—Depleted Uranium*.

Heather Cottin has been a high-school teacher for 32 years. For 40 years she has been active in the civil rights, anti-war, and women's movements, and supported the Chilean and Central American liberation struggles and the anti-apartheid movement. She is the widow of Sean Gervasi and mother of their 13-year-old daughter. She is a union activist and member of the Jewish-Serbian Friendship Society.

Thomas Deichmann is a free-lance journalist and researcher living in Frankfurt, Germany. His articles about the Yugoslav crisis have appeared in numerous European publications and he has become an internationally recognized specialist and critic of the Western media. In 1996 he appeared as an expert witness at the International War Crimes Tribunal for the former Yugoslavia in the defense of Dusko Tadic. His email address is: Thomas.Deichmann@t-online.de.

Alvin Dorfman is an attorney and former Democratic Party State Committeeman (18th AD). A former member of the National Governing Council of the American Jewish Congress, he is president of the Holocaust Survivors Association and the Generation After, and board member and treasurer of the Central American Refugee Center on Long Island. He was president of Long Island's Coordinating Committee for Civil Rights and the Committee in Support of the Mississippi Freedom Democratic Party.

Gregory Elich is a political activist and independent researcher who has published over two dozen articles on the Balkans and Southeast Asia. He works as a database administrator and is a Serbian-American.

Sara Flounders is a co-coordinator of the International Action Center. She has organized opposition to the U.S. use of military force and economic sanctions in Bosnia, Panama, Somalia, and Iraq. She is the organizer of the IAC's Depleted Uranium Project and East Coast co-ordinator of the Anti-Sanctions Project. She frequently speaks to campus and community organizations.

Lenora Foerstel has been North American Coordinator of Women for Mutual Security since 1990 and is on the board of the Women's Strike for Peace. She is a cultural historian and has written numerous articles, produced films, and recently edited a book entitled *Creating Surplus Population: The Effect of Military and Corporate Policies on Indigenous Peoples.*

Sean Gervasi was an economist, political analyst, and activist. He taught at Cambridge, Oxford, the London School of Economics, the University of Paris, and Brooklyn College. He helped start the British anti-Vietnam war movement. He worked at the United Nations with Sean McBride in the Committee Against Apartheid and the Commission on Namibia. He worked in Zimbabwe, Mozambique, and Zambia, and with the liberation movements of Angola and South Africa. Forced out of the UN during the Reagan era, he began to investigate the destabilization of Eastern Europe and the Soviet Union. He died in 1996 in Belgrade, Yugoslavia, while working to expose U.S.-German-NATO plans to recolonize the region.

Barry Lituchy teaches modern European history at Kingsborough Community College, CUNY. He has written numerous articles on the Yugoslav crisis and has appeared as a commentator on a number of TV and radio programs. In 1995 he filmed interviews with refugees from the Krajina and Serbian political figures during the NATO bombings. In October 1997 he organized, along with Bernard Klein, the First International Conference and Exhibition on the Jasenovac Concentration Camp at Kingsborough.

Sam Marcy is a Marxist theoretician, organizer, and former trade unionist who has contributed his talents to the socialist and workers' movement since the 1920s. Since 1959, he has been a regular contributor to *Workers World* newspaper. Marcy has written extensively on the problems of the socialist countries, including the pamphlet *Imperialist Intrigue in the Breakup of Yugoslavia*. Among his books are *Perestroika: a Marxist Critique* and *High Tech, Low Pay*. His writings have been translated into several languages.

Nadja Tesich, filmmaker, novelist, and playwright, was born in Yugoslavia and has returned regularly for the past 30 years. She made even more frequent visits in the last six years. She has incorporated her own eyewitness observations with those of many other European journalists with her on her trips. She speaks all the languages of the area as well as French, Russian, and English. Her new novel *Native Land* is to appear soon.

Gary Wilson is a journalist and researcher who has written extensively on the breakup of Yugoslavia. His articles appear regularly in the New York-based weekly *Workers World* newspaper and have been reprinted in newspapers in Europe and Asia.

Introduction

This book began as a small pamphlet in October 1995 entitled *Bosnia Tragedy: The unknown role of the U.S. government and Pentagon*. It was published by the International Action Center. The pamphlet received a great deal of attention among a current of anti-war activists who suspect U.S. government motives and from Serbian people and others from the region who were shocked at being demonized.

Many people caught up in the war in Bosnia had assumed the U.S. government would be their friend and protector. In Europe there was greater understanding of Germany's historic role in the Balkans and in the breakup of Yugoslavia. A perspective on the complex U.S. role met with great interest. The pamphlet was reprinted in whole or in part in French, Italian, Dutch, German, Serbian, and Bulgarian.

As the Pentagon role in the Balkans expanded, so has the need for information to challenge its military occupation. Over the past five years the International Action Center in New York and San Francisco has produced videos, fact sheets, leaflets, and press releases. Rallies, picket lines, teach-ins, and meetings were organized to counter a barrage of media propaganda clamoring for U.S. intervention. Extensive use of the Internet, videos for cable-access programs, and many radio talk shows helped disseminate this information.

Most of the chapters in the present collection, *NATO in the Balkans*, were written over the past two to three years as the Pentagon blueprint for control of the Balkans unfolded. The authors write from various perspectives. Each contributor to the book is known as outspoken and has developed a consistent position. All share a history of opposition to U.S. intervention.

From their vantage points, they describe the real U.S. aims in the region and the rivalries among competing major powers.

Several chapters focus on the role of the media in providing sophisticated "Big Lie" war propaganda. It serves to cloak the real motives for military intervention and suppress popular debate and opposition. Other chapters deal with the economic leverage exerted by the International Monetary Fund and the World Bank and the strangling effect of sanctions.

This book is produced with the confidence that it will help to arm a new generation of anti-war militants who will surely emerge as the full implications of this pernicious policy sink in. All the king's horses and all the king's men can't control every aspect of life in Bosnia—even though these outside forces take charge of the parliamentary elections and physically seize radio and TV stations.

The occupation of Bosnia by U.S.-led NATO forces takes its toll not only on the peoples who are subjugated militarily. It also exacts a silent price here in the U.S. The Pentagon is soaking up every available dollar that could feed or heal or educate or provide employment. And with every dollar it absorbs, this military monstrosity grows ever more powerful, arrogant, and aggressive.

This is the danger inherent in the military-industrial complex. Its goal is to control the destiny of the planet—militarily, politically, and economically. It is driven by a ravenous appetite for profits.

The first person to name it and warn how perilous its growth could be was not a radical or a leftist. He was the architect of the fusion of industrial production with the military, one who nurtured its rise with war profits.

In 1946 Gen. Dwight D. Eisenhower, Chief of Staff of the U.S. Army, drafted a policy statement to the heads of the armed forces. It laid the basis for linking together the military, industry, science, technology, universities, and virtually all other spheres of economic and social life. But he was not unaware of the dangers lurking in what he had helped to shape.

Eisenhower went on to become president of the United States. In his last speech before leaving office, he issued a warning: "In the councils of government we must guard against the acquisition of unwarranted influence, whether sought or unsought, by the military-industrial complex. The potential for the disastrous rise of misplaced power exists and will exist."

Today the gargantuan proportions to which the military-industrial complex has swelled might shock even Eisenhower. In a time of "peace," half of all the tax monies in the federal budget are earmarked to feed the military machine. The expenses of preparing for and making war are funded at the cost of every needed social program. Like the sorcerer's appentice, forces have been conjured up that cannot be controlled and now have a life of their own.

DREAMS OF GLOBAL MASTERY

Not only the unchecked size of the Pentagon is menacing. Equally fearful are its stated goals—goals that are treated as an acceptable cost of "stability."

Its aims were articulated unabashedly and arrogantly in a Pentagon document entitled "The Defense Planning Guide." The forty-six-page policy statement was excerpted in a prominent *New York Times* article on March 8, 1992. This major policy document asserts that the only possible course for the U.S. to pursue is complete world domination—militarily and politically. And it adds that no other country has the right to aspire to a role of leadership, even as a regional power. While this document was quoted extensively, no U.S. official denied or denounced the report. None even distanced themselves from it. This Pentagon policy paper states:

> Our first objective is to prevent the re-emergence of a new rival. . . . First, the U.S. must show the leadership necessary to establish and protect a new order that holds the promise of convincing potential competitors that they need not aspire to a greater role or

pursue a more aggressive posture to protect their legitimate interests.

We must account sufficiently for the interests of the advanced industrial nations to discourage them from challenging our leadership or seeking to overturn the established political and economic order. Finally, we must maintain the mechanism for deterring potential competitors from even aspiring to a larger regional or global role.

The document then specifically addresses the Pentagon's designs on Europe:

It is of fundamental importance to preserve NATO as the primary instrument of Western defense and security as well as the channel for U.S. influence and participation in European security affairs. . . . We must seek to prevent the emergence of European-only security arrangements which would undermine NATO.

What is most important to maintain is:

. . . the sense that the world order is ultimately backed by the U.S. . . . The U.S. should be postured to act independently when collective action cannot be orchestrated.

The wording of this policy directive for world domination could not be clearer or more threatening. But the U.S. conduct in the civil war in Bosnia brings that language to life.

DAYTON—PAX AMERICANA

Several chapters in this book were written before the "peace" accords were signed at Wright Patterson Air Force Base near Dayton, Ohio, on November 21, 1995. They predicted that the intense but covert U.S. involvement in Bosnia was inexorably headed toward a larger military and political commitment.

The Dayton Accords exposed how far Washington had been willing to go to sabotage peace in order to maintain decisive military control. The documents signed were almost identical to two previous "peace" agreements that the U.S. had opposed. But what presumably made the Dayton Accords different was that they were to be implemented by NATO—a U.S.-led military force.

The first accord that the U.S. government openly sabotaged had been signed by all the same parties in Lisbon, Portugal, in March 1992. The problem was that this agreement was brokered by the European Union. Had this agreement, signed before the civil war began, been allowed to be implemented, how many lives, homes, and futures would have been saved?

Nor are the Dayton Accords much different than the Vance-Owen plan signed in May 1993. That plan was negotiated by former U.S. Secretary of State Cyrus Vance and former British Foreign Secretary Lord David Owen, the latter representing the European Union and the United Nations. Owen has publicly stated that Washington undermined the agreement after it was negotiated. The words of the Defense Planning Guide haunt these efforts to forestall war: "We must seek to prevent the emergence of European-only security arrangements which would undermine NATO."

As the ink dried on the Dayton Accords, *Newsweek* magazine of December 4, 1995, described the agreement as "less a peace agreement than a declaration of surrender." The U.S.-led NATO forces, *Newsweek* continued, "will have nearly colonial powers."

Indeed, the Dayton Accords explicitly defined the colonial administration of Bosnia. At its head sits an appointed High Representative with full executive powers in all civilian affairs. The International Monetary Fund is empowered to appoint and run the Bosnian Central Bank in this artificially fabricated state. The European Bank for Reconstruction and Development directs the restructuring of the public sector as it sells off assets of the state and society.

The Pentagon is currently engaged in a "train and equip" program based in the Bosnian-Croat federation. This army will be equipped with U.S. tanks, armored vehicles, artillery, laser sights, trucks, and small arms. No European NATO country is involved in this project, according to an Agence France-Presse report of September 5, 1997. The "train and equip" program comes with a price tag of $100 million.

As this book goes to press, the U.S.—through its leading role in the NATO occupation—is still exerting its military prowess in an attempt to control Bosnia and the Balkans as a whole. Its troops are intervening in municipal elections and threatening to destroy any radio or television station or newspaper that criticizes NATO's presence in Bosnia. NATO commanders have overruled decisions by Serbia's High Court and have overturned the very parliament whose election they presided over.

Now NATO Commander General Wesley K. Clark has announced that U.S. "peace-keepers" will use lethal force against Serbians who throw stones at the occupying troops.

SLIPPING INTO THE VIETNAM QUAGMIRE

In 1995, President Clinton promised that U.S. soldiers stationed in Bosnia would be home by December 1996. Now they are slated to stay in place until at least July 1998. And, in a carefully crafted campaign with letters and ads, pro-Pentagon organizations, think tanks, and so-called humanitarian groups are pressuring for a military presence in Bosnia far past that date.

How reminiscent these hollow promises to "bring the troops home" are of another president and another war. Three decades ago, then-U.S. President Lyndon Johnson swore the troops would be back from Vietnam by Christmas. His empty assurances were followed by a decade of bloody war, the devastation of all Indochina, casualties totaling three million Vietnamese and fifty-eight thousand U.S. soldiers, and countless injuries.

U.S. troops in Bosnia mean a large new NATO base in Hungary, just over the border. The price tag for building and maintaining this base is in addition to the $5.5 billion cost of maintaining troops in Bosnia. NATO troops are now based in Croatia, Macedonia, and Albania. Tens of thousands of U.S. troops remain in Germany. An "Air Expeditionary Force" of eighteen F-16 fighter bombers is stationed at the NATO base in Aviano, Italy. The bombers are positioned to resume the 4,400 bombing sorties that forced the Serbs to accept the Dayton Accords.

THE COST OF JOINING THE CLUB

The overall cost of the expansion of NATO is estimated to cost $60 to $100 billion. A bonanza for the military contractors. Who will pay? Old Warsaw Pact weapons are considered obsolete. Tanks, aircraft, and communications systems must be interchangeable with NATO equipment. The new NATO members—Poland, Hungary, and the Czech Republic—will fork over half of their annual national budgets for the next decade for weapons procurement.

No other regional powers will be tolerated. That was the message delivered by NATO war "games" held in the Black Sea in July 1996. The ships, marine units, and assault helicopters used in the Kazakhstan war "games" on September 15, 1997, underlined the point. "The message I would leave is that there is no nation on the face of the earth that we cannot get to," blustered NATO Commander General John Sheehan.

WHO ARE THE WAR CRIMINALS?

But U.S. finance capital doesn't expect to rule the region with guns and troops alone. Along with the military occupation, the U.S. is establishing a new legal framework that bolsters its moves to dominate the globe: the War Crimes Tribunal.

Several chapters in this book deal with the issue of war crimes. The authors discuss how the charge of war crimes served to justify U.S. intervention.

The UN Security Council, acting for the prosecution, can now arrest and kidnap anyone in any country. It can decide who can run for office, and even remove government officials. Individuals facing charges have no right to block their extradition, to cross-examine their accusers—or even know their identity. The tribunal is empowered to demand of any country that it hand over any one of its citizens—even heads of state.

This tribunal was established as a subcommittee of the United Nations Security Council, in which the U.S. rules the roost. It is not under the aegis of the General Assembly, the World Court, or any other more representative body.

The Security Council now claims the right to decide in which countries it will set up tribunals, to define the charges, and to select the judges. This enormous power eclipses the sovereign rights of nations, tramples international law, and overrides any standard of civil rights.

Because of their veto power on the Security Council, the very imperialist powers most responsible for war crimes in the past fifty years since the creation of the United Nations will be immune to prosecution.

Any activist who took to the streets to oppose U.S. genocide in Vietnam, its massive bombardment of Iraq, and its invasions of Panama, Grenada, Lebanon, and Somalia will be outraged at the very idea of a court that places oppressed peoples in the dock for war crimes while granting immunity to the world's most powerful aggressor.

The Pentagon generals insist they can fight two or three wars on different fronts at the same time. But they station U.S. troops and weapons in a hundred countries around the globe. They have no interest in substantially improving the lives of the people there. Instead, they expect to control the globe through repressive force and destabilization. Their objective is simply to secure the investments of U.S. corporations.

The NATO military presence will increasingly be a target of angry demonstrations, not only in Bosnia but throughout the whole region. The area is in an upheaval, experiencing the chaos of the capitalist market. Millions of dollars being spent on war games and military maneuvers may only enrage a population where millions of people have gone without a paycheck for months. For example, in August of 1997 thousands demonstrated in the Ukraine against NATO maneuvers.

The Pentagon generals should look at their history books to see how ineffective even a large and brutal military occupation can be. The massive Nazi occupation of the Balkans during World War II could not crush the resistance once it started. The experience of the Pentagon in Vietnam, Lebanon, and Somalia only confirms this. Today's Pentagon generals will be taught the same historical lesson. They will reap the whirlwind of popular resistance.

We hope that *NATO in the Balkans* will help to fuel the imperative demand: "U.S. out of the Balkans—now!"

Sara Flounders
November 1997

PART ONE

WHAT IS NATO PLANNING?

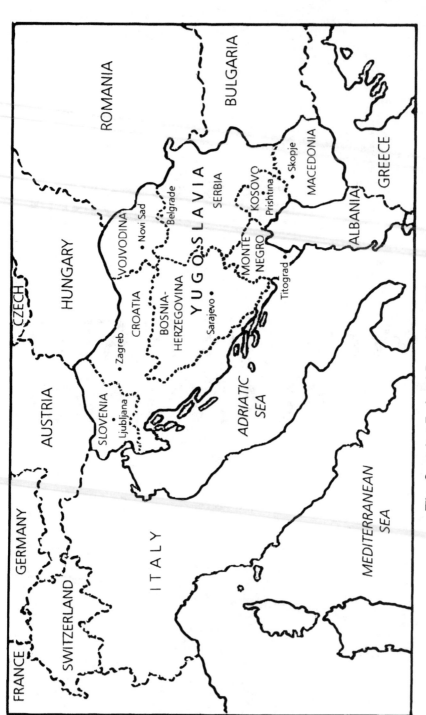

The Socialist Federal Republic of Yugoslavia

1 U.S. and NATO plans to divide Yugoslavia

RAMSEY CLARK [*]

The first time I went to Yugoslavia—as it was then called—I got shot at, literally. It was 1946, and it was either August or September. I was an eighteen-year-old Marine getting ready to be discharged and flying courier service. The week I went in, two C47s had been shot down by ground anti-aircraft fire. We were flying in and you looked out and there were bursts all around. And you think, my God, these are belligerent people down there. What was going on? What the hell was I doing there?

Today I had a meeting for about an hour with a Bulgarian lawyer. He had started out in human rights and had actually been justice minister in the early 1990s for about a year. As we talked and he told me his perception of what was going on today, I realized they were right, back in 1946. They *should* have been shooting at me. It wasn't anything personal, but they knew what they were doing. They just didn't have enough guns to do it, that's all.

This Bulgarian, who is quite an interesting man, was appalled at what the United States was doing. He couldn't believe

---

[*] This chapter is adapted from a speech given at a teach-in on the U.S. role in Bosnia sponsored by the International Action Center and held in New York, October 1995.

the sanctions on Yugoslavia. They've affected Bulgaria pretty drastically. I've driven from Sophia, Bulgaria, to Belgrade twice in the last couple of years. It's a beautiful and easy drive—about three hours. And they feel the pressure constantly, physically and psychologically. In fact, sanctions have affected the whole area all the way down through Greece. Sixty percent of all Greece's exports were trucked into or through Yugoslavia before the war.

The bombing absolutely appalled this Bulgarian lawyer. But the most depressing thing he said was, "We just can't understand what's going on." Sadly, I think it's pretty easily understood, if you can get the pieces together. We need to look at the region and the people. They're a sturdy people, they've been through a lot for much longer than Europeans have been in this country, and they've never been subdued.

They're a creative and energetic people. They're overwhelmingly a happy people. They make good wine and good music, and good talk—if you've got a translator, in my case. They love to sit around and talk in the evening.

There's a book I find helpful in understanding Yugoslavia. It deals with the history of the region from the time that the Ottomans came in. It's told in an ingenious way—through the history and story of a bridge. The building of the bridge, the lives on the bridge, the loves of the bridge, the suicides off the bridge, the fights on the bridge—and the final dynamiting of the bridge at the beginning of World War I. It's called *A Bridge on the Drina* and was written by Ivo Andric, Nobel Laureate. Most Nobel Laureates are and should be forgotten. But here's a man who really understood the history and the people and wanted to give us some sense of what it was like.

The people lived together through Ottoman power and Austro-Hungarian power—five hundred years. They did and can live together. That didn't mean it was all a bed of roses, but in terms of internal violence, it was peaceful compared to what we see now.

Yugoslavia was an idea. There are not too many countries that are created as an idea—other than those the oil companies created. But the idea was, we need a federation. In this little microcosm of so many peoples and cultures of the world, we need a way to function together and live together and prevail together.

It was a strange idea and it was hard to work with. The idea had many enemies from the beginning, because that would make the area hard to exploit. If the Caribbean can't do it and Central America can't—then those small countries have no chance, in my opinion, except total exploitation. They face a future of free trade zones like Bob Herbert wrote about in the *New York Times*, where women work ten to twelve hours a day and can't feed their children or themselves. The Gap and Liz Claiborne and other corporations are selling the stuff they're putting together for slave wages and aren't paying any taxes there.

Yugoslavia had one of the worst experiences in World War II. It's not commonly told. But there was a major killing camp—concentration camp, as we tend to call them—at Jasenovac in the Nazi state of Croatia, according to a very detailed, elaborately researched book called *The Yugoslav Auschwitz*. It's by Vladimir Dedijer, a really interesting man I've had the good fortune to know for many years. He was vice chairman of the Bertrand Russell War Crimes Tribunal and also wrote a major biography of Tito, with some understanding of what was accomplished in the Yugoslav Federation after World War II. His research on the slaughter of the Serbs came out in a new reprint in the United States recently.

It is a document of basic historic importance. Many of the children of those killed, and even some of those interned, are still alive. Without a federation to protect them living with each other, it wouldn't be easy, and everybody knew that.

Don't think that NATO isn't planning the map of Europe every day, knowing exactly what it wants it to look like. Don't think they don't know the composition of the peoples, the physical terrain and the natural resources, the industry and all the rest. They're working on it constantly.

And if you think a country is too small for them to be interested in, you just haven't seen anything. Was Grenada bigger? There's never been a military engagement in history where so many armed troops went so far to attack so few. A people with no defense. The Pentagon inflicted more casualties per capita on the Grenadian population than the United States lost in World War II.

Don't think there's not a purpose to it. Not long after Tito died, as the influence of the Soviet Union declined and its capacity to intervene in anything became negligible—which made the Gulf War possible—the plans to divide Yugoslavia were under way. There can't be any doubt about that. Just look at our legislation, look at what so many people have said in memoirs and other things. The plans were under way.

And there are lots of interests in there. In Slovenia there are over one million Italians. Slovenia and Croatia are the richer parts of the country. We can talk about the success of the federation in terms of the basic quality of life. The people had food, clothing, education, housing, and things like that. In terms of per capita income it was a Third World nation, richer in the north than in the south. Slovenia had about $9,500 per capita income, Croatia over $7,000, Serbia $3,500, Bosnia less than that. Go a bit further south and it's a poor, underdeveloped country.

The purposes of dismantling Yugoslavia have to be understood. Germany obviously had a keen interest. Everybody knew when it was dismantled there would be hell to pay. The United States used ways to direct the violence, and for four or five years now the violence has been directed in the way the United States likes to fight a war—"You and them fight."

It's the same way that the Iran-Iraq war went. Remember Kissinger's famous statement when the war began: "I hope they kill each other." He did everything he could to see that they did. And about a million young men—some very young, thirteen to fourteen years old—lost their lives.

In Yugoslavia, the purpose is, among others, to consolidate NATO and European control in the richer northern part of the former Yugoslavia, to cripple for a long time the Serbian people, and to debilitate as deeply as possible the Muslims.

One of the real ironies of United States' treachery is in the Muslim world. There are a billion and a half Muslims on the planet. They cheer U.S. aid and Israeli support, as they see it, for the Muslims in Bosnia. But who's getting killed? Who's getting the living daylights bombed out of them?

It's not as bad as all that. General Charles G. Boyd, a full four-star general and former deputy European commander for U.S. forces, wrote in *Foreign Affairs* that in 1994 in Sarajevo—which we think of as one of the most violent places in the world today—the total number of deaths from gunfire on all sides, friendly fire, unfriendly fire, whatever it is, is lower than the murder rate in Washington, D.C. I don't mean to put that down, that's tragic, but we have to have a sense of proportion, and that's the fact.

General Boyd pointed out, "Half of the Slavs [Serbs] have been driven out of what we call Bosnia." They're gone. A good many are dead, and a good many are refugees in all kinds of uncomfortable places, exiled from their homeland. We have to realize what is happening. We're coming toward a NATO-developed buffer that will include northern-oriented, Austro-Hungarian participants as a part of the north, and a vast debilitation of Muslims and a vaster debilitation of Serbs.

We don't think much about the sanctions, but the sanctions are more deadly than the bombing in this war. The same was true in the Gulf War. The United States dropped 88,500 tons of bombs in Iraq—one every thirty seconds for forty-two days. But that killed far fewer people than the sanctions have. There are four million people in Iraq today on the brink of death because of the sanctions. Already, seven hundred thousand people have died from the sanctions.

If you look at the people in Belgrade and other cities and towns of Serbia, Yugoslavia, you see deprivation and severe malnutrition. But there is no malnutrition in Sarajevo, according to General Boyd. Of course, he's right.

That's how you really break the country down. What happens to all those undersized children that survive, who didn't get enough nutrition before and after birth?

Gun supplies to Muslims are restricted. They come through Croatia, which is heavily armed. Peter Galbraith is the U.S. ambassador there, and he's calling a lot of the shots for this over-all plan. He pushed the Serbs down as far as you can, and it's related geopolitically as much if not more than economically.

There's been a lot of talk about the economics of it. Fortress Europe is coming back because the rich countries are getting richer and the poor countries are getting poorer. It's the greatest problem on the planet today, just as the rich are getting richer here in our country and the poor are getting poorer. They're concerned about the teeming hordes, and they want barriers to immigration.

NATO is more concerned, as is the United States, about Islamic fundamentalism, domestically and internationally, than any other single threat, probably. That's what the FBI said constantly in Sheik Omar Abdel-Rahman's case. That's the number one priority for the CIA and the FBI. They're terrified about these people, they're true believers.

What the United States is doing is consolidating the position of Europe, fortifying it, breaking down not just Serbs, but Slavic people as much as possible. Slavs are by far the largest ethnic group in Europe, bigger than the French, the Germans, or anybody else. And they are looked down upon almost racially by northern Europe and by too many Americans.

We have to recognize that these things don't just happen, that this is planned and controlled attrition. It will be a major policy. There won't be a real cease-fire. You want them to kill a few more people. You want them to take it down and down and down. Then you send a garrison force in, and the people will be miserable. But they'll be rebellious, and there won't be peace. We'll have more trouble.

And we'll have mothers over here like the mothers of British Tommies in the north of Ireland. They're getting their sons home in boxes and wondering what in the world they were doing there anyway, because they should never have been there. And the U.S. should never have been planning these things. It should never have participated in these things. Those of us who live here have an absolute moral obligation to see that it ends now—there and everywhere.

We knew what's coming out now about Central America, but no one could prove it. Battalion 316 in Honduras, trained here, directed from here, killing people all over the place to undermine the FSLN in Nicaragua, to support the contras and all the rest. The systematic carnage in Guatemala, which we have generally attributed to the Guatemalan elite, had the direct participation of the U.S. CIA. They thought: How do you take care of these restless natives if you don't control them and kill them and impoverish them?

There will be a billion more people on the planet in the next four to five years. And the vast majority are going to have beautiful, dark skin and live short, miserable lives of violence and hunger and sickness and poverty, unless we act radically here. In Bosnia obviously we've got to move for a major federation of the whole Balkan peninsula that can give them an opportunity to construct their own lives in the way they choose without outside interference. But because of the tragic history that others have imposed on them, we will need a Marshall Plan of enormous magnitude to help them rebuild their lives. If we do that, we can hope to have some bearable conscience in some peaceable future.

2 Why is NATO in Yugoslavia?

*SEAN GERVASI**

The North Atlantic Treaty Organization has recently sent a large task force into Yugoslavia, ostensibly to enforce a settlement of the Bosnian war arrived at in Dayton, Ohio, at the end of 1995. This task force is said to consist of some sixty thousand men, equipped with tanks, armor, and artillery. It is backed by formidable air and naval forces. In fact, if one takes account of all the support forces involved, including forces deployed in nearby countries, it is clear that on the order of one hundred and fifty thousand troops are involved. This figure has been confirmed by U.S. defense sources.[1]

By any standards, the sending of a large Western military force into Central and Eastern Europe is a remarkable enterprise, even in the fluid situation created by the supposed end of the Cold War. The Balkan task force represents not only the first major NATO military operation, but a major operation staged "out of area," that is, outside the boundaries originally established for NATO military action.

However, the sending of NATO troops into the Balkans is the result of enormous pressure for the general extension of NATO eastwards.

---

*This chapter is based on a paper presented to a conference in Prague, Czech Republic, on 13-14 January 1996.

If the Yugoslav enterprise is the first concrete step in the expansion of NATO, others are planned for the near future. Some Western powers want to bring the Visegrad countries[2] into NATO as full members by the end of the century. There was resistance to the pressures for such extension among certain Western countries for some time. However, the recalcitrants have now been bludgeoned into accepting the alleged necessity of extending NATO.

The question is: Why are the Western powers pressing for the expansion of NATO? Why is NATO being renewed and extended when the "Soviet threat" has disappeared? There is clearly much more to it than we have so far been told. The enforcement of a precarious peace in Bosnia is only the immediate reason for sending NATO forces into the Balkans.

There are deeper reasons for the dispatch of NATO forces to the Balkans, and especially for the extension of NATO to Poland, the Czech Republic, and Hungary in the relatively near future. These have to do with an emerging strategy for securing the resources of the Caspian Sea region and for "stabilizing" the countries of Eastern Europe—ultimately for "stabilizing" Russia and the countries of the Commonwealth of Independent States. This is, to put it mildly, an extremely ambitious and potentially self-contradictory policy. And it is important to pose some basic questions about the reasons being given for pursuing it.

The idea of "stabilizing" the countries which formerly constituted the socialist bloc in Europe does not simply mean ensuring political stability there, ensuring that the regimes which replaced socialism remain in place. It also means ensuring that economic and social conditions remain unchanged. And, since the so-called transition to democracy in the countries affected has in fact led to an incipient deindustrialization and a collapse of living standards for the majority, the question arises whether it is really desirable.

The question is all the more pertinent since "stabilization," in the sense in which it is used in the West, means reproducing in the former socialist-bloc countries economic and social conditions which are similar to the economic and social conditions currently prevailing in the West. The economies of the Western industrial nations are, in fact, in a state of semi-collapse, although the governments of those countries would never really acknowledge the fact. Nonetheless, any reasonably objective assessment of the economic situation in the West leads to this conclusion. And that conclusion is supported by official statistics and most analyses coming from mainstream economists.

It is also clear, as well, that the attempt to "stabilize" the former socialist-bloc countries is creating considerable tension with Russia, and potentially with other countries. Not a few commentators have made the point that Western actions in extending NATO even raise the risks of nuclear conflict.[3]

It is enough to raise these questions briefly to see that the extension of NATO which has, *de facto*, begun in Yugoslavia and is being proposed for other countries is to a large extent based on confused and even irrational reasoning. One is tempted to say that it results from the fear and willfulness of certain ruling groups. To put it most bluntly, why should the world see any benefit in the enforced extension to other countries of the economic and social chaos which prevails in the West, and why should it see any benefit in that when the very process itself increases the risks of nuclear war?

The purposes of this paper are to describe what lies behind the current efforts to extend NATO and to raise some basic questions about whether this makes any sense, in both the narrow and deeper meanings of the term.

NATO IN YUGOSLAVIA

The North Atlantic Treaty Organization was founded in 1949 with the stated purpose of protecting Western Europe from possible military aggression by the Soviet Union and its allies.

With the dissolution of the Communist regimes in the former socialist bloc in 1990 and 1991, there was no longer any possibility of such aggression, if there ever really had been. The changes in the former Communist countries made NATO redundant. Its raison d'être had vanished. Yet certain groups within the NATO countries began almost immediately to press for a "renovation" of NATO and even for its extension into Central and Eastern Europe. They began to elaborate new rationales which would permit the continuation of business as usual.

The most important of these was the idea that, with the changes brought about by the end of the Cold War, the Western countries nonetheless faced new "security challenges" outside the traditional NATO area which justified the perpetuation of the organization. The spokespersons for this point of view argued that NATO had to find new missions to justify its existence.

The implicit premise was that NATO had to be preserved in order to ensure the leadership of the United States in European and world affairs. This was certainly one of the reasons behind the large-scale Western intervention—in which the participation of U.S. NATO partners was relatively meager—in Kuwait and Iraq in 1990 and 1991. The coalition which fought against Iraq was cobbled together with great difficulty. But it was seen by the United States government as necessary for the credibility of the U.S. within the Western alliance as well as in world affairs.

The slogan put forward by the early supporters of NATO enlargement was "NATO: out of area or out of business," which made the point, although not the argument, as plainly as it could be made.[4]

Yugoslavia has also been a test case, and obviously a much more important one. The Yugoslav crisis exploded on the edge of Europe, and the Western European nations had to do something about it. Germany and the United States, on the other hand, while seeming to support the idea of ending the civil wars in Yugoslavia, in fact did everything they could to prolong

them, especially the war in Bosnia. Their actions perpetuated
and steadily deepened the Yugoslav crisis.

It is important to recognize that almost from the beginning of the Yugoslav crisis, NATO sought to involve itself. That
involvement was obvious in 1993 when NATO began to support United Nations Protection Force (UNPROFOR) operations
in Yugoslavia, especially in the matter of the blockade against
the Federal Republic of Yugoslavia and the enforcement of a
no-fly zone in Bosnian airspace.

That involvement, however, had much smaller begin-
nings, and it must be remembered that NATO as an organization was involved in the war in Bosnia-Herzegovina at a very
early stage. In 1992, NATO sent a group of about 100 personnel to Bosnia-Herzegovina, where they established a military
headquarters at Kiseljak, a short distance from Sarajevo. Ostensibly, they were sent to help United Nations forces in Bosnia.

It was obvious, however, that there was another purpose. A NATO diplomat described the operation to *Intelligence
Digest* in the following terms at the time:

> This is a very cautious first step, and we are defi-
> nitely not making much noise about it. But it could be
> the start of something bigger. . . . You could argue
> that NATO now has a foot in the door. Whether we
> manage to open the door is not sure, but we have
> made a start.[5]

It seems clear that NATO commanders were already
anticipating the possibility that resistance to U.S. and German
pressures would be overcome and that NATO's role in Yugoslavia would be gradually expanded.

Thus NATO was working to create a major "out-of-
area" mission almost from the beginning of the war in Bosnia-
Herzegovina. The recent dispatch of tens of thousands of troops
to Bosnia, Austria, Hungary, Croatia, and Serbia is thus simply
the culmination of a process that began almost four years ago. It
was not a question of proposals and conferences. It was a question of inventing operations which, with the backing of key

countries, could eventually lead to NATO's active engagement "out of area," and thus to its own renovation.

EASTWARD EXPANSION OF NATO

NATO had never carried out a formal study on the enlargement of the alliance until quite recently, when the Working Group on NATO Enlargement issued its report. No doubt there were internal classified studies, but nothing is known of their content to outsiders.

Despite the lack of clear analysis, however, the engines for moving things forward were working hard from late 1991. At the end of that year, NATO created the North Atlantic Co-operation Council. NATO member nations then invited nine Central and East European countries to join the NACC in order to begin fostering cooperation between the NATO powers and former members of the Warsaw Pact.

This was a first effort to offer something to East European countries wishing to join NATO itself. The NACC, however, did not really satisfy the demands of those countries, and in the beginning of 1994 the U.S. launched the idea of a Partnership for Peace. The PFP offered nations wishing to join NATO the possibility of cooperating in various NATO activities, including training exercises and peacekeeping. More than twenty countries, including Russia, are now participating in the PFP.

Many of these countries wish eventually to join NATO. Russia obviously will not join. It believes that NATO should not be moving eastwards. According to the Center for Defense Information in Washington, a respected independent research center on military affairs, Russia is participating in the PFP "to avoid being shut out of the European security structure altogether."[6]

The movement toward the enlargement of NATO has therefore been steadily gathering momentum. The creation of the North Atlantic Cooperation Council was more or less an expression of sympathy and openness toward those aspiring to

NATO membership. But it did not carry things very far. The creation of the Partnership for Peace was more concrete. It actually involved former Warsaw Pact members in NATO itself. It also began a "two-track" policy toward Russia, in which Russia was given a more or less empty relationship with NATO simply to allay its concerns about NATO expansion.

However, despite this continuous development, the public rationale for this expansion has for the most part rested on fairly vague premises. And this leads to the question of what has been driving the expansion of NATO during the last four years. The question must be posed for two areas: the Balkans and the countries of Central Europe. For there is an important struggle going on in the Balkans, a struggle for mastery of the southern Balkans in particular. And NATO is now involved in that struggle. There is also, of course, a new drift back to Cold War policies on the part of certain Western countries. And that drift is carrying NATO into Central Europe.

STRUGGLE FOR MASTERY IN THE BALKANS

We have been witnessing, since 1990, a long and agonizing crisis in Yugoslavia. It has brought the deaths of tens of thousands, driven perhaps two million people from their homes, and caused turmoil in the Balkan region. And in the West it is generally believed that this crisis, including the civil wars in Croatia and Bosnia-Herzegovina, was the result of internal Yugoslav conflicts, and specifically of conflicts among Croats, Serbs, and Bosnian Muslims. This is far from the essence of the matter.

The main problem in Yugoslavia, from the first, was foreign intervention in the country's internal affairs. Two Western powers, the United States and Germany, deliberately contrived to destabilize and then dismantle the country. The process was in full swing in the 1980s and accelerated as the present decade began. These powers carefully planned, prepared, and assisted the secessions which broke Yugoslavia apart. And they did almost everything in their power to expand and prolong the civil wars which began in Croatia and then continued in Bosnia-

Herzegovina. They were involved behind the scenes at every stage of the crisis.

Foreign intervention was designed to create precisely the conflicts which the Western powers decried. For they also conveniently served as an excuse for overt intervention once civil wars were under way.

Such ideas are, of course, anathema in Western countries. That is only because the public in the West has been systematically misinformed by war propaganda. It accepted almost from the beginning the version of events promulgated by governments and disseminated through the mass media. It is nonetheless true that Germany and the U.S. were the principal agents in dismantling Yugoslavia and sowing chaos there.

This is an ugly fact in the new age of realpolitik and geopolitical struggles which has succeeded the Cold War order. Intelligence sources have begun recently to allude to this reality in a surprisingly open manner. In the summer of 1995, for instance, *Intelligence Digest*, a respected newsletter published in Great Britain, reported that "The original U.S.-German design for the former Yugoslavia [included] an independent Muslim-Croat dominated Bosnia-Herzegovina in alliance with an independent Croatia and alongside a greatly weakened Serbia."[7]

Every senior official in most Western governments knows this description to be absolutely accurate. And this means, of course, that the standard descriptions of "Serbian aggression" as the root cause of the problem, the descriptions of Croatia as a "new democracy," etc., are not just untrue but actually designed to deceive.

But why? Why should the media seek to deceive the Western public? It was not simply that blatant and large-scale intervention in Yugoslav affairs had to be hidden from public view. It was also that people would ask questions about why Germany and the U.S. deliberately created havoc in the Balkans. Inevitably, they would want to know the reasons for such actions. And these had to be hidden even more carefully than the destructive actions of great powers.

At root, the problem was that the United States had an extremely ambitious plan for the whole of Europe. It is now stated quite openly that the U.S. considers itself a "European power." In the 1980s, this assertion could not be made so easily. That would have caused too much dissension among Western allies. But the U.S. drive to establish its domination in Europe was nonetheless a fact. And the United States was already planning what is now openly talked about.

Quite recently, Richard Holbrooke, the Assistant Secretary of State for European Affairs, made the official position clear. In a recent article in the influential journal *Foreign Affairs*, he not only described the United States as a "European power" but also outlined his government's ambitious plans for the whole of Europe. Referring to the system of collective security, including NATO, which the U.S. and its allies created after World War II, Mr. Holbrooke said,

> This time, the United States must lead in the creation of a security architecture that includes and thereby stabilizes all of Europe—the West, the former Soviet satellites of Central Europe and, most critically, Russia and the former republics of the Soviet Union.[8]

In short, it is now official policy to move towards the integration of all of Europe under a Western political and economic system, and to do so through the exercise of "American leadership." This is simply a polite, and misleading, way of talking about the incorporation of the former socialist countries into a vast new empire.[9]

It should not be surprising that the rest of Mr. Holbrooke's article is about the necessity of expanding NATO, especially into Central Europe, in order to ensure the "stability" of the whole of Europe. Mr. Holbrooke states that the "expansion of NATO is an essential consequence of the raising of the Iron Curtain."[10]

Thus, behind the repeated interventions in the Yugoslav crisis, there lay long-term strategic plans for the whole of Europe.

As part of this evolving scheme, Germany and the U.S. originally determined to forge a new Balkan order, one based on the market organization of economies and parliamentary democracy. They wanted to put a definitive end to socialism in the Balkans.[11] Ostensibly, they wanted to "foster democracy" by encouraging assertions of independence, as in Croatia. In reality, this was merely a ploy for breaking up the Balkans into small and vulnerable countries. Under the guise of "fostering democracy," the way was being opened to the recolonization of the Balkans.

By 1990, most of the countries of Eastern Europe had yielded to Western pressures to establish what were misleadingly called "reforms." Some had accepted all the Western conditions for aid and trade. Some, notably Bulgaria and Romania, had only partially accepted them.

In Yugoslavia, however, there was resistance. The 1990 elections in Serbia and Montenegro kept a socialist or social-democratic party in power. The federal government thus remained in the hands of politicians who, although they yielded to pressures for "reforms" from time to time, were nevertheless opposed to the recolonization of the Balkans. And many of them were opposed to the fragmentation of Yugoslavia. Since the third Yugoslavia, formed in the spring of 1992, had an industrial base and a large army, that country had to be destroyed.

From the German point of view, this was nothing more than the continuation of a policy pursued by the Kaiser and then by the Nazis.

Once Yugoslavia was dismantled and thrown into chaos, it was possible to begin reorganizing this central part of the Balkans. Slovenia, Croatia, and Bosnia-Herzegovina were to be brought into a German sphere of interest. Germany acquired access to the sea on the Adriatic, and potentially, in the event that the Serbs could be overwhelmed, to the new Rhine-Danube canal, a route which can now carry three-thousand-ton ships from the North Sea into the Black Sea. The southern reaches of Yugoslavia were to fall into an American sphere of interest. Macedonia, which commands the only east-west and north-south passages across the Balkan mountains, was to be the centerpiece of an American region.

But the American sphere would also include Albania and, if those regions could be stripped away from Serbia, the Sanjak and Kosovo. Some American planners have even talked of the eventual emergence of a Greater Albania, under U.S. and Turkish tutelage, which would comprise a chain of small Muslim states, possibly including Bosnia-Herzegovina, with access to the Adriatic.

Not surprisingly, Germany and the U.S., although they worked in concert to bring about the dismantling of Yugoslavia, are now struggling for control of various parts of that country, notably Croatia and Bosnia-Herzegovina. In fact, there is considerable jockeying for influence and commercial advantage throughout the Balkans.[12] Most of this competition is between Germany and the U.S., the partners who tore Yugoslavia apart. But important companies and banks from other European countries are also participating. The situation is similar to that created in Czechoslovakia by the Munich Agreement in 1938. Agreement was reached on a division of the spoils in order to avoid clashes which would lead immediately to war.

NEW 'GREAT GAME' IN THE CASPIAN SEA

Yugoslavia is significant not just for its own position on the map, but also for the areas to which it allows access. And influential American analysts believe that it lies close to a zone of vital U.S. interests, the Black Sea-Caspian Sea region.

This may be the real significance of the NATO task force in Yugoslavia.

The United States is now seeking to consolidate a new European-Middle Eastern bloc of nations. It is presenting itself as the leader of an informal grouping of Muslim countries stretching from the Persian Gulf into the Balkans. This grouping includes Turkey, which is of pivotal importance in the emerging new bloc. Turkey is not just a part of the southern Balkans and an Aegean power. It also borders on Iraq, Iran, and Syria. It thus connects southern Europe to the Middle East, where the U.S. considers that it has vital interests.

The U.S. hopes to expand this informal alliance with Muslim states in the Middle East and southern Europe to include some of the new nations on the southern rim of the former Soviet Union.

The reasons are not far to seek. The U.S. now conceives of itself as being engaged in a new race for world resources. Oil is especially important in this race. With the war against Iraq, the U.S. established itself in the Middle East more securely than ever. The almost simultaneous disintegration of the Soviet Union opened the possibility of Western exploitation of the oil resources of the Caspian Sea region.

This region is extremely rich in oil and gas resources. Some Western analysts believe that it could become as important to the West as the Persian Gulf.

Countries like Kazakhstan have enormous oil deposits. Its recoverable reserves probably exceed nine billion barrels. Kazakhstan could probably pump seven hundred thousand barrels a day. The problem, as in other countries of the region, at least from the perspective of Western countries, has been to get the oil and gas resources out of the region and to the West by safe routes.

The movement of this oil and gas is not simply a technical problem. It is also political. It is of crucial importance to the U.S. and to other Western countries today to maintain friendly relations with countries like Kazakhstan. It is even more important that they know that any rights acquired, to pump petroleum or to build pipelines to transport it, will be absolutely respected since the amounts projected for investment in the region are very large.

What this means is that Western producers, banks, pipe-line companies, etc., want to be assured of "political stability" in the region. They want to be assured that there will be no politi-cal changes which would threaten their new interests or poten-tial ones.

An important article in the *New York Times* recently de-scribed what has been called a new "great game" in the region, drawing an analogy to the competition between Russia and Great Britain in the northwest frontier of the Indian subconti-nent in the nineteenth century. The authors of the article wrote that

> Now, in the years after the cold war, the United States is again establishing suzerainty over the empire of a former foe. The disintegration of the Soviet Un-ion has prompted the United States to expand its zone of military hegemony into Eastern Europe (through NATO) and into formerly neutral Yugoslavia. And —most important of all—the end of the cold war has permitted America to deepen its involvement in the Middle East."[13]

Obviously, several reasons prompted Western leaders to seek the expansion of NATO. One of these, and an important one, has clearly been commercial.

This becomes more evident as one looks more closely at the parallel development of commercial exploitation in the Cas-pian Sea region and the movement of NATO into the Balkans.

On 22 May 1992, the North Atlantic Treaty Organiza-tion issued a remarkable statement regarding the fighting then going on in Transcaucasia. This read in part as follows:

> [The] Allies are profoundly disturbed by the continu-ing conflict and loss of life. There can be no solution to the problem of Nagorno-Karabakh or to the differ-ences it has caused between Armenia and Azerbaijan by force. Any action against Azerbaijan's or any other state's territorial integrity or to achieve political goals by force would represent a flagrant and unac-

ceptable violation of the principles of international law. In particular we [NATO] could not accept that the recognized status of Nagorno-Karabakh or Nakhichevan can be changed unilaterally by force.[14]

This was a remarkable statement by any standards. For NATO was in fact issuing a veiled warning that it might have to take "steps" to prevent actions by governments in the Caspian Sea region which it construed as threatening vital Western interests.

Two days before NATO made this unusual declaration of interest in Transcaucasian affairs, an American oil company, Chevron, had signed an agreement with the government of Kazakhstan for the development of the Tengiz and Korolev oil fields in the western part of the country. The negotiations for this agreement had been under way for two years prior to its being signed. And reliable sources have reported that they were in danger of breaking down at the time because of Chevron's fears of political instability in the region.[15]

At the time that NATO made its declaration, of course, there would have been little possibility of backing up its warning. There was, first of all, no precedent at all for any large, out-of-area operation by NATO. NATO forces, furthermore, were far removed from Transcaucasia. It does not take a long look at a map of the Balkans, the Black Sea, and the Caspian Sea to realize that the situation is changing.

NEXT STAGE: 'STABILIZING' THE EAST

The current pressure for the enlargement of NATO to Central and Eastern Europe is part of an effort to create what is mistakenly called "the new world order." It is the politico-military complement of the economic policies initiated by the major Western powers and designed to transform Central and East European society.

The United States, Germany, and some of their allies are trying to build a truly global order around the North Atlantic Basin economy. There is actually nothing very new about the kind of order they are trying to establish. It is to be founded on capitalist institutions. What is new is that they are trying to extend "the old order" to the vast territories which were thrown into chaos by the disintegration of communism. They are also trying to incorporate into this "order" countries which were previously not fully a part of it.

In a word, they are trying to create a functioning capitalist system in countries which have lived under socialism for decades, or in countries, such as Angola, which were seeking to break free of the capitalist system.

As they try to establish a "new world order," the major Western powers must also think about how to preserve it. So, in the final analysis, they must think about extending their military power toward the new areas of Europe which they are trying to attach to the North Atlantic Basin. Hence the proposed role of NATO in the new European order.

The two principal architects of what might be a new, integrated and capitalist Europe are the United States and Germany. They are working together especially closely on East European questions. In effect, they have formed a close alliance in which the U.S. expects Germany to help manage not only West European but also East European affairs. Germany has become, as George Bush put it in Mainz in 1989, a "partner in leadership."

This close relationship ties the U.S. to Germany's vision of what German and American analysts are now calling Central Europe. It is a vision which calls for: 1) the expansion of the European Union to the East; 2) German leadership in Europe; and 3) a new division of labor in Europe.

It is the idea of a new division of labor which is particularly important. In the German view, Europe will in the future be organized in concentric rings around a center, which will be Germany. The center will be the most developed region in every sense. It will be the most technically developed and the wealthiest. It will have the highest levels of wages, salaries, and per capita income. And it will undertake only the most profitable economic activities, those which put it in command of the system. Thus Germany will take charge of industrial planning, design, the development of technology, etc., of all the activities which will shape and coordinate the activities of other regions.

As one moves away from the center, each concentric ring will have lower levels of development, wealth, and income. The ring immediately surrounding Germany will include a great deal of profitable manufacturing and service activity. It is meant to comprise parts of Great Britain, France, Belgium, the Netherlands, and northern Italy. The general level of income would be high, but lower than in Germany. The next ring would include the poorer parts of Western Europe and parts of Eastern Europe, with some manufacturing, processing, and food production. Wage and salary levels would be significantly lower than at the center.

It goes without saying that, in this scheme of things, most areas of Eastern Europe will be in an outer ring. Eastern Europe will be a tributary of the center. It will produce some manufactured goods, but not primarily for its own consumption. Much of its manufacturing, along with raw materials, and even food, will be shipped abroad. Moreover, even manufacturing will pay low wages and salaries. And the general level of wages and salaries, and therefore of incomes, will be lower than they have been in the past.

In short, most of Eastern Europe will be poorer in the new, integrated system than it would have been if East European countries could make their own economic decisions about what kind of development to pursue. The only development possible in societies exposed to the penetration of powerful foreign capital and hemmed in by the rules of the International Monetary Fund is dependent development.

This will also be true of Russia and the other countries of the Commonwealth of Independent States—the former Soviet Union. They will also become tributaries of the center, and there will be no question of Russia pursuing an independent path of development. There will obviously be some manufacturing in Russia, but there will be no possibility of balanced industrial development. For the priorities of development will be increasingly dictated by outsiders. Western corporations are not interested in promoting industrial development in Russia, as the foreign investment figures show.

The primary Western interest in the CIS is in the exploitation of its resources. The breakup of the Soviet Union was thus a critical step in opening the possibility of such exploitation. The former republics of the USSR became much more vulnerable once they became independent. Furthermore, Western corporations are not interested in developing CIS resources for local use. They are interested in exporting them to the West. This is especially true of gas and petroleum resources. Much of the benefit from the export of resources would therefore accrue to foreign countries. Large parts of the former Soviet Union are likely to find themselves in a situation similar to that of Third World countries.

What Germany is seeking, then, with the support of the U.S., is a capitalist rationalization of the entire European economy around a powerful German core. Growth and high levels of wealth in the core are to be sustained by subordinate activities in the periphery. The periphery is to produce food and raw materials, and manufacture exports for the core and overseas markets. Compared to the (Western and Eastern) Europe of the 1980s, then, the future Europe will be very different, with lower and lower levels of development as one moves away from the German center.

Thus many parts of Eastern Europe, as well as much of the former Soviet Union, are meant to remain permanently underdeveloped areas, or relatively underdeveloped areas. Implementation of the new division of labor in Europe means that they must be locked into economic backwardness.

For Eastern Europe and the countries of the CIS, the creation of an "integrated" Europe within a capitalist framework will require a vast restructuring. This restructuring could be very profitable for Germany and the U.S. It will mean moving backwards in time for the parts of Europe being attached to the West.

The nature of the changes under way has already been prefigured in the effects of the "reforms" implemented in Russia from the early 1990s. It was said, of course, that these "reforms" would eventually bring prosperity. This was, however, a hollow claim from the beginning. For the "reforms" implemented at Western insistence were nothing more than the usual restructuring imposed by the World Bank and the International Monetary Fund on Third World countries. And they have had the same effects.

The most obvious is the precipitous fall in living standards. One third of the population of Russia is now trying to survive on income below the official poverty line. Production since 1991 has fallen by more than half. Inflation is running at an annual rate of 200 percent. The life expectancy of a Russian male fell from 64.9 years in 1987 to 57.3 years in 1994.[16] These figures are similar to those for countries like Egypt and Bangladesh. And, in present circumstances, there is really no prospect of an improvement in economic and social conditions in Russia. Standards of living are actually likely to continue falling.

Clearly there is widespread and justified anger in Russia and in other countries about the collapse of living standards which has accompanied the early stages of restructuring. This has contributed to a growing political backlash inside Russia and other countries. The most obvious recent example may be found in the results of the December parliamentary elections in Russia. It is also clear that the continuing fall in living standards in the future will create further angry reactions.

Thus the extension of the old world order into Eastern Europe and the CIS is a precarious exercise, fraught with uncertainty and risks. The major Western powers are extremely anxious that it should succeed, to some extent because they see success, which would be defined in terms of the efficient exploitation of these new regions as a partial solution to their own grave economic problems. There is an increasingly strong tendency in Western countries to displace their own problems, to see the present international competition for the exploitation of new territories as some kind of solution to world economic stagnation.

Western analysts rightly suppose that the future will bring political instability. So, as Senator Bill Bradley put it recently, "The question about Russia is whether reform is reversible."[17] Military analysts draw the obvious implication: the greater the military power which can potentially be brought to bear on Russia, the less the likelihood of the "reforms" being reversed. This is the meaning of the following extraordinary statement by the Working Group on NATO Enlargement:

> The security task of NATO is no longer limited to maintaining a defensive military posture against an opposing force. There is no immediate military security threat to Western Europe. The political instability and insecurity in Central and Eastern Europe, however, greatly affect the security of the NATO area. NATO should help to fulfill the Central and Eastern European desires for security and integration into Western structures, thus serving the interests in stability of its members.[18]

This represents an entirely new position on the part of NATO. It is a position which some NATO countries thought imprudent not long ago. And it is alarming, because it does not confront the real reasons behind the present pressure for NATO's extension. However evasive and sophistic the reasoning of the Working Group may be, it appears that the debate in many countries is now closed. It would, of course, be much better if the real issues could be debated publicly. But for the moment they cannot be, and the pressure for NATO enlargement is going to continue.

DANGERS OF EXTENDING NATO

The current proposal to expand NATO eastward creates many dangers.

It should be stated that many leaders in Western countries oppose the expansion of NATO, and they have repeatedly explained the dangers of such expansion. It is important to recognize that despite the official position of NATO and the recent report of the Working Group, there is strong opposition to NATO's moving eastward. Nonetheless, for the moment those in favor of NATO expansion have won the day.

Four dangers of NATO expansion in particular require discussion here.

The first is that the expansion of NATO will bring new members under the NATO umbrella. This will mean, for instance, that the United States and other Western members are obliged to defend, say, Slovakia against an attack. Where will an attack come from? Is NATO really prepared to defend Slovakia in the event of a conflict with another East European country? In a country like the United States, this would be very unpopular. As Senator Kassebaum put it in October of 1995:

> Are the American people prepared to pledge, in the words of the North Atlantic Treaty, that an armed attack against one or more of these potential new members will be considered an attack against all?[19]

The issue of extending the umbrella is a critical one. For the NATO powers are nuclear powers. The Working Group report stated that, in appropriate circumstances, the forces of NATO allies could be stationed on the territory of new members. And the Working Group did not rule out, as it should have, the stationing of nuclear weapons on the territory of new members. The failure to rule out such a possibility means that NATO is embarking on a dangerous path, a path that increases the risks of nuclear war.

The Working Group's silence on this matter cannot fail to be taken as a threat by those who are not joining NATO. And clearly the most important of these is Russia, because it too possesses nuclear weapons—as do the Ukraine and Kazakhstan.

The second danger is that expansion will jeopardize relations between the United States and Russia, or even lead to a second Cold War. While NATO countries present the organization as a defensive alliance, Russia sees it quite differently. For more than forty years, the Soviet Union considered NATO as an offensive alliance aimed at all the members of the Warsaw Pact. The general opinion in Russia is still that NATO is an offensive alliance. The former Foreign Minister, Mr. Kozyrev, made this quite clear to NATO members. How can Russia possibly see things differently in the future?

The expansion of NATO is inevitably perceived by Russia as encirclement. It is seen as assuming that Russia will inevitably again become an aggressive state. This, however, is much more likely to push Russia toward belligerence than to do anything else. It will certainly not calm Russia's fears about NATO's intentions in moving into Eastern Europe. Referring to the recent NATO decision on expansion, the Director of the Institute of U.S.A and Canada Studies of the Russian Academy of Sciences stated recently that:

> Russia is still a military superpower with a huge area and a large population. It is a country with enormous economic capabilities which has extraordinary potential for good or ill. But now it is a humiliated country in search of identity and direction. To a certain extent, the West and its position on NATO expansion will determine what direction Russia chooses. The future of European Security depends on this decision.[20]

The third danger in extending NATO is that it will undermine the implementation of the START I Treaty and the ratification of the START II Treaty, as well as other arms control and arms limitation treaties designed to increase European security. The Russians, for instance, have made it clear that they will go ahead with the implementation of the Conventional

Armed Forces in Europe (CFE) Treaty "if the situation in Europe is stable." The expansion of NATO into Eastern Europe, however, significantly changes the present equilibrium in Europe. So NATO countries are risking many of the achievements of the last twenty-five years in the field of disarmament. Some argue convincingly that NATO expansion will undermine the nuclear Non-Proliferation Treaty.

Such consequences will hardly make Europe or the globe safer in the future.

The fourth principal danger in NATO expansion is that it will unsettle the situation in Eastern Europe. NATO claims its expansion will help to ensure stability. But Eastern Europe, particularly after the changes of the last five years, is already unstable. The piecemeal expansion of NATO into Eastern Europe will increase tensions between new members and those left outside. It cannot fail to do so. Those left outside NATO are bound to feel more insecure when NATO has established itself in a neighboring country. This would place them in a buffer zone between an expanding NATO and Russia. They are bound to react in a fearful and even hostile manner. The piecemeal expansion of NATO could even trigger an arms race in Eastern Europe.

WEAKNESS OF THE WESTERN POSITION

When closely considered, the proposal to extend NATO eastward is not just dangerous. It also seems something of a desperate act. It is obviously irrational, for it can become a self-fulfilling prophecy. It can lead to a second Cold War between the NATO powers and Russia, and possibly to nuclear war. It must be assumed that no one really wants that.

Why, then, would the NATO countries propose such a course of action? Why would they be unable to weigh the dangers of their decision objectively?

Part of the answer is that those who have made this decision have looked at it in very narrow terms, without seeing the larger context in which NATO expansion would take place. In that larger context, the proposal to expand NATO is obviously irrational.

Consider the larger context. NATO proposes to admit certain countries in Central Europe as full members of the alliance in the near future. Other East European countries are being considered for later admission. This extension has two possible purposes. The first is to prevent "the failure of Russian democracy," that is, to ensure the continuation of the present regime, or something like it. The second is to place NATO in a favorable position if a war should ever break out between Russia and the West.

In an age of nuclear weapons, pursuing the second purpose is perhaps even more dangerous than it was during the years of the Cold War, since there are now several countries with nuclear weapons which could potentially be targeted against NATO. The argument that NATO should be expanded eastward in order to ensure the West an advantage in the event of a nuclear war is not very convincing. And it would certainly not be convincing to Central European countries if it were openly discussed. Those countries would be most likely to suffer in the first stages of such a war. Their situation would be similar to that of Germany during the Cold War, as the German anti-war movement began to understand in the 1980s.

The main purpose of expanding NATO, as almost everyone has acknowledged, is to make sure that there is no reversal of the changes which have taken place in Russia during the last five years. Were such a reversal to happen, it would end the dream of a three-part Europe united under the capitalist banner and close a very large new space for the operation of Western capital. A NATO presence in Central and Eastern Europe is simply a means of maintaining new pressure on those who would wish to change the present situation in Russia.

However, as has been seen, this also means locking Russia, and other countries of the CIS, into a state of underdevelopment and continuous economic and social crisis in which millions of people will suffer terribly, and in which there is no possibility of society seeking a path of economic and social development in which human needs determine economic priorities.

What is horribly ironic about this situation is that the Western countries are offering their model of economic organization as the solution to Russia's problems. The realistic analysts, of course, know perfectly well that it is no such thing. They are interested only in extending Western domination further eastward. And they offer their experience as a model for others only to beguile. But the idea that "the transition to democracy," as the installation of market rules is often called, represents progress is important in the world battle for public opinion. It has helped to justify and sustain the policies which the West has been pursuing toward the countries of the CIS.

The Western countries themselves, however, are locked in an intractable economic crisis. Beginning in the early 1970s, profits fell, production faltered, long-term unemployment began to rise, and standards of living began to fall. Within this larger picture there were, of course, the ups and downs of the business cycle. But what was important was the trend. The trend of gross-domestic-product growth in the major Western countries has been downward since the major recession of 1973-1975. In the United States, for instance, the rate of growth fell from about 4 percent per year in the 1950s and the 1960s, to 2.9 percent in the 1970s, and then to about 2.4 percent in the 1980s. Current projections for growth are even lower.

The situation was not very different in other Western countries. Growth was somewhat faster, but unemployment was significantly higher. The current rates of unemployment in Western Europe average about 11 percent, and there is more unemployment hidden in the statistics as a result of various government pseudo-employment plans.

Both Western Europe and North America have experienced a prolonged economic stagnation. And capitalist economies cannot sustain employment and living standards without relatively rapid growth. In the twenty-five years after World War II, most Western countries experienced rapid growth, on the order of 4 and 5 percent per year. It was that growth which made it possible to maintain high levels of employment, the rise in wages, and the advance of living standards. And there is no doubt that the Western countries made great advances in the postwar period. Large numbers of working class people were able to achieve decent living standards. The middle and upper classes prospered; indeed, many of them reached a standard of living which can only be called luxurious.

The postwar honeymoon, however, is clearly over. The great "capitalist revolution" touted by the Rockefellers is no more. "Humanized capitalism" is no more. Declining growth has now returned us to the age of "le capitalisme sauvage." It has triggered economic and social crisis in every Western country. It is undermining the principal achievements of the postwar period. In Europe, the welfare state has been under attack for fifteen years by those who would shift the burden of crisis onto the shoulders of the less fortunate. In the United States, a relatively meager "social net" to protect the poor is now being shredded by the aggressive and ignorant defenders of corporate interests, who also want to be sure that those who can least afford it bear the brunt of the system's crisis of stagnation.

The West, then, is itself locked in crisis. This is not a transient crisis or a "long cycle," as academic apologists would have it. It is a systemic crisis. The market system can no longer produce anything like prosperity. The markets which drove the capitalist economy in the postwar period—automobiles, consumer durables, construction, etc.—are all saturated, as sheaves of government statistics in every country demonstrate. The system has not found new markets which could create an equivalent wave of prosperity. Moreover, the acceleration of technical progress in recent years has begun to eliminate jobs everywhere at a staggering rate. There is no possible way of compensating for its effect, for creating new employment in sufficient quantity and at high wage levels.

Government and industry leaders in the West are fully aware of the situation in one sense. They know what the statistics are. They know what the problems are. But they are not able to see that the source of the problem is the fact that, having achieved very high levels of production, income, and wealth, the present capitalist system has nowhere to go. Half-way solutions could be found, but Western leaders are unwilling to make the required political concessions. In particular, the large concentrations of capital in Western countries are led by people who are constitutionally incapable of seeing that something fundamental is wrong. That would require them to agree to the curtailing of their power.

Therefore, the leaders of government and industry drive blindly on, not wishing to see, not prepared to accept policies that might set the present system on a path of transition to some more rational and more human way of organizing economic life. It is this blindness, grounded in confusion and fear, which has clouded the ability of Western leaders to think clearly about the risks of extending NATO into Eastern Europe. The Western system is experiencing a profound economic, social, and political crisis. And Western leaders apparently see the exploitation of the East as the only large-scale project available which might stimulate growth, especially in Western Europe.

They are therefore prepared to risk a great deal for it. The question is: will the world accept the risks of East-West conflict and nuclear war in order to lock into one region economic arrangements which are already collapsing elsewhere?

[1] *Defense News*, 25 November 1995; see also Gary Wilson, "Anti-War Activists Demand: No More U.S. Troops to the Balkans," Workers World News Service, 7 December 1995.

[2] As of 1996, the Visegrad countries were the Czech Republic, the Slovak Republic, Hungary, and Poland.

[3] See, for instance, "NATO Expansion: Flirting with Disaster," *Defense Monitor*, November/December 1995, Center for Defense Information, Washington, D.C.

[4] Senator Richard Lugar, "NATO: Out of Area or Out of Business," remarks delivered to the Open Forum of the U.S. State Department, 2 August 1993, Washington, D.C.

[5] "Changing Nature of NATO," *Intelligence Digest*, 16 October 1992.

[6] *Defense Monitor*, loc. cit., p. 2.

[7] "Bonn's Balkans-to-Teheran Policy," *Intelligence Digest*, 11-25 August 1995.

[8] Richard Holbrooke, "America, a European Power," *Foreign Affairs*, March/April 1995, p. 39.

[9] The crucial point is that Eastern Europe and the countries of the former USSR are to adopt the institutions prevailing in Western Europe, i.e., capitalism and parliamentary democracy.

[10] Holbrooke, loc. cit., p. 43.

[11] See National Security Decision Directive, "United States Policy Toward Yugoslavia," Secret Sensitive (declassified), The White House, Washington, D.C., 14 March 1984.

[12] Joan Hoey, "The U.S. 'Great Game' in Bosnia," *The Nation*, 30 January 1995.

[13] Jacob Heilbrunn and Michael Lind, "The Third American Empire," *New York Times*, 2 January 1996.

[14] "The Commercial Factor Behind NATO's Extended Remit," *Intelligence Digest*, 29 May 1992.

[15] Idem.

[16] Senator Bill Bradley, "Eurasia Letter: A Misguided Russia Policy," *Foreign Policy*, Winter 1995-1996, p. 89.

[17] Ibid., p. 93.

[18] Draft Special Report of the Working Group on NATO Enlargement, May 1995. This statement did not appear in the final version of the report dated September 1995.

[19] Quoted in *Defense Monitor*, loc. cit., p. 5.

[20] Dr. Sergei Rogov, Director of the Russian Academy of Sciences' Institute of USA and Canada Studies, quoted in *Defense Monitor*, loc. cit., p. 4.

3   Bosnia tragedy: The unknown role of the Pentagon

SARA FLOUNDERS[*]

The recurring media image of Yugoslavia in the United States and Europe is of desperate people fleeing local war and ethnic hatred or living a precarious existence dependent on United Nations convoys for their next meal.

According to the UN High Commission on Refugees, this is the largest refugee population in the world. By 1994, there were over 3.7 million war refugees in the former Yugoslavia. The war has taken its toll on all participants in the struggle. Of the refugees, 44 percent are Muslim, 36 percent are Serbs, and 20 percent are Croatian. The enormous human suffering represented in these cold statistics cannot be calculated.

The very names Bosnia and Serbia are now associated with "ethnic cleansing," mass rape, atrocities, and age-old national hatreds. U.S. involvement, UN troops, and NATO forces are depicted as neutral forces or peacekeepers carrying out humanitarian or diplomatic missions. When UN officials, NATO generals, and U.S., British, French, or German diplomats meet,

---

[*] This chapter is adapted from the pamphlet *Bosnia Tragedy: the unknown role of the U.S. government & Pentagon* (New York: World View Forum, 1995) by Sara Flounders.

it's to discuss the newest "peace plan." The motive for every new military measure is always described as deep concern over how to end the fighting.

Is the civil war raging in Yugoslavia a case of spontaneous combustion caused by "ancient ethnic hatreds" burning out of control? Is the U.S. government an innocent bystander? Is the real problem presidential indecision about how to defend a small, oppressed, Bosnian Moslem government targeted by the "new fascists" of the 1990s—the Serbs?

A closer examination of the root causes of the incredibly destructive civil war raging in the region yields a completely different picture. Age-old ethnic hatred among small nationalities didn't just explode into modern-day barbarism. Rather, war exists in the region as a result of the intervention of outside powers. In this process the U.S. has been neither an innocent bystander nor a neutral party. The reality is that the U.S. government lit the fire in the Balkans. At every stage Washington has acted as an arsonist pouring gasoline on the flames.

The greatest responsibility for the dismemberment of Yugoslavia and the resulting civil war lies with the U.S. government. It was not an accident or an oversight. It was a policy decision. Each step the U.S. has taken has widened the war and increased divisions in the region.

ORIGINS OF THE BREAKUP—A U.S. LAW

A year before the breakup of the Socialist Federal Republic of Yugoslavia, on Nov. 5, 1990, the U.S. Congress passed the 1991 Foreign Operations Appropriations Law 101-513.* This bill was a signed death warrant. One provision in particular was so lethal that a CIA report predicting a bloody civil war referred to this law.[1]

A section of Law 101-513 suddenly and without previous warning cut off all aid, credits, and loans from the U.S. to Yugoslavia within six months. Conducting trade without credits

---

* See Appendix for full text of the Yugoslav portion of this law.

is virtually impossible in the modern world—especially for an indebted country lacking hard currency. The law also demanded separate elections in each of the six republics that make up Yugoslavia, requiring State Department approval of election procedures and results before aid to the separate republics would be resumed. The legislation further required U.S. personnel in all international financial institutions such as the World Bank and the International Monetary Fund to enforce this cut-off policy for all credits and loans.

There was one final provision. Only forces that the U.S. State Department defined as "democratic" would receive funding. This meant an influx of funds to small, right-wing, nationalist parties in a financially strangled region suddenly thrown into crisis by the overall funding cut-off. The impact was, as expected, devastating.

The Yugoslav federal government was unable to pay the enormous interest on its foreign debt or even to arrange the purchase of raw materials for industry. Credit collapsed and recriminations broke out on all sides.

At the time there was no civil war. No republic had seceded. The U.S. was not engaged in a public dispute with Yugoslavia. The region was not even in the news. World attention was focused on the international coalition the Bush administration was assembling to destroy Iraq—a war that reshaped the Middle East at a cost of half a million Iraqi lives.

What was behind the sweeping legislation directed at Yugoslavia, especially when U.S. policy makers themselves predicted that the sudden unraveling of the region would lead to civil war?

With the collapse of the Soviet Union, U.S. big business was embarking on an aggressive march to reshape all of Europe. Nonaligned Yugoslavia was no longer needed as a buffer state between NATO and the Warsaw Pact. A strong, united Europe was hardly desirable. Washington policy makers considered both to be relics of the Cold War.

CONTROL OF THE PURSE STRINGS

This one piece of legislation—Law 101-513—demonstrates the U.S. government's enormous power. It was one part of annual legislation that defines in detail policies to be pursued in every region of the globe. This law implements U.S. corporate control through major funding to international financial institutions—such as the Inter-American Development Bank, the Asian Development Bank, the African Development Bank—and through direct assistance to individual countries.

The deadly restrictions on Yugoslavia took a mere twenty-three lines. Compare this to the more than nine pages that detail sanctions to be imposed on Iraq. As of December 1994, the U.S.-UN sanctions on Iraq had killed more than half a million children. This projection is from Thomas Ekfal, the United Nations Children's Fund representative in Baghdad.[2]

The 1991 Foreign Appropriations Law also prescribed various forms of economic strangulation for several other countries deemed enemies, including Angola, Cambodia, Cuba, Iran, Iraq, Libya, Syria, Korea (DPRK), and Vietnam. On the other hand, countries moving hastily toward a capitalist market economy in 1990, such as Poland, were to receive special funding. In all the expressions of concern and sympathy for refugees and displaced people in countries all over the globe, but especially in the former Yugoslavia, no U.S. official ever mentions the terrible suffering caused by U.S. economic strangulation.

Of course, financial strings were hardly new to Yugoslavia in 1990. Yugoslavia had become utterly dependent on loans from Western banks. The increasingly onerous conditions had dislocated the economy. A year earlier, the price of continued U.S. loans and credits was a brutal austerity program that devalued the currency, froze wages, cut subsidies, closed many state industries deemed unprofitable for capitalist investors, and increased unemployment to 20 percent. The result was strikes, walkouts, a sharp increase in political and economic tension, and, above all, an upsurge in national antagonisms on all sides.

Once the U.S. acted so decisively toward Yugoslavia in 1990, the European powers were hardly willing to be bystanders to the enforced breakup of a country in their own backyard. The U.S. Foreign Appropriations Law sent a clear message to the European powers that Yugoslavia and the whole Balkan region were again up for grabs. On their own they might never have dared to act. Now they dared not be out of the action.

EUROPEAN INTERVENTION

By February 1991 the Council of Europe followed the U.S. measure with its own political demands and explicit economic intervention in the internal affairs of the Yugoslav Federation. Their demand was similar: that Yugoslavia hold multi-party elections or face economic blockade.

Right-wing and fascist organizations not seen in forty-five years—since the defeat of the Nazi occupation by the anti-fascist Partisan movement—were suddenly revived and began receiving covert support. These fascist organizations had been maintained in exile in the U.S., Canada, Germany, and Austria. Now they became the main conduit for funds and arms. By March 1991, Croatian fascists were organizing attacks and demonstrations calling for the overturn of the socialist federation and the expulsion of all Serbs from Croatia.

On May 5, 1991, the date of the six-month deadline imposed by U.S. Foreign Operations Law 101-513, Croatian separatists staged violent demonstrations and besieged a military base in Gospic. The Yugoslav federal government, under attack, ordered the army to intervene. The civil war had begun. Slovenia and Croatia declared independence on June 25, 1991.

In Croatia the right-wing party, the Croatian Democratic Union (HDZ), came to power using fascist symbols and slogans from the era of Nazi occupation and the quisling Ustasha party.[3] Its program guaranteed a return to capitalist property relations and denied citizenship, jobs, pensions, passports, and land ownership to all other nationalities, but especially targeted the large Serbian minority. In the face of armed expropriations and mass expulsions, the Serbs in Croatia began to arm themselves. The experience of World War II—when almost a million people, primarily Serbs, but also Jews, Romani, and tens of thousands of others died in Ustashi death camps—fueled the mobilization.

As the largest nationality and the one that opposed the breakup of the Yugoslav federation, the Serbs became the target and the excuse for Western intervention. History was turned on its head as the media portrayed the Serbs as fascists. In 1991, right-wing nationalist parties swept the elections in Slovenia and Croatia. However, in Serbia and in Montenegro the mass mood was overwhelmingly for the federation and also against further privatization or other capitalist inroads. This was an unexpected resistance to the political collapse sweeping Eastern Europe at the time.

The tactic of targeting the Serbs with UN resolutions, imposing brutal sanctions, and freezing all credit and trade also served as a veiled threat against Russia. The breakup and dismemberment of the Soviet Union has been encouraged by the same forces that encouraged the breakup of Yugoslavia.

Reunited Germany moved aggressively into the region to consolidate its position. It was the first to openly grant diplomatic recognition to the break-away republics.

The U.S. State Department's position after Croatia and Slovenia seceded was official support for a continued federation. But this flew in the face of the demands and the process set in motion by the U.S. Foreign Operations Law passed in 1990 before the Yugoslav civil war began.

REWRITING HISTORY

The rationale behind Western intervention in Yugoslavia is based on rewriting history. Every debate about drawing and redrawing the map of Bosnia assumes the right of the Western powers as outside "neutral" forces to carve up and decide the fate of the region in the interests of "peace." The implied justification is that the small, barbaric nations of the Balkans are so torn by ethnic hatred that they are incapable of deciding anything themselves.

There is a bloody history in the Balkans—but it's not the one that's being connected to the present-day struggle. It's much more fundamental. It's the history of the major imperialist powers battling for control and domination of this strategic crossroads of Europe and the Middle East.

The history of modern Europe sometimes seems to revolve around carving and recarving the Balkans. It is a history of continually redrawing borders and defining regions of influence, of arming mercenary bands and holding international conferences in Paris, in Berlin, in London, and at the Hague to confer about which power would be in control of what region. All this was always without any consultation with the many small nationalities whose fate hung in the balance.

The Austro-Hungarian Empire, Ottoman Turkey, Czarist Russia, Britain, France, Germany, and Italy have all considered the Balkans their rightful "sphere of influence." World War I began in Sarajevo. Although the competition and rivalry for markets extended globally—far beyond the Balkans—this small region has always been a tinderbox for the big powers.

In World War II the resistance movement to Nazi German occupation led by Marshal Tito and the League of Yugoslav Communists united the small nations of the Balkans into an explosive political force. From scattered bands of guerrillas it grew into the largest partisan movement in Europe, more than a million strong. Forty-three German divisions could not destroy the movement. This experience shaped Yugoslavia's history and laid the basis for the socialist federation. It remains a powerful heritage.

Today, the capitalist media speak endlessly of "ancient ethnic hatreds" but never of this revolutionary partisan movement and the long tradition of struggles to unite the South Slav peoples against outside domination.

For forty-five years the Yugoslav federation—six republics and two autonomous regions—was able to hold the

Western powers at bay. It was able to develop industry in an impoverished, underdeveloped area and raise the standard of living. The fact that the IMF and U.S. banks were able again to strangle and dismember it does not negate its historical accomplishment.

CASTING THE SERBS AS FASCISTS

How did the Serbs come to be viewed as fascists in this conflict? This characterization has now become an accepted fact, an issue beyond debate. It makes U.S. motives seem unimpeachable and on the side of good against evil.

In April 1993 Jacques Merlino, associate director of French TV 2, interviewed James Harff, director of Ruder Finn Global Public Affairs, a Washington, D.C.-based public relations firm. The interview shows the role of the corporate media in shaping a political issue.

Harff bragged of his services to his clients—the Republic of Croatia, the Republic of Bosnia-Herzegovina, and the parliamentary opposition in Kosovo, an autonomous region of Serbia. Merlino described how Harff uses a file of several hundred journalists, politicians, representatives of humanitarian associations, and academics to create public opinion. Harff explained: "Speed is vital . . . it is the first assertion that really counts. All denials are entirely ineffective."

In the interview, Merlino asked Harff what his proudest public relations endeavor was. Harff responded:

"To have managed to put Jewish opinion on our side. This was a sensitive matter, as the dossier was dangerous looked at from this angle. President Tudjman was very careless in his book, *Wastelands of Historical Reality*. Reading his writings one could accuse him of anti-Semitism. [Tudjman claimed the Holocaust never happened—S.F.] In Bosnia the situation was no better: President Izetbegovic strongly supported the creation of a fundamentalist Islamic state in his book, *The Islamic Declaration*.

"Besides, the Croatian and Bosnian past was marked by real and cruel anti-Semitism. Tens of thousands of Jews perished in Croatian camps, so there was every reason for intellectuals and Jewish organizations to be hostile toward the Croats and the Bosnians. Our challenge was to reverse this attitude and we succeeded masterfully.

"At the beginning of July 1992, *New York Newsday* came out with the article on Serb camps. We jumped at the opportunity immediately. We outwitted three big Jewish organizations—the B'nai B'rith Anti-Defamation League, The American Jewish Committee and the American Jewish Congress. In August, we suggested that they publish an advertisement in the *New York Times* and organize demonstrations outside the United Nations.

"That was a tremendous coup. When the Jewish organizations entered the game on the side of the [Muslim] Bosnians, we could promptly equate the Serbs with the Nazis in the public mind. Nobody understood what was happening in Yugoslavia. The great majority of Americans were probably asking themselves in which African country Bosnia was situated.

"By a single move we were able to present a simple story of good guys and bad guys which would hereafter play itself. We won by targeting the Jewish audience. Almost immediately there was a clear change of language in the press, with use of words with high emotional content such as ethnic cleansing, concentration camps, etc., which evoke images of Nazi Germany and the gas chambers of Auschwitz. No one could go against it without being accused of revisionism. We really batted a thousand in full."

Merlino replied, "But between 2 and 5 August 1992, when you did this, you had no proof that what you said was true. All you had were two *Newsday* articles."

"Our work is not to verify information," said Harff. "We are not equipped for that. Our work is to accelerate the circulation of information favorable to us, to aim at judiciously chosen targets. We did not confirm the existence of death

camps in Bosnia, we just made it widely known that *Newsday*
affirmed it. . . . We are professionals. We had a job to do and
we did it. We are not paid to moralize."[4]

THE RAPE CHARGE

One charge against the Serbs has aroused the anger and shaped
the view of millions of people who previously had little interest
or involvement in the Balkans. The charge is rape—rape as a
systematic weapon of war, a planned deliberate strategy. The
media asserts that rapes were a conscious policy and the responsibility of the Bosnian Serb leadership.

Between the fall of 1992 and spring of 1993 sensational
news reports claimed that at least twenty thousand and up to
one hundred thousand Muslim women had been raped by units
of the Bosnian Serb Army. This crystallized the view that the
Serbs were the aggressors and the Muslims the victims.

Women are the first victims in every war. Rape and the
degrading abuse of women are all too often carried out as a
stamp of conquest by invading armies imbued with patriarchal
possessive attitudes. But the charge of rape has many times
been consciously used as an essential prop of war propaganda.
The purported defense of women is used to mobilize armies and
galvanize blind hatred.

The sensational charges of rape were used to a cynical
extent by the major corporate media, especially in the U.S., with
no attempt to examine the sources. The foreign minister of
Bosnia-Herzegovina, Haris Silajdzic, first raised the charge at
peace talks in Geneva that thirty thousand women and girls had
been raped. *Ms.* magazine ran a cover story that accused
Bosnian Serb forces of raping for the purpose of producing
pornographic films. No such films were ever found and the
charges were not supported by the findings of Helsinki Watch
or Human Rights Watch.

In January 1993 the Warburton Report, authorized by
the European Community, estimated twenty thousand Muslim
women had been raped as part of a Serb strategy of conquest.

This report was widely cited as an independent, authoritative source. No coverage was given to a dissenting member of the investigative team, Simone Veil, a former French minister and president of the European Parliament. She revealed that the estimate of twenty thousand victims was based on actual interviews with only four victims—two women and two men.

The Croatian Ministry of Health in Zagreb was the main source upon which the Warburton Report based its figure of twenty thousand.[5]

Newsweek magazine reported that up to fifty thousand Muslim women had been raped in Bosnia.[6] Tom Post, a contributor to the article, explained that the estimate of fifty thousand rapes was based on interviews with twenty-eight women. This estimate was the result of an extrapolation—multiplying each charge of rape by a certain factor because historically rape has been and continues to be an under-reported crime.

French television reporter Jerome Bony explained the problem. "When I was fifty kilometers from Tuzla, I was told: 'Go to the Tuzla high school grounds. There are four thousand raped women.' At twenty kilometers this figure dropped to four hundred. At ten kilometers only forty were left. Once at the site, I found only four women willing to testify."

The *New York Times* carried a photo story with the caption: "A two-month-old baby girl born to a teen-age Muslim woman after she was raped in a Serbian detention camp."[7] *USA Today* told the story of a five-month-old baby, presumably the product of systematic Serbian rape.[8] At that time, the war was not yet nine months old.

Women's organizations understandably outraged by these lurid reports demanded that the U.S. and the European powers take action. However, many of these same women ought to be aware that U.S. troops do not protect women. In every U.S. military operation an entire sex industry is created and tens of thousands of women are forced into sexual slavery and prostitution. Consider the experience of Vietnam, Thailand, Korea, and the Philippines. Even U.S. women in the military experience rape and sexual abuse, then cover-ups and denial, as the Tailhook scandal and subsequent exposes so graphically demonstrated.

CONTROL THROUGH DIVISION IN BOSNIA

The divisive U.S. role in Bosnia, the most multi-ethnic of the regions, raises other questions. Does the U.S. seek, through the breakup of Yugoslavia, not only to position itself in the region but to advance a more complex, hidden agenda? Certainly U.S. conduct has involved many maneuvers that have prolonged the war and increased the rivalry among Britain, France, and Germany. Turkey, Greece, and Italy have also historically been involved in the region and are again maneuvering.

On March 18, 1992, a negotiated agreement for a unified state brokered by the European Community was reached in Lisbon among the Bosnian Muslim, Croatian, and Serb forces. This agreement of all three parties would have prevented the disastrous civil war that began that same year. It would have saved the hundreds of thousands of refugees whose lives have been destroyed by war. Washington sabotaged this original agreement by telling the Bosnian regime of Alija Izetbegovic that it could get much more—possibly domination of the whole region—with U.S. backing. The U.S. role in destroying this carefully crafted agreement is acknowledged by all sides. Even the *New York Times* described Washington's role.[9] The U.S. government officially encouraged Izetbegovic, the head of the right-wing Party for Democratic Action, to unilaterally declare a sovereign state under his presidency.

Muslim groups in two separate areas of Bosnia have challenged the government led by Alija Izetbegovic. They dispute Izetbegovic's claim that he represents the interests of the Muslim community. They want a policy of cooperation and trade with the other nationalities of the region. Both groups have condemned Izetbegovic for right-wing nationalist policies and reliance on U.S. military aid.

The elected Bosnian Muslim government in the city of Tuzla, one of the wealthiest industrial centers in Yugoslavia before it was dismembered, claims that the U.S.-supervised rewrite of the Bosnian constitution gave power only to the most extreme right-wing nationalist forces of Izetbegovic's Party for Democratic Action and neo-fascist Franjo Tudjman's Croatian Democratic Union. Other political forces were excluded, even among Muslims.

A Bosnian Muslim group in the northwest Bihac area led by Fikret Abdic declared its autonomy from the U.S.-backed government based in Sarajevo. In retaliation, the Izetbegovic government launched a military attack against these Muslim forces that wanted peace with their Serbian and Croatian neighbors. This attack on an elected Moslem Bosnian government was organized by the U.S. As reported in November 1994 in Britain in such newspapers as the *Guardian*, the *Observer* and the *Independent*, as well as in newspapers in France and Germany, six U.S. generals took part in planning the offensive in June of that year. The attack violated the cease-fire and a UN-declared safe area.

The Izetbegovic government's U.S.-backed offensive was at first successful in the Bihac region. But the Bosnian Serbs, in alliance with Serbs in Croatia and Bosnian Moslem forces led by Fikret Abdic, reorganized and began a strong push back. U.S. bombers under NATO command then came to Izetbegovic's defense.

In the U.S. media, neither the U.S. role in planning the offensive nor the fact that the U.S.-backed forces were the ones to violate the cease-fire was examined. The Bosnian Muslim forces opposing the Izetbegovic government based in Sarajevo have received only scant mention as "renegade forces."

Retired U.S. Air Force Gen. Charles G. Boyd, deputy commander in chief of the U.S. European Command from 1992 to 1995, wrote in *Foreign Affairs* magazine that Abdic's government in Bihac was "one of the few examples of successful multi-ethnic cooperation in the Balkans." Further, Boyd wrote,

"Abdic, a powerful local businessman, was a member of the Bosnian collective presidency. He outpolled Izetbegovic in national elections and had been expelled from the government when Sarajevo [Izetbegovic's headquarters] rejected an internationally brokered peace agreement."[10]

U.S. backing of Izetbegovic's attack on other Bosnian Muslim forces exposes just how cynically the Pentagon is using right-wing Muslim forces in order to prolong and widen the war. Those who call on the Pentagon to come to the defense of Muslim people should recall the U.S. role in the Middle East. The U.S. government has demonized Muslim people and made war on the people of Palestine, Lebanon, Iraq, and Iran—as well as on Libya, Somalia, and Afghanistan. Muslim people in Bosnia will be the greatest losers in this war-torn region as a result of the alliance of the narrow, right-wing Izetbegovic grouping and the Pentagon.

CIA ROLE IN BOSNIA

The European press has been much more candid on what the U.S. was doing in Bosnia than the media in this country. Here are some headlines from British newspapers:

"CIA agents training Bosnian army"—*The Guardian*, November 17, 1994

"America's secret Bosnia agenda"—*The Observer*, November 20, 1994

"How the CIA helps Bosnia fight back"—*The European*, November 25, 1994

"Allies facing split over Bosnia"—*The Independent*, November 12, 1994

"Europe braces for more rows with U.S."—*The Guardian*, November 12, 1994

These few headlines expose both the CIA role in Bosnia and the depth of the growing dispute in NATO. The media in France, Germany, and Italy have carried similar exposés of large-scale CIA involvement in the widening war in Bosnia. Coverage has included information on tactical operations, sharing satellite information, and controlling local air traffic. Units of both the Croatian and Bosnian armies have reportedly been trained within the region and in the United States. U.S.-based forces have provided assistance in building airstrips and organizing large weapons shipments through Croatia to the Bosnian forces.

The debate in the European press—complete with Pentagon denials and "clarification"—has received scant coverage in the U.S. media. This avoidance of an issue receiving wide coverage in Britain and France raises further questions of why the major U.S. media are aiding and abetting this operation and why the European media are exposing this information.

The exposés follow months of increasingly sharp criticisms and veiled charges by UN officials that the U.S. has sabotaged each agreement, peace plan, and even the cease-fires.

It is clear that the civil war in Yugoslavia has broken the growing unity of the European powers. They are at each other's throats over how to proceed. The struggle between the use of UN peacekeepers versus NATO bombing reflects these divisions.

UN LEAKS INFORMATION ON U.S. ROLE

Occasionally the debate makes it into the pages of U.S. newspapers. In April 1994 the *Washington Post* cited two senior UN officials—a general and a civilian—who blame the U.S. "for the continuation of the war in Bosnia because it has given the Muslim-led Bosnian government the false impression that Washington's military support was on the way."[11]

The article explained that the officials interviewed were two of the highest-ranking UN representatives in Bosnia. Yet they feared using their names lest they be expelled from Bosnia. However, both claimed that U.S. moral and financial support of the Izetbegovic regime was prolonging the war.

The officials accused the U.S. of leading on Izetbegovic's forces by promising full-scale NATO intervention on his side. U.S. Gen. John Shalikashvili, chair of the U.S. Joint Chiefs of Staff, had gone to Sarajevo to meet with Bosnian military leaders. It was a powerful incentive to keep fighting. And it was reinforced when, in an impassioned speech at the opening of the new U.S. Embassy in Sarajevo, U.S. Ambassador to the UN Madeleine Albright said, "Your future and America's future are inseparable."

The *New York Times* described the new supplies, including heavy weapons, flooding into Bosnia since the U.S. organized the Croatian-Bosnian alliance.[12]

Each "peace proposal" or map defining the areas of Moslem or Serb control divides the area into dependent, unsustainable enclaves needing constant resupply, which would require a military presence for many years. Industrial centers and the major roads in this mountainous region are partitioned so the Bosnian government based in Sarajevo controls them. The Bosnian Serbs have been allocated the poorest rural and mountainous regions with no connecting roads or corridors between them. The Bosnian Serbs cannot survive under these plans. Their situation is untenable. They are driven to resist.

USE OF WAR PROPAGANDA

The siege of Gorazde in the spring of 1994 is one of the clearest examples of the U.S. propaganda barrage to justify and demand measures that would widen the war and give the U.S. military a blank check. Nightly news broadcasts about Gorazde focused on the Serbian bombing of a hospital and claimed casualties in the thousands. Then, after days of gory stories in the media and heavy U.S. pressure, U.S. planes flying under NATO auspices bombed Serb positions. A heated UN Security Council debate and vote, however, blocked the full-scale NATO air strikes that the U.S. was demanding.

After the siege was lifted, the commander of UN troops in Bosnia, British Army Lt. Gen. Michael Rose, told visiting U.S. Rep. John P. Murtha, chair of the House Appropriations Committee subcommittee on defense, that reports of damage and casualties were greatly exaggerated. The Bosnian casualties around Gorazde "were closer to two hundred than two thousand." The media had wildly exaggerated casualties in order to promote a war climate and justify NATO intervention.

The UN officials found that the hospital in Gorazde, which had been repeatedly described as all but destroyed by the Serbs, basically needed a broom to clear up the rubbish. It was still functioning. The hospital had been damaged because the Izetbegovic government forces had established their military headquarters next door.

After the siege ended, the *New York Times* referred to a giant munitions factory in Gorazde under Bosnian Muslim control.[13] The Pobjeda Munitions Factory included "a honeycomb of underground tunnels and storage bunkers." It held "enough explosives in the factory to flatten a city." Throughout the siege the public had been bombarded with countless stories on the plight of unarmed Bosnian Muslim forces versus a well-armed Bosnian Serb army.

World sympathy for the government of Izetbegovic has been built mainly through horror stories of brutal Serbian attacks on unarmed civilians in Sarajevo. One of the most gruesome was an attack on an open-air market on February 5, 1994, that left sixty-eight people dead. As the rift between the U.S. forces and the British and French forces under the UN flag grows more heated, these widely publicized "Serb atrocities" are being disputed. A UN analysis of the crater showed that the Izetbegovic regime's forces were responsible for the explosion at the market.[14] Later, the UN publicly released a crater analysis of another shell that exploded, wounding a child, as proof that Izetbegovic's Bosnian army had fired on its own civilians to gain sympathy.[15]

Just a few weeks earlier, U.S. war propaganda had reached new depths with gory descriptions of carnage, mass rapes, disembowelments, even massacres of children when the Bosnian government pulled out of Srebrenica. However, a UN investigative team reported on July 24, 1995, that they could not find a single eyewitness to any atrocity.

Hubert Wieland, personal representative of the UN High Commission for Human Rights, traveled with a team of investigators to Srebrenica and to Tuzla, the Bosnian city to which almost all the refugees were taken. Although his team spoke with scores of Muslims at the main refugee camp and at other collection centers, no eyewitness could be found.

U.S. SUPPORTS CROAT INVASION OF KRAJINA

In contrast to the storm of outrage in the media when the Serbs moved into the town of Srebrenica, there was no such coverage two weeks later when, in a blitzkrieg attack on August 3, 1995, Croatian forces with U.S. backing launched the biggest and bloodiest offensive in four years of civil war.

Within a week, two hundred thousand new refugees were fleeing the Croatian army. However, there was no coverage of these old people being driven from their homes or the chaos of thousands fleeing the bombing of their villages. There was no sympathy and there was no talk of sanctions on Croatia. Secretary of State Warren Christopher declared that the crushing military offensive was "to our advantage."

Pentagon support amounted to far more than just a nod of approval. According to the London *Independent*, "The rearming and training of Croatian forces in preparation for the present offensive are part of a classic CIA operation: probably the most ambitious operation of its kind since the end of the Vietnam war."[16]

The London *Times* reported that "the rearming of Croatia remains one of the biggest untold stories of the Yugoslav war. American officials strenuously deny any involvement in this operation but the region is teeming with former generals who unconventionally chose the Balkans, rather than Florida, for their well-earned retirement."[17]

'SAFE AREAS' LAUNCHING PADS FOR U.S. WAR

On a daily basis news coverage in the U.S. refers to Serb violations of UN-declared "safe areas," six towns held by the Bosnian government and surrounded by Serb-held territory. This term reinforces the popular misconception that the "safe areas" are neutral, demilitarized, civilian havens removed from the civil war. U.S. military support has made this term a cynical fraud. The excuse for every NATO bombing of the Bosnian Serb forces has been an alleged Serb attack on a "safe area." But it is U.S. military intervention that has made these "safe areas" unsafe. The "safe areas" are really staging areas for U.S.-backed Bosnian army offensives against the Bosnian Serb forces. UN Secretary General Boutros Boutros-Ghali confirmed this in a report to the UN Security Council on May 30, 1995:

> In recent months [the U.S.-backed Bosnian] government forces have considerably increased their military activity in and around most safe areas, and many of them, including Sarajevo, Tuzla and Bihac, have been incorporated into the broader military campaign of the [Bosnian] government's side.
>
> The headquarters and the logistics installations of the Fifth Corps of the [Bosnian] government army are located in the town of Bihac and those of the Second Corps in the town of Tuzla.
>
> The government also maintains a substantial number of troops in Srebrenica (in this case a violation of a demilitarization agreement), Gorazde and Zepa, while Sarajevo is the location of the General Command of the government army and other military installations. There is also an ammunition factory in Gorazde.
>
> The Bosnian Serb forces' reaction to offensives launched by the [U.S.-backed Bosnian] government army from safe areas have generally been to respond against military targets within those areas.[18]

PRETEXT FOR NATO BOMBS

Still another explosion on August 28, 1995, at a small enclosed marketplace in Sarajevo killed thirty-seven people. It became the U.S. pretext for the most massive military action in Europe since World War II. More than four thousand U.S.-NATO military air sorties were carried out.

New York Times Washington correspondent David Binder reported in the *Nation* magazine that the explosion came the day after Assistant Secretary of State Richard Holbrooke promised more active NATO air strikes. Only an excuse was needed. Binder quotes four different military sources disputing the immediate UN report that blamed the Bosnian Serbs for the explosion.[19]

Russian artillery officer Col. Andrei Demurenko went on television in Sarajevo to denounce the UN report on the explosion as a falsification. He announced that the probability of hitting a street less than thirty feet wide from Serb artillery positions one to two miles away was "one in one million."

A Canadian specialist with extensive service in Bosnia told Binder that the fuse of the mortar shell recovered from the marketplace crater "had not come from a mortar tube at all." Two unidentified U.S. administration officials in Sarajevo explained to Binder that based on the trajectory, the shallowness of the crater, and the absence of any high-pitched distinct whistle, the shell was either fired from very close range or dropped from a nearby roof into the crowd. Although Binder is a regular correspondent for the *New York Times*, he had to go to the *Nation* with this story.

The U.S. media's outrage over the marketplace explosion in Sarajevo stands in sharp contrast to the great approval for the U.S. launch of thirteen Tomahawk cruise missiles targeting the city of Banja Luka. Banja Luka is behind the Bosnian Serb lines. It is the second-largest city in Bosnia—and the city with the most refugees of all of the former Yugoslavia. In the U.S.-NATO attack many civilians were killed and one hospital was bombed.

'END ARMS EMBARGO' MEANS WIDEN WAR

The demand to "end the arms embargo" is raised as a simple slogan of the Bosnian government's right to defend itself. Like the term "safe areas," the reality is far different. "End the arms embargo" means to legitimize thousands of U.S. troops technically training the Bosnian army in advanced military equipment, securing airports and roads for landing, and moving heavy equipment. It further involves U.S. surveillance flights and ground cover in a mountainous region where a dependent, isolated minority government currently controls small enclaves. This would greatly expand Pentagon involvement beyond the CIA training and supply level of today and the NATO air cover of more than forty thousand sorties over the past three years.

There's a struggle within the summits of U.S. power between those who want to rely on U.S./NATO bombing missions to destroy the Bosnian Serb forces and those who feel the only way to decisively control and reshape the region is through U.S. ground troops and an end to the arms embargo. Both sides of the debate seek to expand and widen the war. Both sides of the debate assert the right of U.S. finance capital to impose its solution.

WAR IS CALLED PEACE

The newly formed Action Council for Peace in the Balkans best reflects the cynical double-speak where peace means war. It is composed of the bipartisan forces of U.S. militarism that are framing the debate. Members of the Executive Council include Zbigniew Brzezinski, national security advisor under Carter; Frank Carlucci, a national security advisor and secretary of defense under Reagan; Hodding Carter, a state department spokesperson under Carter; Max Kampelman, who headed Reagan's nuclear arms team; and Jeane Kirkpatrick, Reagan's United Nations ambassador.

On July 12, 1995, this Council for Peace in the Balkans issued a call for "an end to the arms embargo against Bosnia, the withdrawal of the UN forces from Bosnia, and an effective NATO air campaign." This "peaceful" group asserts that the "air campaign" should be "strategic and sustained," not "pinprick strikes." The statement concludes, "A failure to act will be disastrous for the people of Bosnia, for the U.S., and for our vital interests in Europe."

INTER-IMPERIALIST RIVALRY

CIA and Pentagon involvement in the civil war in the Balkans has positioned the U.S. militarily in a strategic region. At the same time it has frayed the developing unity among its European imperialist rivals. These U.S. rivals bear the increasing burden of hundreds of thousands of destitute refugees, thousands of ground troops in position, and the bitter acrimony of competing interests. What appears to be a bureaucratic dispute between NATO and UN officials is in reality a struggle between the imperialist ruling class of the U.S. and its European rivals, who fear being drawn into a protracted war. Each defends its right to carve up this strategic region in accordance with its own interests. But the Europeans have troops on the ground. If their forces take casualties while the U.S. calls the shots, opposition at home will rise.

There seems to be a great deal of information on close German-U.S. collaboration at the expense of British and French interests. But even this cooperation may change. The fact that the U.S. arms and trains the Croatian troops may be a sign that Washington is asserting itself in Croatia also.

The debate on U.S.-controlled NATO forces helping to evacuate UN "peacekeepers" reflects an expanding effort to make the U.S. the only power deciding the fate of the Balkans. The determination of both France and Britain to be bigger powers in Europe now that the Cold War is over is reflected in their large commitment of troops under the UN flag throughout Bosnia. But the Pentagon has been able to frustrate the mission of the British and French troops by encouraging the Bosnian government, which is totally dependent on the U.S., to sabotage any agreements.

Washington's November 1994 decision to unilaterally end support for the UN Security Council arms embargo was the most open statement to date that it would pursue its own agenda in Bosnia at the expense of the Europeans. This decision was also at the expense of the hundreds of thousands of uprooted and displaced people caught in the crossfire.

SANCTIONS: ECONOMIC DOMINATION OF THE REGION

The UN Security Council voted to impose a sanctions blockade on the remains of the Yugoslav federation (Serbia and Montenegro) on May 30, 1992. The UN Security Council vote was rushed through to pre-empt a UN report published two days later saying that the Federal Republic of Yugoslavia was in full compliance with the UN demands that all Yugoslav Federal Army troops be withdrawn from Bosnia.

These sanctions strangling all economic life were imposed only on the Serbs, in spite of the fact that the World Court in The Hague ruled that the Federal Republic of Yugoslavia was not the aggressor in the conflict in Bosnia. UN sanctions have not been imposed on Washington's client states in the region, the Croatian and Bosnian governments. The UN Security Council did not even discuss imposing sanctions on the Croatian government in response to its August 1995 massive attack on the Krajina section of Croatia and its expulsion or "ethnic cleansing" of over two hundred thousand Serbs there.

Although the stated aim of sanctions is to end arms shipments from Serbia to the Serbs in Bosnia, U.S. and Western powers used the opportunity of enforcing the sanctions to gain control of all the roads, waterways, and communications in this strategic part of Europe. All approaches to seaports and airports are sealed off. The Pentagon now controls all navigation on the mighty Danube River—major thoroughfare of the Balkans and Eastern Europe. All shipping is restricted. The Danube is more important for Europe than the Mississippi River is for commerce in the U.S. All countries of the Danube Basin—not only Serbia but Romania, Bulgaria, Hungary, and Slovakia—thus have effectively been put under the blockade.

The Western capitalist powers are the only ones that stand to benefit from the resulting economic dislocation in a number of formerly socialist countries that are now forcibly going through privatization of their major industries and resources. Entire industrial complexes, no longer able to be competitive in the world market or even to receive raw material for production or ship their goods, can be bought for a song by multinational corporations.

Although medical and humanitarian goods are supposedly exempted, the sanctions disrupt the entire supply system— its markets, foreign trade, communications, and transport. Funds, bank accounts, and credit are frozen. Yugoslavia is a country with limited resources that is forced to cope with a flood of at last four hundred thousand refugees displaced from Croatia and Bosnia. More than 40 percent of the refugees are under eighteen years old. Basic medicines, food, fuel for cooking, heating, and running industries, and sanitation are at crisis levels.

All the imperialist powers, but particularly the U.S., recognize that Yugoslavia sets precedents for intervention in the former republics of the Soviet Union. In early December 1994, the summit of the Organization for Security and Cooperation in Europe met. Its first military action was to authorize a "peacekeeping mission" to Nagorno-Karabakh, the enclave disputed by Armenia and Azerbaijan. The stated purpose of the forces going into Nagorno-Karabakh is to prevent a Bosnia-like situation. Their track record is not encouraging.

What is at stake is ownership and control of the industries and natural resources to be privatized. In a war-torn region, all this can be bought at bargain prices. Who will control the markets, the rich resources, the rebuilding, and the new investments? Military control of the situation will be decisive. Diplomacy is only a cover for the military struggle.

THE PENTAGON PLAN

The U.S. is determined to be the dominant power in the Balkans. This thinking is best reflected in an extraordinary forty-six-page Pentagon document excerpted by the *New York Times*. The document, leaked by Pentagon officials, asserts the need for complete U.S. world domination in both political and military terms and threatens other countries that even *aspire* to a greater role. The public threats seem to be aimed at the European powers and Japan. Why else would the document be released with no disavowal by the Pentagon? This Pentagon policy document states:

> Our first objective is to prevent the re-emergence of a new rival. . . . First, the U.S. must show the leadership necessary to establish and protect a new order that holds the promise of convincing potential competitors that they need not aspire to a greater role or pursue a more aggressive posture to protect their legitimate interests.

> We must account sufficiently for the interests of the advanced industrial nations to discourage them from seeking to overturn the established political and economic order. Finally, we must maintain the mechanism for deterring potential competitors from even aspiring to a larger regional or global role.

The document goes on to specifically address Europe:

> It is of fundamental importance to preserve NATO as the primary instrument of Western defense and security. . . . We must seek to prevent the emergence of European-only security arrangements which would undermine NATO.[20]

No senior U.S. official has ever denounced or renounced this document. When then-President George Bush was asked directly about it, he said that while he hadn't read the report, "We are the leaders and we must continue to lead."

OPERATION BALKAN STORM

Just how little U.S. involvement has to do with "aiding poor Bosnia" is best seen in an opinion piece in the *New York Times* by retired Air Force Chief of Staff Gen. Michael J. Dugan entitled "Operation Balkan Storm: Here's a Plan."[21]

Dugan is best remembered for an unusually candid interview before the Gulf War where he laid out very precise plans for the destruction of Iraq. He was relieved of his command for being too frank in describing the Pentagon's war plans at a time when the U.S. was claiming to the UN that it wanted to impose sanctions on Iraq to pursue a diplomatic solution. However, four months later the war unfolded almost exactly as Dugan had described.

"A win in the Balkans would establish U.S. leadership in the post-Cold War world in a way that Operation Desert Storm never could," Dugan crowed. He laid out a scenario of coalition building, if possible, with Britain, France, and Italy on an ad-hoc basis, since the UN Security Council is deadlocked on the use of force by NATO. He described arming the pro-U.S. Bosnian forces such as those around Izetbegovic and use of "unconventional" operations in Bosnia to suspend UN humanitarian operations. Then, he said, massive air power should be used against Serbs in Bosnia and Serbia. This Air Force general likes to brag about U.S. death technology. Dugan suggested using aircraft carriers, F-15s, F-16s, F-18s, and F-111s, Tomahawk missiles, and the JSTARS surveillance system to destroy Serbia's electricity grid, refineries, storage facilities, and communications. "But the U.S. costs in blood and treasure would be modest compared with that of Bosnian trauma."

Whether it was the original U.S. legislation of November 1990, or the recognition of an independent Bosnia under a right-wing U.S.-backed government rather than the compromise government acceptable to all sides in March 1992, or the U.S.-brokered Croatian-Muslim federation of March 1994—U.S. intervention at each stage in the growing conflict in the Balkans has fanned the flames of war. Whether it is the early 1993

Vance-Owen plan to cantonize Bosnia into tiny enclaves or the Vance-Stoltenberg Plan of late 1993 for a three-way partition of Bosnia—each proposal is an assertion of U.S. determination to dominate the region and keep its imperialist rivals off guard.

Despite the many grim warnings of difficult terrain and low cloud cover, the Clinton administration has offered to send twenty-five thousand troops as a "peacekeeping" force if a U.S. plan presented in late August 1995 is imposed on the people of the region. Massive use of air power began in September 1995. Once committed, more and more troops are required in a war that can quickly escalate. There is a heated debate today in ruling military, corporate, and government circles. But it is not about how to negotiate peace. It is about how to insure U.S. domination of a strategic region.

THE ONLY SOLUTION—U.S. OUT

The analogy to U.S. CIA advisors in Vietnam followed by twenty-five thousand troops to prop up the U.S. puppet Ngo Dinh Diem comes to mind all too quickly. The war that is unfolding will not be fought in a Hollywood fantasy in front of computer screens, as the rank-and-file soldiers of other U.S. wars know so well. The trauma for millions of refugees from Southeast Asia continues to this day. It will cost much more in "blood and treasure" than General Dugan so callously estimates. A further exposé of U.S. war plans and involvement in the Balkans is desperately needed in order to open a debate and build a powerful opposition to the latest episode in the Pentagon's plans for world domination.

Concerned people of every political persuasion, when confronted with the gruesome images of the war, ask, "Doesn't the U.S. government have a responsibility to do something to stop the bloodshed?" Or the question is posed, "How can the U.S. bring peace?"

The U.S. economy today is completely dependent on and intertwined with militarism. U.S. military spending is larger than the military budgets of all the other countries of the world combined. Most U.S. corporations are dependent in one way or another on the profits of war and militarism. More than $250 billion a year is spent on militarism. This is the only area of the federal budget not facing drastic cuts.

The implications of greater and greater military involvement are not discussed with working and poor people here in the U.S. Yet the decisions will impact on the lives of every one in this country, in the form of further cutbacks in desperately needed social services.

All the many nationalities of the former Yugoslavia have shown from past experience that they are capable of resolving their differences. They lived together in peace and harmony for forty-five years under a socialist federation. Although more than one million people died and millions were uprooted during World War II, driving out the imperialist invaders became a unifying force that galvanized all the many divided nationalities.

U.S. involvement in the Balkans is not about helping any of the people in the region—Muslims, Croats, Serbs, or Albanians. The only interest of the Pentagon is in creating weak, dependent puppet regimes in order to dominate the entire region economically and politically. Only the giant multinational corporations will benefit.

The only demand for those genuinely concerned with peace is, "U.S. out, NATO out." The involvement of the Pentagon can only bring wider war, more death and destruction, shattered lives, and hundreds of thousands of additional refugees. The same demand needs to be raised by the anti-war movements in each of the West European countries—Germany, France, Britain, and Italy. They and the U.S. are imperialist powers, meaning that the highest profits of the corporations of these capitalist countries come from their investments and economic control of other less developed countries.

It is not an easy task to build an anti-war movement. It must combat all the lies of the corporate media. But it has been done before. As the war widens and the cutbacks in education, health care, and housing continue here in the U.S., this idea will take root.

The only way to end the Vietnam war was for the U.S. to get out. The years and years of negotiations were only an excuse to widen the war, continue the bombing, and further the intervention. By the end of the war, all of Indochina lay in ruins, the landscape pockmarked with bomb craters and poisoned with Agent Orange. Getting the U.S. and the other imperialists out of the Balkans is the only way to keep this war from escalating into an even wider struggle that would engulf the whole region.

---

[1] CIA report described in the *New York Times*, Nov. 28, 1990.

[2] *New York Newsday*, 19 December 1994.

[3] See p. 134 of Gregory Elich's essay in this book.

[4] Jacques Merlino, *Les Vérités yugoslaves ne sont pas toutes bonnes à dire* (*The Truth from Yugoslavia Is Not Easy to Report*) (Paris: Editions Albin Michel S.A., 1993). Unofficial translation.

[5] *New York Times*, 19 October 1993.

[6] *Newsweek*, 4 January 1993.

[7] *New York Times*, 15 January 1993.

[8] *USA Today*, 13 January 1993.

[9] *New York Times*, 17 June 1993.

[10] Gen. Charles G. Boyd, "Making Peace with the Guilty: The Truth about Bosnia," *Foreign Affairs*, September/October 1995, p. 22.

[11] *Washington Post*, 30 April 1994.

[12] *New York Times*, 24 June 1994.

[13] *New York Times*, 24 April 1994.

[14] Reuters, 18 February 1994.

[15] *New York Times*, 10 November 1994.

[16] *Independent*, 6 August 1995.

[17] *Times*, 5 August 1995.

[18] UN Document S/1995/444, 30 May 1995.

[19] David Binder, "Bosnia's Bombers," *The Nation*, 2 October 1995.

[20] Excerpted in the *New York Times*, 8 March 1992.

[21] *New York Times*, 29 November 1992.

PART TWO

BACKGROUND TO THE BREAKUP OF YUGOSLAVIA

4 Dismantling Yugoslavia, colonizing Bosnia

MICHEL CHOSSUDOVSKY[*]

As heavily armed U.S. and NATO troops enforce the peace in Bosnia, the press and politicians alike portray Western intervention in the former Yugoslavia as a noble, if agonizingly belated, response to an outbreak of ethnic massacres and human rights violations. In the wake of the November 1995 Dayton peace accords, the West is eager to touch up its self-portrait as savior of the Southern Slavs and get on with "the work of rebuilding" the newly sovereign states. But following a pattern set early on, Western public opinion has been misled. The conventional wisdom holds that the plight of the Balkans is the outcome of an "aggressive nationalism," the inevitable result of deep-seated ethnic and religious tensions rooted in history.[1] Likewise, commentators cite "Balkan power-plays" and the clash of political personalities to explain the conflicts.[2]

Lost in the barrage of images and self-serving analyses are the economic and social causes of the conflict. The deep-seated economic crisis which preceded the civil war is long forgotten.

---

[*] This article appeared originally in *Covert Action Quarterly*, No. 56, Spring 1996.

The strategic interests of Germany and the U.S. in laying the groundwork for the disintegration of Yugoslavia go unmentioned, as does the role of external creditors and international financial institutions. In the eyes of the global media, Western powers bear no responsibility for the impoverishment and destruction of a nation of twenty-four million people.

But through their domination of the global financial system, the Western powers, in pursuit of national and collective strategic interests, helped bring the Yugoslav economy to its knees and stirred simmering ethnic and social conflicts. Now it is the turn of Yugoslavia's war-ravaged successor states to feel the tender mercies of the international financial community.

As the world focuses on troop movements and cease fires, the international financial institutions are busily collecting former Yugoslavia's external debt from its remnant states, while transforming the Balkans into a safe-haven for free enterprise. With a Bosnian peace settlement holding under NATO guns, the West has unveiled a "reconstruction" program that strips that brutalized country of sovereignty to a degree not seen in Europe since the end of World War II. It consists largely of making Bosnia a divided territory under NATO military occupation and Western administration.

NEOCOLONIAL BOSNIA

Resting on the Dayton Accords, which created a Bosnian "constitution," the U.S. and the European Union have installed a full-fledged colonial administration in Bosnia. At its head is their appointed High Representative, Carl Bildt, a former Swedish prime minister and European Union representative in Bosnian peace negotiations.[3] Bildt has full executive powers in all civilian matters, with the right to overrule the governments of both the Bosnian Federation and the Republika Srpska (Serbian Bosnia). To make the point crystal clear, the accords spell out that "The High Representative is the final authority in theater regarding interpretation of the agreements."[4] He will work with NATO's Military High Command of the Implementation Force/Operation Joint Endeavor (IFOR) as well as creditors and donors.

The UN Security Council has also appointed a "commissioner" under the High Representative to run an international civilian police force. Irish police official Peter Fitzgerald, with previous UN policing experience in Namibia, El Salvador, and Cambodia,[5] presides over some 1,700 policemen from fifteen countries. The police will be dispatched to Bosnia after a five-day training program in Zagreb.[6]

The new constitution hands the reins of economic policy over to the Bretton Woods institutions and the London-based European Bank for Reconstruction and Development (EBRD). The IMF is empowered to appoint the first governor of the Bosnian Central Bank, who, like the High Representative, "shall not be a citizen of Bosnia and Herzegovina or a neighboring State."[7]

Under the IMF regency, the Central Bank will not be allowed to function as a Central Bank: "For the first six years . . . it may not extend credit by creating money, operating in this respect as a currency board." Neither will Bosnia be allowed to have its own currency (issuing paper money only when there is full foreign exchange backing), nor permitted to mobilize its internal resources.[8] Its ability to self-finance its reconstruction through an independent monetary policy is blunted from the outset.

While the Central Bank is in IMF custody, the European Bank for Reconstruction and Development heads the Commission on Public Corporations, which supervises operations of all public sector corporations, including energy, water, postal services, telecommunications, and transportation. The EBRD president appoints the commission's chair and will direct public sector restructuring, meaning primarily the sell-off of state and socially-owned assets and the procurement of long term investment funds.[9] Western creditors explicitly created the EBRD "to give a distinctively political dimension to lending."[10]

As the West trumpets its support for democracy, actual political power rests in the hands of a parallel Bosnian "state" whose executive positions are held by non-citizens. Western creditors have embedded their interests in a constitution hastily written on their behalf. They have done so without a constitutional assembly, without consultations with Bosnian citizens' organizations and without providing a means of amending this "constitution." Their plans to rebuild Bosnia appear more suited to sating creditors than satisfying even the elementary needs of Bosnians.

And why not? The neocolonization of Bosnia is the logical culmination of long Western efforts to undo Yugoslavia's experiment in market socialism and workers' self-management and impose in its place the diktat of the free market.

SHAPE OF THINGS TO COME

Multi-ethnic, socialist Yugoslavia was once a regional industrial power and economic success. In the two decades prior to 1980, annual GDP growth averaged 6.1 percent, medical care was free, the literacy rate was of the order of 91 percent, and the life expectancy was seventy-two years.[11] But after a decade of Western economic ministrations and five years of disintegration, war, boycott, and embargo, the economies of the former Yugoslavia are prostrate, their industrial sectors dismantled.

Yugoslavia's implosion was in part due to U.S. machinations. Despite Belgrade's non-alignment and its extensive trading relations with the European Community and the U.S., the Reagan administration targeted the Yugoslav economy in a "Secret Sensitive" 1984 National Security Decision Directive (NSDD 133), "United States Policy toward Yugoslavia." A censored version declassified in 1990 largely elaborated on NSDD 54 on Eastern Europe, issued in 1982. The latter advocated "expanded efforts to promote a 'quiet revolution' to overthrow Communist governments and parties" while reintegrating the countries of Eastern Europe into a market-oriented economy.[12]

The U.S. had earlier joined Belgrade's other international creditors in imposing a first round of macroeconomic reform in 1980, shortly before the death of Marshal Tito. Successive IMF-sponsored programs since then continued the disintegration of the industrial sector and the piecemeal dismantling of the Yugoslav welfare state. Debt restructuring agreements increased foreign debt, and a mandated currency devaluation also hit hard at Yugoslavs' standard of living.

This initial round of restructuring set the pattern. Throughout the 1980s, the IMF prescribed further doses of its bitter economic medicine periodically as the Yugoslav economy slowly lapsed into a coma. Industrial production declined to a negative 10 percent growth rate by 1990[13]—with all its predictable social consequences.

MR. MARKOVIC GOES TO WASHINGTON

In autumn 1989, just before the fall of the Berlin Wall, Yugoslav federal Premier Ante Markovic met in Washington with President George Bush to cap negotiations for a new financial aid package. In return for assistance, Yugoslavia agreed to even more sweeping economic reforms, including a new devalued currency, another wage freeze, sharp cuts in government spending, and the elimination of socially-owned, worker-managed companies.[14] The Belgrade nomenklatura, with the assistance of Western advisors, had laid the groundwork for the prime minister's mission by implementing beforehand many of the required reforms, including a major liberalization of foreign investment legislation.

"Shock therapy" began in January 1990. Although inflation had eaten away at earnings, the IMF ordered that wages be frozen at their mid-November 1989 level. Prices continued to rise unabated, and real wages collapsed by 41 percent in the first six months of 1990.[15]

The IMF also effectively controlled the Yugoslav central bank. Its tight money policy further crippled federal Yugoslavia's ability to finance its economic and social programs. State revenues that should have gone as transfer payments to the republics and provinces went instead to service Belgrade's debt with the Paris and London clubs. The republics were largely left to their own devices.

In one fell swoop, the reformers engineered the final collapse of Yugoslavia's federal fiscal structure and mortally wounded its federal political institutions. By cutting the financial arteries between Belgrade and the republics, the reforms fueled secessionist tendencies that fed on economic factors as well as ethnic divisions and virtually ensured the de facto secession of the republics. The IMF-induced budgetary crisis created an economic fait accompli that paved the way for Croatia's and Slovenia's formal secession in June 1991.

CRUSHED BY THE INVISIBLE HAND

The reforms demanded by Belgrade's creditors also struck at the heart of Yugoslavia's system of socially-owned and worker-managed enterprises. As one observer noted:

> The objective was to subject the Yugoslav economy to massive privatization and the dismantling of the public sector. The Communist Party bureaucracy, most notably its military and intelligence sector, was canvassed specifically and offered political and economic backing on the condition that wholesale scuttling of social protections for Yugoslavia's work force was imposed. [16]

It was an offer that a desperate Yugoslavia could not refuse. Advised by Western lawyers and consultants, Markovic's government passed financial legislation that forced "insolvent" businesses into bankruptcy or liquidation. Under the new law, if a business were unable to pay its bills for 30 days running, or for thirty days within a forty-five-day period, the government would launch bankruptcy procedures within the next fifteen days.

The assault on the socialist economy also included a new banking law designed to trigger the liquidation of the socially owned "Associated Banks." Within two years, more than half the country's banks had vanished, to be replaced by newly-formed "independent profit-oriented institutions."

These changes in the legal framework, combined with the IMF's tight money policy toward industry and the opening of the economy to foreign competition, accelerated industrial decline. From 1989 through September 1990, more than a thousand companies went into bankruptcy. By 1990, the annual rate of growth of GDP had collapsed to *minus* 7.5 percent. In 1991, GDP declined by a further 15 percent, while industrial output shrank by 21 percent.[17]

The IMF package unquestionably precipitated the collapse of much of Yugoslavia's well-developed heavy industry. Other socially-owned enterprises survived only by not paying workers. More than half a million workers still on company payrolls did not get regular paychecks in late 1990. They were the lucky ones. Some six hundred thousand Yugoslavs had already lost their jobs by September 1990, and that was only the beginning. According to the World Bank, another 2,435 industrial enterprises, including some of the country's largest, were slated for liquidation. Their 1.3 million workers—half the remaining industrial work force—were "redundant."[18]

As 1991 dawned, real wages were in free fall, social programs had collapsed, and unemployment ran rampant. The dismantling of the industrial economy was breathtaking in its magnitude and brutality. Its social and political impact, while not as easily quantified, was tremendous. "The pips are squeaking," as London's patrician *Financial Times* put it.[19]

Less archly, Yugoslav President Borisav Jovic warned that the reforms were "having a markedly unfavorable impact on the overall situation in society. . . . Citizens have lost faith in the state and its institutions. . . . The further deepening of the economic crisis and the growth of social tensions has had a vital impact on the deterioration of the political-security situation."[20]

POLITICAL ECONOMY OF DISINTEGRATION

Some Yugoslavs joined together in a doomed battle to prevent the destruction of their economy and polity. As one observer found, "Worker resistance crossed ethnic lines, as Serbs, Croats, Bosnians and Slovenians mobilized ... shoulder to shoulder with their fellow workers."[21] But the economic struggle also heightened already tense relations among the republics—and between the republics and Belgrade.

Serbia rejected the austerity plan outright, and some 650,000 Serbian workers struck against the federal government to force wage hikes.[22] The other republics followed different and sometimes self-contradictory paths.

In relatively wealthy Slovenia, for instance, secessionist leaders such as Social Democratic party chair Joze Pucnik supported the reforms: "From an economic standpoint, I can only agree with socially harmful measures in our society, such as rising unemployment or cutting workers' rights, because they are necessary to advance the economic reform process."[23]

But at the same time, Slovenia joined other republics in challenging the federal government's efforts to restrict their economic autonomy. Both Croatian leader Franjo Tudjman and Serbia's Slobodan Milosevic joined Slovene leaders in railing against Yugoslavia's attempts to impose harsh reforms.[24]

In the multi-party elections in 1990, economic policy was at the center of the political debate as separatist coalitions ousted the Communists in Croatia, Bosnia and Slovenia. Just as economic collapse spurred the drift toward separation, the separation in turn exacerbated the economic crisis. Cooperation among the republics virtually ceased. And with the republics at each others' throats, both the economy and the nation itself embarked on a vicious downward spiral.

The process sped downward as the republics' leaderships deliberately fostered social and economic divisions to strengthen their own hands: "The republican oligarchies, who all had visions of a 'national renaissance' of their own, instead of choosing between a genuine Yugoslav market and hyperinflation, opted for war which would disguise the real causes of the economic catastrophe."[25] The simultaneous appearance of militias loyal to secessionist leaders only hastened the descent into chaos. These militias, with their escalating atrocities, not only split the population along ethnic lines, they also fragmented the workers' movement.[26]

WESTERN HELP

The austerity measures had laid the basis for the recolonization of the Balkans. Whether that required the breakup of Yugoslavia was subject to debate among the Western powers, with Germany leading the push for secession and the U.S., fearful of opening a nationalist Pandora's box, originally arguing for Yugoslavia's preservation.

Following the decisive victory of Franjo Tudjman and the rightist Democratic Union in Croatia in May 1990, German Foreign Minister Hans Dietrich Genscher, in almost daily contacts with his counterpart in Zagreb, gave his go-ahead for Croatian secession.[27] Germany did not passively support secession; it "forced the pace of international diplomacy" and pressured its Western allies to recognize Slovenia and Croatia. Germany sought a free hand among its allies "to pursue economic dominance in the whole of Mitteleuropa."[28]

Washington, on the other hand, favored "a loose unity while encouraging democratic development. . . . Secretary of State] Baker told Tudjman and [Slovenia's President] Milan Kucan that the United States would not encourage or support unilateral secession . . . but if they had to leave, he urged them to leave by a negotiated agreement."[29]

Instead, Slovenia, Croatia, and finally, Bosnia fought bloody civil wars against "rump" Yugoslavia (Serbia and Montenegro) or Serbian nationalists or both. But now, the U.S. has belatedly taken an active diplomatic role in Bosnia, strengthened its relations with Croatia, and Macedonia, and positioned itself to play a leading role in the region's economic and political future.

THE POST-WAR REGIME

Western creditors have now turned their attention to Yugoslavia's successor states. As with the demise of Yugoslavia, the economic aspects of post-war reconstruction remain largely unheralded, but the prospects for rebuilding the newly independent republics appear bleak. Yugoslavia's foreign debt has been carefully divided and allocated to the successor republics,[30] which are now strangled in separate debt rescheduling and structural adjustment agreements.

The consensus among donors and international agencies is that past macroeconomic reforms adopted under IMF advice had not quite met their goal and further shock therapy is required to restore "economic health" in Yugoslavia's successor states. Croatia and Macedonia have followed the IMF's direction. Both have agreed to loan packages—to pay off their shares of the Yugoslav debt—which require a consolidation of the process begun with Ante Markovic's bankruptcy program. The too familiar pattern of plant closings, induced bank failures, and impoverishment continues apace.

And global capital applauds. Despite an emerging crisis in social welfare and the decimation of his economy, Macedonian Finance Minister Ljube Trpevski proudly informed the press that "the World Bank and the IMF place Macedonia among the most successful countries in regard to current transition reforms."[31]

The head of the IMF mission to Macedonia, Paul Thomsen, agreed. He avowed that "the results of the stabilization program were impressive" and gave particular credit to "the efficient wages policy" adopted by the Skopje government. Still, his negotiators added, even more budget cutting will be necessary.[32]

But Western intervention is making its most serious inroads on national sovereignty in Bosnia. The neocolonial administration imposed by the Dayton Accords, supported by NATO's firepower, ensures that Bosnia's future will be determined in Washington, Bonn, and Brussels—not Sarajevo.

RECONSTRUCTION COLONIAL-STYLE

If Bosnia is ever to emerge from the ravages of war and neocolonialism, massive reconstruction will be essential. But judging by recent Balkan history, Western assistance is more likely to drag Bosnia into the Third World rather than lift it to parity with its European neighbors.

The Bosnian government estimates that reconstruction costs will reach $47 billion. Western donors have pledged $3 billion in reconstruction loans, yet only $518 million have so far been granted. Part of this money is tagged to finance some of the local civilian costs of IFOR's military deployment and part to repay international creditors.[33]

Fresh loans will pay back old debt. The Central Bank of the Netherlands has generously provided "bridge financing" of $37 million to allow Bosnia to pay its arrears with the IMF, without which the IMF will not lend it fresh money. But in a cruel and absurd paradox, the sought-after loans from the IMF's newly created "Emergency Window" for "post-conflict countries" will not be used for post-war reconstruction. Instead, they will repay the Dutch Central Bank, which had coughed up the money to settle IMF arrears in the first place.[34] Debt piles up, and little new money goes for rebuilding Bosnia's war-torn economy.

While rebuilding is sacrificed on the altar of debt repayment, Western governments and corporations show greater interest in gaining access to strategic natural resources. With the discovery of energy reserves in the region, the partition of Bosnia between the Federation of Bosnia-Herzegovina and the Bosnian-Serb Republika Srpska under the Dayton Accords has taken on new strategic importance. Documents in the hands of Croatia and the Bosnian Serbs indicate that coal and oil deposits have been identified on the eastern slope of the Dinarides Thrust, retaken from rebel Krajina Serbs by the U.S.-backed Croatian army in the final offensives before the Dayton Accords. Bosnian officials report that Chicago-based Amoco was

among several foreign firms that subsequently initiated explora-
tory surveys in Bosnia.[35]

"Substantial" petroleum fields also lie in the Serb-held
part of Croatia just across the Sava river from Tuzla, the headquarters for the U.S. military zone.[36] Exploration operations
went on during the war, but the World Bank and the multina-
tionals which conducted the operations kept local governments
in the dark, presumably to prevent them from acting to grab
potentially valuable areas.[37]

With their attention devoted to debt repayment and potential energy bonanzas, the Western powers have shown little
interest in rectifying the crimes committed under the rubric of
ethnic cleansing. The seventy thousand NATO troops on hand
to "enforce the peace" will accordingly devote their efforts to
administering the partition of Bosnia in accordance with Western economic interests rather than restoring the status quo ante.

While local leaders and Western interests share the
spoils of the former Yugoslav economy, they have entrenched
socio-ethnic divisions in the very structure of partition. This
permanent fragmentation of Yugoslavia along ethnic lines
serves to thwart a united resistance of Yugoslavs of all ethnic
origins against the recolonization of their homeland.

But what's new? As one observer caustically noted, all
of the leaders of Yugoslavia's successor states have worked
closely with the West: "All the current leaders of the former
Yugoslav republics were Communist Party functionaries and
each in turn vied to meet the demands of the World Bank and
the International Monetary Fund, the better to qualify for investment loans and substantial perks for the leadership."[38]

Western-backed neoliberal macroeconomic restructuring
helped destroy Yugoslavia. Yet, since the onset of war in 1991,
the global media has carefully overlooked or denied its central
role. Instead, it has joined the chorus singing praises of the free
market as the basis for rebuilding a war-shattered economy. The
social and political impact of economic restructuring in Yugoslavia has been carefully erased from our collective understand-

ing. Opinion-makers instead dogmatically present cultural, ethnic, and religious divisions as the sole cause of the crisis. In reality, they are the consequence of a much deeper process of economic and political fracturing.

This false consciousness not only masks the truth, it also prevents us from acknowledging precise historical occurrences.

Ultimately it distorts the true sources of social conflict. When applied to the former Yugoslavia, it obscures the historical foundations of South Slavic unity, solidarity and identity. But this false consciousness lives worldwide, where the only possible world is one of shuttered factories, jobless workers, and gutted social programs, and "bitter economic medicine" is the only prescription.

At stake in the Balkans are the lives of millions of people. Macroeconomic reform there has destroyed livelihoods and made a joke of the right to work. It has put basic needs such as food and shelter beyond the reach of many. It has degraded culture and national identity. In the name of global capital, borders have been redrawn, legal codes rewritten, industries destroyed, financial and banking systems dismantled, social programs eliminated. No alternative to global capital, be it market socialism or "national" capitalism, will be allowed to exist.

But what happened to Yugoslavia—and now continues in its weak successor states—should resonate beyond the Balkans. Yugoslavia is a mirror for similar economic restructuring programs in not only the developing world but also in the U.S., Canada and Western Europe.

The Yugoslav reforms are the cruel reflection of a destructive economic model pushed to the extreme.

---

[1] See, e.g., former U.S. Ambassador to Yugoslavia Warren Zimmerman, "The Last Ambassador, A Memoir of the Collapse of Yugoslavia," *Foreign Affairs*, v. 74, n. 2, 1995.

[2] For a critique, see Milos Vasic, *et al.*, "War Against Bosnia," *Vreme News Digest Agency*, 13 April 1992.

[3] Testimony of Richard C. Holbrooke, Assistant Secretary of State, Bureau of European and Canadian Affairs, before the Senate Appropriations Committee, Subcommittee on Foreign Operations, 19 December 1995.

[4] *Dayton Peace Accords*, "Agreement on High Representative," Articles I and II, 15 December 1995.

[5] United Nations General Secretariat, *Curriculum Vitae of Thomas Peter Fitzgerald*, n.d. (1995).

[6] *Dayton Peace Accords*, "Agreement on International Police Task Force," Article II.

[7] *Ibid.*, "Agreement on General Framework," Article VII.

[8] *Ibid.*

[9] *Ibid.*, "Agreement on Public Corporations," Article I.

[10] "Stabilising Europe," *The Times* (London), 22 November 1990.

[11] World Bank, *World Development Report 1991*, Statistical Annex, Tables 1 and 2, 1991.

[12] Sean Gervasi, "Germany, the U.S., and the Yugoslav Crisis," *Covert Action*, n. 43, Winter 1992-93, p. 42.

[13] World Bank, *Industrial Restructuring Study: Overview, Issues, and Strategy for Restructuring*, Washington, DC, June 1991, pp. 10, 14.

[14] Gervasi, *op. cit.*, p. 44.

[15] World Bank, *Restructuring, op. cit.*, p. viii.

[16] Ralph Schoenman, "Divide and Rule Schemes in the Balkans," *The Organizer* (San Francisco), 11 September 1995.

[17] Judith Kiss, "Debt Management in Eastern Europe," *Eastern European Economics*, May-June 1994, p. 59.

[18] Already laid-off and "redundant" workers constituted fully two-thirds of the industrial workforce. World Bank, *Restructuring, op. cit.*, Annex I.

[19] Jurek Martin, "The road to be trodden to Kosovo," *Financial Times*, 13 March 1991.

[20] British Broadcasting Service, "Borisav Jovic Tells SFRY Assembly Situation Has 'Dramatically Deteriorated,'" 27 April 1991.

[21] Schoenman, *op. cit.*

[22] Gervasi, *op. cit.*, p. 44.

[23] Federico Nier-Fischer, "Eastern Europe: Social Crisis," *InterPress Service*, 5 September 1990.

[24] Klas Bergman, "Markovic Seeks to Keep Yugoslavia One Nation," *Christian Science Monitor*, 11 July 1990, p. 6.

[25] Dimitrije Boarov, "A Brief Review of Anti-Inflation Programs: the Curse of the Dead Programs," *Vreme News Digest Agency*, 13 April 1992.

[26] *Ibid.*

[27] Gervasi, *op. cit.*, p. 65.

[28] *Ibid.*, p. 45.

[29] Zimmerman, *op. cit.*

[30] In June 1995, the IMF, acting on behalf of creditor banks and Western governments, proposed to redistribute that debt as follows: Serbia and

Montenegro, 36 percent; Croatia, 28 percent; Slovenia, 16 percent; Bosnia-Herzegovina, 16 percent; and Macedonia, 5 percent.

[31] *Macedonian Information Liaison Service News*, 11 April 1995.

[32] *Ibid.*

[33] "The Government of the Republic of Bosnia and Herzegovina shall provide, free of cost, such facilities NATO needs for the preparation and execution of the Operation" (Annex 1-A). Under the accord, NATO personnel will pay no Bosnian taxes, including sales taxes.

[34] *United Press International*, "IMF to admit Bosnia on Wednesday," 18 December 1995.

[35] Frank Viviano and Kenneth Howe, "Bosnia Leaders Say Nation Atop Oil Fields," *San Francisco Chronicle*, 28 August 1995; Scott Cooper, "Western Aims in Ex-Yugoslavia Unmasked," *The Organizer*, 24 September 1995.

[36] Viviano and Howe, *ibid.*

[37] Cooper, *op. cit.*

[38] Schoenman, *op. cit.*

5 How imperialism broke up the Yugoslav Socialist Federation

SAM MARCY[*]

It is impossible to seriously consider the Yugoslav situation without first taking into account some pertinent aspects of history and politics.

The imperialist conspiracy to break up the Socialist Federation of Yugoslavia didn't start yesterday. It didn't start with the UN Security Council voting for sanctions. It didn't start with the earlier meeting of the European Economic Community in Spain. It started a long time ago, when the Anti-Fascist Council of National Liberation of Yugoslavia (AVNOJ), led by Tito (Josip Broz) and the Communist Party, defeated the royalist and reactionary forces of Col. Draza Mihajlovic and his Chetniks.

The front mobilized the workers, peasants, progressive intellectuals, and thousands of middle-class people into the Par-

---

[*] This article originally appeared in *Workers World* newspaper, 11 June 1992.

tisan guerrilla army that defeated the German Nazi and Italian fascist invaders and their quisling regimes.

The U.S. and the British until 1943 recognized Mihajlovic and his royalist, reactionary coalition and refused recognition to the representatives of the Yugoslav people organized in the AVNOJ. Then, seeing that the progressive and revolutionary forces were on the verge of scoring a historic victory, the imperialists suddenly changed sides and began to give token support to the Partisans. They did so largely to disrupt the socialist solidarity between the Yugoslav leaders and the Soviet Union.

The very same forces that fought in Yugoslavia against the revolution, particularly the royalist riffraff and pro-fascist groupings, have all these years been promoted, secured, cultivated, and supported financially by the U.S. and European imperialists. Now they are being pushed forward as an authentic leadership to replace the Yugoslav government in Belgrade.

MONARCHIST DEMOCRATS?

In recent days, the imperialist press have written about a "democratic opposition" in Serbia. Who are they?

There is the "Democratic Movement of Serbia, which embraces the old monarchy and enjoys the support of many Serbian traditionalists."[1] What are these monarchist traditions? Suppression of the Serbian people! These idle rich have for decades been living it up in the decadent casinos and watering places of Europe.

"Crown Prince Alexander—the son of the last king of Yugoslavia who was forced into exile during World War II— met recently in Washington with senior White House and State Department officials. This week he expressed his willingness to preside over a constitutional monarchy in cooperation with the democratic movement and spoke of a coalition government that would fall into the mainstream of European democracy. It seems likely that the opposition will win the backing of the

Serbian Orthodox Church, which reportedly has dispatched senior clerics to meet with the prince."[2]

This stooge, who is ordered around by U.S. imperialism like an errand boy, has expressed his willingness to head up a "democratic government." And giving him their blessing are the reactionary clergy that supported the Mihajlovic forces. This "Democratic Movement of Serbia" is nothing but the old reactionaries in a new form. They are now boycotting the elections in Serbia because they haven't got the forces to contest them. The sanctions against Serbia just passed* by the UN Security Council—the same council that okayed sanctions and then outright imperialist war against Iraq—are timed to coincide with and disrupt the elections.

An editorial headed "Popular Opposition" (!) in the *Financial Times* of London calls for the isolation of Serbia: "The demonstration inside Belgrade by some fifty thousand anti-war protesters was an indication that popular opposition to [Serbian leader Slobodan Milosevic's] policies is growing, at least in the capital. However, the peace movement in Serbia is mainly middle-class based."[3] In other words, it's a bourgeois, pro-capitalist, pro-imperialist opposition. The demonstrations seem to be precisely timed to undermine the government of Milosevic.

"It would be an illusion to believe," concedes the London big business paper, "that it finds much of an echo in the rural Serb and Montenegrin population, not least the Serbs in Bosnia who look on the Belgrade government as their main protector and champion." A valuable admission from the mouth of the enemy. What's missing here is any word on the attitude of the workers. Notwithstanding the political confusion caused by the maneuvers of the principal imperialist powers involved in the current struggle, the workers are supporting the Yugoslav government.

Most deeply involved among the European imperialist powers are the Germans and Austrians and, to a lesser extent,

---

* On May 30, 1992.

France and Italy. That's who dominated the European Community conference on the Balkans held recently in Spain. The U.S. at first feigned disinterest in this struggle. Back on March 31, 1991, "U.S. President George Bush wrote to Ante Markovic, the [Yugoslav] federal premier, expressing his support for a united Yugoslavia and warning that those who seceded unilaterally would not be rewarded by the U.S., a warning clearly directed against Croatia and Slovenia."[4] However, "On June 25, first Croatia and then Slovenia proclaimed its independence. Two days later, the [Yugoslav army] attacked Slovene border posts that had been taken over by the Slovene Territorial Army and customs officials. Fighting extended to other parts of Slovenia. . . ."[5] Germany then "set off a campaign to recognize Croatian independence."[6]

The U.S. seemed to be outmaneuvered and to have lost interest in this struggle, in which Germany was the principal actor through the medium of the European Community. However, the apparent ambiguity of the U.S. was ended when in September Cyrus Vance, U.S. Secretary of State under President Jimmy Carter, was appointed special UN envoy to Yugoslavia. Now Washington was fully in it. Germany made it clear it would recognize Slovenia and Croatia. By December 23, 1991, Bosnia-Herzegovina and Macedonia indicated they, too, were moving toward secession.

IMPERIALISM AND SELF-DETERMINATION

What is the Leninist point of view in a case like this? Is the secession of these republics from Yugoslavia an example of self-determination?

Each and every nation has a right to determine its destiny. This can mean integration; it can mean joining in a federation; it can also mean exercising the right to leave, to secession. In any case, it has to express the will of the nation or nationality. But when the choice is the product of external imperialist pressures of an economic, political, and even military character, that is another matter.

Was the president of Croatia defending genuine self-determination when he openly called for the U.S. Sixth Fleet to come to Dubrovnik?[7]

The strategy of the imperialists has been to lure the republics away from the Yugoslav federation. But they are not united. There is a struggle between Germany and the U.S. over who will get the dominant position in the entire Balkan area. Each has its own forum. Germany and the U.S. are both seeking to make pawns of the republics. The U.S. may at one time support the Yugoslav Federal Republic but later come out against it; Germany may support Croatia and Slovenia at one point and later change. It all depends strictly on the military and political exigencies of the situation. But each is attempting to win overall control for itself.

RICH VS. POOR REPUBLICS

As in so many other areas of the world, there is a more developed so-called northern part of Yugoslavia where the bourgeoisie is stronger, and a southern, poorer part. Slovenia and Croatia are more developed, whereas Bosnia-Herzegovina, Macedonia and Montenegro, as well as the province of Kosovo in Serbia, are less developed.

As of 1975, Croatia was the most industrialized and prosperous. "More than one-third of Croatia is forested and lumber is a major export. The region is the leading coal producer of Yugoslavia and also has deposits of bauxite, copper, petroleum and iron ore. The republic is the most industrialized and prosperous area of Yugoslavia."[8] Since then, Slovenia has overtaken Croatia as the most developed.

Henry Kamm wrote in the *New York Times* about the rich-poor split in Yugoslavia. "The southern republics—Bosnia-Herzegovina, Macedonia, Montenegro as well as the province of Kosovo—are subsidized by the more prosperous areas through a federal fund and direct contributions. . . . Slovenia [is aware] that its 2 million people have the highest level of economic development among the republics and provinces that make up the federal country of 23 million. Slovenia is a small Slavic republic. The economic crisis has sharpened the contrast between the rich and the poor."[9]

Kamm interviewed people in Slovenia who resented the southern republics. Milos Kobe said, "Fantastic sums go to the south and they don't know how to use them economically." A man named Kmecl told the U.S. reporter, "We cannot invest in renewal because our capital is going for the development of the underdeveloped. A small country like this cannot afford this. After forty years of this policy, [the southern republics] are still not developed and we can't maintain the pace. We're immobilized. A technologically highly developed society like Slovenia needs always more for its own science and culture while the underdeveloped need more for social protection than they produce."

We have heard this refrain before. It sounds just like the rich bourgeois elements in any capitalist country who complain that they have to subsidize the poor. They forget that their riches come from the sweat and blood of the workers in every one of these republics and that they became industrialized only because of the socialization of the means of production and centralized planning. This is what protected them from the ravages of imperialist penetration. The federation was like a security blanket that helped them develop.

The imperialists have lured the bourgeois elements of Slovenia and Croatia in particular with the promise of becoming an integral part of the European Community and sharing in its alleged prosperity. They think they'll get a market for their products and be able to deal with the West Europeans on an equal basis, without being "encumbered" by the poorer republics in the federation. All of them, including Serbia, are being lured to invest their foreign exchange in Europe or America, thereby becoming (they hope) a prosperous part of the imperialist system.

The imperialists have already succeeded in getting the Yugoslavs to invest large sums in the West. "The central bank of Yugoslavia won an important battle in a lawsuit against Drexel, Burnham, Lambert and some of its top executives," writes the *New York Times*. The Yugoslav bank "contended it had been tricked by Drexel into providing $70 million that had been used in a failed effort to shore up the failed firm."[10]

The Europeans' strategy is to promise the bourgeois elements all sorts of things once they are part of the European Community. And while Washington wants to win these republics over to itself, it would still prefer that they be with the Europeans than that they remain in a Yugoslavia with the potential for reconstituting a socialist federation.

The *Financial Times* of London editorialized to its fellow imperialists on the Continent: "[W]hatever action is finally decided, it is essential that it should be taken by the international community as a whole, including the U.S., which alone has the clout to bring the transgressors of international law to heel. Anything less, as has been proved conclusively, is doomed to failure."[11] In other words, Wall Street is the boss and you'd better include them in any move against Yugoslavia.

SOCIALIST FEDERATION A GREAT BREAKTHROUGH

It is impossible to understand the situation in Yugoslavia if we accept the imperialist premise that what has happened is merely the surfacing of national antagonisms that had been smothered or driven underground following the Yugoslav Revolution.

The establishment of the socialist federation of Yugoslavia was a historic victory. For the first time, a united front of the Balkan countries was formed that was able to detach them from imperialist domination, either Allied or Axis. It was the product of a revolutionary upsurge that engulfed the working-class movements of Europe. The federation developed over a period of years. Its collective presidency was a progressive new political conception. Each republic had an opportunity to run the federation for a specified time and in rotation. The same concept prevailed in the structure of the Communist parties.

They were also organized on the basis of the collective principle that the party in each republic had an opportunity to run the federated Communist Party.

What opened the gates to imperialism? Unquestionably, a contributing factor was the unfortunate and ill-considered split between Yugoslavia and the Soviet Union. Yugoslavia was expelled from the Cominform in 1948 and thereafter isolated from the socialist camp. Years later an attempt was made by the USSR leadership to repair the situation so Yugoslavia could exist without leaning on or getting aid from imperialism. But the socialized, centralized economy of Yugoslavia had already been damaged.

The gates to imperialism opened wide when Yugoslavia established its so-called workers' control of management. This sounded highly democratic—a step away from the rigid, centralized control that stifled the creative energy of the working class. Now the workers' talents and abilities to manage Yugoslavia's affairs would be utilized.

Workers' control as a step away from capitalism is progressive. But it's a backward step when it leads away from centralized socialist planning. The concept of workers' control soon degenerated into managerial control and the abandonment of centralized planning. Yugoslavia fell into the coils of the International Monetary Fund and the World Bank. By 1981, it was completely dominated by world finance capital. It had opened wide the gates to so-called free enterprise.

DECENTRALIZATION, THEN DISMEMBERMENT

This development intensified competition among the various enterprises in each republic and among the republics themselves in a thoroughly bourgeois manner. Under such conditions, socialist solidarity was lost and, more significantly, the standard of living plummeted to such an extent that workers were no longer able to purchase basic necessities. By 1991, the new government had acquired a debt of $31 billion. Unemployment was over a million and inflation was 200 percent.

From free enterprise, the necessity arose for free, sovereign, independent republics. Economic decentralization soon led to political decentralization. The dismemberment of Yugoslavia had already begun. This was not an automatic, spontaneous development. No sooner had there developed the greater autonomy of the republics than the imperialists began to funnel funds into the republics with a view to encouraging and promoting separatist and secessionist objectives. It is they who unloosed the forces of virulent national hatred. The stimulation of national hatred is a byproduct of imperialist finance capital's investment in Yugoslavia.

Slobodan Milosevic, the Serbian leader, is also a product of that tendency. From the earliest days of his ascendancy to leadership in the Socialist Party of Serbia, the imperialist press played him up as a "charismatic personality." They supported his nationalist demagogy. It was only later that they found it might become disadvantageous to them if he went too far.

It must be taken into account that there was no unified policy of the imperialists in Yugoslavia. Germany, Italy, France, and the U.S. had divergent views on how to approach the situation. Each had its own sordid material interests, which often were hidden. Their policies can also be mistaken. It is not an easy task to stimulate, promote, and finance nationalist tendencies in the republics and then get them to carry out the wishes of individual imperialist countries without arousing all sorts of internecine struggles. The very forces that they stimulated and brought into motion got out of control.

Each imperialist power, even if it has no direct economic interest in Yugoslavia, is inevitably drawn into the struggle so as not to be left out of the picture. Each tries to find a basis for a relationship with Yugoslavia that will bring it advantage. It is no wonder that the U.S. State Department did not always know what to do. But one thing they were expert at: financing the counterrevolution.

It is true that earlier they had tangentially supported the Yugoslav regime. They felt a so-called nonaligned entity was useful in the struggle against the USSR. But after Tito died there was no basis for tolerating any remaining communist experiments. Then the dismantling began in earnest—not overtly, but covertly. Secret diplomacy is one of the most important weapons of imperialism. But the different imperialists often find themselves at loggerheads. While each of the imperialists would want to outdo the others in exerting influence over a dominant Serbia, they are not in favor of a Milosevic who postures as an extreme nationalist and who occasionally flouts European and U.S. intervention.

ROLE OF MILOSEVIC

Milosevic is not very different from any bourgeois nationalist in the oppressed countries. Certainly, communists are opposed to the ideology of a Bonapartist, especially if he has degenerated with the abandonment of communism. But that's no excuse for supporting imperialist intervention.

Really, Milosevic is not much different from Saddam Hussein. His espousal of bourgeois nationalism is no reason for anyone to fall on all fours and allow U.S. imperialism to run roughshod over the country. It reduces itself again to the U.S., Britain, and France—notwithstanding their differences— attempting to do what they have done in so many oppressed countries around the globe. The fact that it is taking place in Europe does not change the situation at all.

It is not inconceivable that Serbia or a coalition of some of the republics will reunify on the basis of socialist conceptions. In any event, a federation, even on a bourgeois basis, is bound to be more progressive and productive, more independent of imperialism, than if it is cut up into small principalities with no real power in the world community.

We in the United States tend to think of the oppressed nations as mainly those in the economically underdeveloped world—Latin America, the Middle East, Africa, and most of Asia. Of course, the bourgeoisie will turn heaven and earth to deny that there is national oppression in the U.S. From kindergarten on, they drum it into the heads of everyone that this is "one nation, indivisible, with liberty and justice for all." But also not well publicized is the fact that national oppression exists in Europe, too.

Just saying that one nationality in the Balkans is more developed industrially than another blurs the relationship of oppressor to oppressed. For instance, Slovenia may be more developed with a higher standard of living, but once it is involved in an internecine war and becomes completely dependent on imperialism, it may well find itself in a position of subordination and potentially of oppression.

The tendency in the capitalist press is to obliterate the relationship between oppressor and oppressed and present the internecine struggle as a purely Balkan affair between the nationalities. Overlooked entirely is that for a period of time there existed a federation that not only increased the standard of living but was able on its own to play a more or less important role, even on the international arena.

Under present conditions, particularly if the war continues, all the nationalities risk being reduced to pawns of the imperialist powers. It may be true that the Yugoslav regime can hold out for a considerable period against imperialist sanctions, but even should it come out victorious, it will have been drained of much of its life blood and material resources, assuming it is able to overcome overt and covert imperialist domination.

Bourgeois radicals tend to neglect the class essence of the struggle in Yugoslavia. No matter how carefully they may try to analyze the relations among the nationalities, if they leave out the relation between the bourgeoisie and the proletariat, between the national bourgeoisie and the imperialist banks and industrialists, they are left completely at the mercy of monopoly capitalism.

PROLETARIAT IS LEADERLESS

Of course, the most important aspect of the situation in Yugoslavia is the position of the proletariat itself. The proletariat at the present time is leaderless, the party having abandoned its vanguard role as leader in the struggle for socialist construction. Only the proletariat can play a consistent internationalist role. The bourgeoisie, on the other hand, by virtue of its overriding interest in overturning socialist and state property and promoting private property, not only sharpens its class relations with the proletariat but promotes and stimulates antagonisms among the nationalities.

No nation in modern times is free from class rule. Every state rules in the interests of either the workers or the bourgeoisie. The mere fact it is small or exploited by an imperialist power may obscure that fact but does not invalidate it. This must be borne in mind in approaching the national question. One can easily get lost in the struggle for nationality, for freedom from oppression, and forget the existence of an exploiting class within the nation.

In the epoch of the bourgeoisie, a nation is merely an instrument of domination by the propertied and exploiting class. Of course, the struggle against the imperialist oppressor must be led by a proletarian vanguard to be effective, and the duty of the vanguard is to mobilize all the progressive elements in society on a democratic and anti-imperialist basis. An excellent example of this was the Yugoslav struggle for liberation.

The current Yugoslav regime is in large measure a product of the recent events in the Soviet Union, beginning with the Gorbachev administration. His reactionary program accelerated all the social antagonisms in Yugoslavia, as elsewhere in Eastern Europe. Certainly, the sweeping bourgeois restorationist measures taken by the new regimes in the East, and particularly the swallowing up of the German Democratic Republic, could not but have a detrimental effect on class and socialist consciousness in Yugoslavia. The leadership, such as it was, panicked under the impact of these events. They not only changed the name of the party, they began to compete with each other over who would go further in bourgeois economic reforms.

The monolithic imperialist media have never had such a clear field in which to lie and deceive the masses, now that they are no longer restrained by the existence of a socialist camp. The absence of a strong and vigorous working class press also facilitates the task of the bourgeoisie. They are riding high. But then comes one of those elemental and spontaneous risings, as happened around the Rodney King beating in Los Angeles, which demonstrate the fragility of bourgeois rule over the working class and the oppressed masses.

Truth crushed to earth will rise again, and, with it, so will the working class.

---

[1] *Washington Post*, 31 May 1992.

[2] Ibid.

[3] *Financial Times*, 2 June 1992.

[4] *Britannica Book of the Year 1992* (Chicago: Encyclopedia Britannica, Inc., 1992).

[5] Ibid.

[6] *Financial Times*, 9 September 1991.

[7] Cable News Network Prime News, 29 May 1992; the Croatian president spoke in English.

[8] *New Columbia Encyclopedia* (New York, 1975).

[9] *New York Times,* 13 July 1987.

[10] *New York Times,* 10 July 1991.

[11] *Financial Times,* 2 June 1992.

6   The role of sanctions in the destruction of Yugoslavia

"The one who chooses this economic, peaceful, quiet, lethal remedy will not have to resort to force. It is not such a painful remedy. It doesn't take a single human life outside the country exposed to boycott, but instead subjects that country to a pressure that, in my view, no modern nation can withstand."
U.S. President Woodrow Wilson, speaking on economic sanctions in Versailles, France, 1919

In 1990, the Yugoslav republic of Serbia had a gross domestic product of about $24 billion. The per capita income was over $3,000, and every person was guaranteed the right to housing, education, quality health care, a job or income, a one-month paid annual vacation, and other benefits. Three years later, Serbia's gross domestic product had dropped to under $10 billion and per capita income was $700. People were dying from the lack of common medicines and were being operated on without anesthesia.

What brought about this catastrophe? In its relative magnitude it far exceeded the impact of the 1929-33 depression in the United States. But unlike the economic crisis of the 1930s—a product of the normal, unconscious functioning of the capitalist business cycle—Yugoslavia's destruction was planned and created with full deliberation. The planning took place not inside the country but in the capitals of the "great" powers— Berlin, London, Paris, Rome, and, above all, Washington.

Yugoslavia's economy was demolished by sanctions. Sanctions is a word with a deceptively mild ring to it. But the sanctions imposed by the United Nations Security Council on Yugoslavia, today a country of ten million people, cut off the country's economic lifeblood. Even in mid-1997, twenty months after some of the harshest sanctions were lifted, it has not really begun to recover.

In 1991-92, Yugoslavia, a socialist federation of six republics and two autonomous regions that had existed since 1945, disintegrated in a horrific civil war. There were internal factors leading to the breakup, but the decisive role was played by the intervention of outside powers. By mid-1992, the Federal Republic of Yugoslavia was reduced to Serbia and Montenegro. Western-backed governments in Slovenia, Croatia, and Bosnia had declared their independence, and Macedonia soon would do likewise.

In the early stages of the breakup of Yugoslavia, Germany and Austria encouraged and gave military support to the secessionist governments in Slovenia and Croatia. The German government, emboldened by its recent swallowing up of East Germany, was looking to extend its empire along familiar lines. Slovenia, Croatia, and, in fact, all of Yugoslavia had been conquered by Nazi Germany a half century earlier.[1] But it wasn't just Germany. The U.S., France, Italy, Britain, and Austria were all contending for influence over, and control of, pieces of the former federation and the other Balkan and East European states. The target of hostility of all these outside powers was the Federal Republic of Yugoslavia and the Serbian forces living outside the now-shrunken borders of Yugoslavia.

The attack on the FRY was justified by a media campaign labeling "the Serbs" as war criminals and violators of human rights. There were undoubtedly war crimes, crimes against humanity, and violations of human rights committed in the civil war by Serbs, and also by Croatians and Muslims. It was a war fought on the basis of nationality against nationality.

The outside powers who wanted to break up the old Yugoslav federation fanned the flames of nationalism and secession, knowing full well what a civil war fought on this basis would mean. These same powers have themselves committed crimes against humanity all over the world, for which they have yet to answer—in Vietnam, the Congo, Algeria, Ireland, Guatemala, Hiroshima and Nagasaki, the slave trade, the genocide of indigenous peoples in the Americas—the list is long indeed. So, when the governments responsible for the historic and contemporary oppression of so much of humanity invoke "human rights" as justification for punishing Yugoslavia (or any country, for that matter), they should be challenged, especially by progressives. The role of sanctions is an important issue for the anti-war and anti-intervention movement, particularly because they are increasingly being used by the U.S. government against developing countries. This chapter will attempt to show how, under the banner of protecting human rights, sanctions were used as a key weapon in destroying Yugoslavia, promoting civil war, and inflicting great suffering on the people in Yugoslavia and throughout the region.

U.S. POSITION IN 1989-90

From the early 1950s, U.S. relations with Yugoslavia had been of a different character than those with the other eastern European countries. Most of eastern Europe was freed from Nazi domination in World War II by the Soviet Red Army. In Yugoslavia, however, a communist-led national liberation movement, AVNOJ, headed by Josip Broz (Tito), defeated the Nazis and their local puppet governments. After the war, the AVNOJ took power and began to re-create Yugoslavia as a socialist society. Great emphasis was put on guaranteeing equality among all the peoples of this multinational state, including Slovenes, Croats,

Serbs, Bosnian Muslims, Albanians, Hungarians, Macedonians, Montenegrins, and others.

A series of disputes between the Soviet Union and Yugoslavia led to the expulsion of Yugoslavia from the socialist bloc in 1948. In the years that followed, the Yugoslav leadership, while maintaining the socialist core of its economy, entered into commercial, financial, and military relationships with the U.S. and other Western powers. Yugoslavia made economic concessions that allowed a level of private enterprise. The country became indebted to international banks in the 1960s and 1970s, causing much economic dislocation in the 1980s.

U.S. support for maintaining Yugoslavia's territorial integrity during this period was primarily for geopolitical reasons: Yugoslavia was seen as a buffer against the Soviet Union. With the collapse of the socialist governments in Eastern Europe and the weakening of the Soviet Union in the late 1980s, Yugoslavia's strategic importance for the U.S. was dramatically reduced. Nevertheless, the U.S. diplomatic position of supporting Yugoslavia's territorial unity officially continued from 1989 to mid-1991, although now for a very different reason. The U.S. ally and rival, the newly reunified Germany, was on the move in Eastern Europe.

The German government was, during the period of 1989-91, an open promoter of breaking up the Yugoslav federation, confident that the richest republics, Croatia and Slovenia, would be swept into Germany's rapidly expanding sphere of influence. While the Bush administration gave diplomatic support to Yugoslavia's territorial integrity at that time, it simultaneously sought to destroy the federation's socialist economic base. The U.S. aim was to become the dominant power in all of a capitalist Yugoslavia. There were strong reasons to think this could soon be a reality.

In 1989, Eastern European socialist governments from Poland to Bulgaria had fallen. The Gorbachev leadership in the USSR, in addition to encouraging the collapse of its Warsaw Pact allies, was carrying out policies which had the effect of chaotically dismantling the Soviet economy. And in Yugoslavia itself, then-Prime Minister Ante Markovic was "known to favor market-oriented reforms."[2] Markovic was described as "Washington's best ally in Yugoslavia."[3]

Markovic launched a program of privatizing or shutting down state industry, cutting back on social programs and subsidies, and freezing wages. The impact was quick and severe. According to a Yugoslav government report, the standard of living declined 18.1 percent between January and October 1990, while industrial production fell 10.4 percent, retail prices doubled, and sales dropped 23.8 percent. Nearly eight hundred enterprises, employing half-a-million workers, went bankrupt.[4]

The sharp economic decline not only raised unemployment to 20 percent, it also heightened tensions among the country's republics. This was no surprise to the leadership. Markovic himself, on a state visit to Washington in late 1989 to get support for his program, had told President Bush that rising tension among nationalities would be a consequence of his austerity/privatization plan.[5] In the midst of this economic crisis, Markovic announced plans in June 1990 for further cuts in government spending. But in October, to the dismay of the U.S., the reforms were halted and Markovic was later ousted as prime minister. Much damage had already been done to the Yugoslav economy.

THREAT OF SANCTIONS; SECESSION OF SLOVENIA AND CROATIA

On November 5, 1990, the U.S. House and Senate passed Foreign Operations Appropriation Law 101-513, calling for the cut-off of aid and credits to Yugoslavia within six months.[6] Three weeks later, the CIA leaked a report to the media predicting that Yugoslavia would disintegrate in civil war, possibly within the next year.[7]

On June 25, 1991, the recently elected right-wing governments in Slovenia and Croatia declared their independence from Yugoslavia. Both did so in violation of the federation's constitution, which contained a specific secession procedure that all republics were bound to follow. The Yugoslav National Army (JNA) deployed units in both republics to prevent the illegal secession. The first fighting broke out in Slovenia, when Slovenian secessionist militia units seized the country's posts on the international borders with Austria, Italy, and Hungary.

The new regimes in Slovenia and Croatia had been emboldened to secede by the support they received from outside powers. Immediately after secession and the outbreak of fighting, the European Community (EC—now known as the European Union or EU), made up of twelve western European states, intervened. With Germany taking the lead, the EC threatened harsh economic reprisals against Yugoslavia if the federation's government defended its territory by military means. The EC would cut off $1 billion in scheduled aid and, more ominously, all economic relations if Yugoslavia did not accept mediation for a "peaceful solution."[8] Sixty percent of all Yugoslav trade was with EC countries.[9]

The EC plan called for: 1) Slovenia and Croatia to suspend their independence for three months; 2) the JNA units to withdraw to their barracks; and 3) the EC foreign ministers to mediate an agreement. This plan looked even-handed on the surface, but it wasn't. While the Yugoslav federal army was prevented from defending its own borders, Slovenia and Croatia were given three months' breathing space to build up their armed forces. Military supplies poured into both republics, primarily from Germany, which had been arming both even before their independence declarations.[10]

Author Sean Gervasi posed this question regarding the EC plan: "How would President Lincoln have treated a similar foreign intervention in the U.S. Civil War?"[11]

Immediately after the EC agreement, the U.S. on July 11, 1991, implemented its law suspending aid and credits that had been passed the previous November.[12] This plus the threat of the EC sanctions was the key factor in the initial breakup of the socialist federation. There is little doubt that the Yugoslav leadership and army would have otherwise fought to preserve the country's unity.

The economy was further devastated by the breakup itself. Yugoslavia was one integrated economy. Now its network of interlocking plants, raw materials supplies, and distribution was torn apart virtually overnight.[13]

Yugoslavia's reprieve from the threatened EC sanctions was to be short-lived. When the three-month waiting period ended in October 1991, Slovenia and Croatia formally declared their independence. Heavy fighting continued between the newly formed Croatian army and its paramilitary allies on one side, and Serbian militias and elements of the JNA on the other.

Serbs numbered six hundred thousand in a Croatian population of 4.3 million, with most living in the Krajina and other concentrated areas. Most Serbs were vehemently opposed to living under Croatian control, for reasons that dated back to World War II. When the Nazi army conquered Yugoslavia in 1941, it established, with its local Ustasha party allies, a puppet Croatian state. During its three-year existence, Croatian fascists slaughtered six hundred thousand to over a million Serbs—the numbers are still disputed among Serbs themselves—and one hundred thousand Jews and Romani people.

The new Croatian president, Franjo Tudjman, expressed his admiration for the Ustasha government and denied that it had carried out genocide. The old Ustasha regime's checkerboard flag became the banner of the new Croatia.[14] A racist campaign was launched in the Croatian mass media, depicting Serbs as sub-humans. Tudjman repeatedly called for German and U.S. intervention in Yugoslavia. On May 29, 1992, CNN Prime News reported that Tudjman, speaking in English, appealed for the U.S. Sixth Fleet to come to the Croatian port of Dubrovnik.

To understand the Serbian response to Croatian independence under Tudjman's leadership, consider what the reaction here would be if part of the U.S. seceded under an avowedly white racist government, raised the Confederate flag, and adopted "Dixie" as its national anthem.

THE FIRST ROUND OF SANCTIONS

The EC and the U.S. moved quickly to support Croatia. On November 8, 1991, EC foreign ministers attending a NATO summit meeting declared broad economic sanctions against Yugoslavia, including suspension of a 1980 trade and cooperation agreement. The EC also banned the import of Yugoslav textiles, and said it would go to the UN to seek an oil embargo against the country.[15] The next day, President Bush announced that the U.S. would implement similar sanctions. The *New York Times* said that while the "measures referred broadly to Yugoslavia, European officials said they were aimed at Serbia and Yugoslavia's Serbian-led army."[16] The sanctions hit hard at the weakened Yugoslav economy.

In January 1992, the EC recognized the independence of Slovenia and Croatia. This recognition gave impetus, not accidentally, to secessionist forces in the republics of Macedonia and Bosnia-Herzegovina.

The newly-elected president of Bosnia was Alija Izetbegovic, whose party had won in an election boycotted by most of the Serbian population of the republic. In Bosnia, no single ethnic group has a majority. The largest groups are Muslims* (44 percent), Serbs (31 percent), and Croats (17 percent). Many people, regardless of ethnic or religious background, regarded themselves as Yugoslavs.

Earlier in his career, Izetbegovic had been a very marginal figure. He was jailed in the early 1980s for inciting racial hatred. For decades, he had been an advocate of making Bosnia an Islamic religious republic, despite the fact that Muslims were a minority of the population.[17] The vast majority of Bosnian Muslims, by all accounts, had no interest in living in an Islamic fundamentalist state and even less in imposing one on others.

---

* The Yugoslav Constitution of 1974 defined Muslims as an ethnic group.

Nor was Izetbegovic the most popular political figure among Bosnian Muslims, much less the population as a whole, when he maneuvered his way into the presidency in 1991. But he had crucial support from outside—particularly from the U.S.—which enabled him to gain power.[18]

Of all the Yugoslav republics, Bosnia had the most diverse and intermingled population. There was no way lines could be drawn on a map in a completely equitable way for all nationalities. It was for this reason that a civil war in Bosnia—fought out on the basis of nationality against nationality—was to prove the bloodiest and most tragic of Yugoslavia's conflicts.

While the Serbian leadership wanted to keep Yugoslavia together as a federation, the actions of Serbian president Slobodan Milosevic intensified the division along nationalist lines. As a leader of the League of Communists of Yugoslavia, Milosevic broke with the tradition of emphasizing Yugoslavian solidarity. Instead, he conducted the struggle by appealing to Serbian nationalism. This precluded appealing to the workers of other nationalities who also opposed the breakup of the federation.[19]

That the breakup of Yugoslavia would ignite a devastating civil war was well-known to the outside powers who were most involved in promoting the country's dismemberment. David Owen, the former British cabinet minister, together with Cyrus Vance of the U.S., authored the failed Vance-Owen peace plan for Bosnia. In his book *Balkan Odyssey*, Owen reprints part of a memo issued by the Dutch government on July 13, 1991, just after Slovenia and Croatia declared independence. The Netherlands was then holding the rotating position of president of the EC. The document attempted to summarize the position of the EC as a whole:

> 1. We seem to agree that it is not possible for Yugoslavia to continue to exist with the present constitutional structure intact. . . .
>
> 2. It is equally difficult to imagine that Yugoslavia could *peacefully dissolve* into six independent repub-

lics within their present borders ... [author's emphasis].

And further:

This example [Bosnia with its diverse population] shows why unilateral declarations of independence of individual republics cannot solve Yugoslavia's problems.[20]

It is also important to note, as Owen himself does, that the borders of the Yugoslav republics were never meant to be international borders.

The socialist government led by Tito went to great lengths to do justice to the smaller nationalities when the republican borders were drawn in 1945. This resulted in substantial numbers of some nationalities, particularly Serbs and to a lesser degree Croats, ending up in republics outside those where they were a majority. As long as there was one federal government with a strong policy of equal rights for all nationalities, committed to actively promoting class rather than national solidarity, this was not such a big problem. But all that changed in 1991-92.

Despite the knowledge that Yugoslavia could not "peacefully dissolve into six independent republics within their present borders," and that "unilateral declarations of independence cannot solve Yugoslavia's borders," the key outside powers proceeded to encourage exactly those policies. And the U.S., exerting its position as the sole superpower, was increasingly becoming the dominant outside force.

Intense negotiations were held in Lisbon, Portugal, on March 18-19, 1992, to prevent civil war in Bosnia. An agreement was reached "to partition the republic along ethnic lines with local communities having broad autonomy."[21] Izetbegovic signed this agreement, known as the Cutileiro plan, but almost immediately reversed himself and rejected it after the U.S. said it was prepared to recognize Bosnia as an independent country.[22] On March 22, the civil war widened to Bosnia. On April 6, the U.S. and the EC recognized the Izetbegovic government as the legitimate government of Bosnia. This step had the effect of pouring gasoline on an already roaring fire.[23] A brutal, multi-sided civil war was underway and would last for more than three years.

THE U.S./UN BLOCKADE

The U.S. moved to assert its domination in the struggle and the Balkans region as a whole. On May 30, 1992, the UN Security Council voted "to follow the Bush administration's lead and impose tough economic sanctions on the Yugoslav government."[24] In Executive Order 12808, issued the same day, Bush declared a national state of emergency, saying: "The grave events in Serbia and Montenegro constitute an unusual and extraordinary threat to the national security, foreign policy, and economy of the United States." How a small and embattled country was able to threaten, from a distance of four thousand miles, the world's only superpower was never explained by the president. Nor was the meaning of "grave events," since there was no war taking place within the borders of the shrunken Yugoslav federation.[25]

UN Resolution 757 authorized:

• An international ban on all exports to, and imports from, Yugoslavia by any country. This specifically included an oil embargo. Yugoslavia produces only about 20 percent of its oil needs.

• An international ban on all foreign investment and commercial contacts with Yugoslavia.

• A freeze by all countries of Yugoslav assets.

• Suspension of all scientific, technical, and cultural exchanges.

• A ban on civilian air travel in or out of Yugoslavia.

• A ban on Yugoslav participation in international sports events.

On September 22, 1992, Yugoslavia became the first country to be expelled from the General Assembly. In May, Slovenia, Croatia, and Bosnia had been admitted to the international body.[26] On November 16, the UN Security Council voted to institute a total naval blockade of the country, including the stopping of all ships approaching Yugoslavia on the Danube River as well as in the Adriatic Sea. On December 15, Yugoslavia was expelled from the International Monetary Fund.

Taken together, these measures represented one of the most comprehensive attempts to isolate an entire country and destroy its economy. The only comparable international sanctions were those imposed on Iraq in 1990, which served as a model for the quarantining of Yugoslavia. At U.S. insistence, the Iraq sanctions remain in place as of this writing, and have taken the lives of an estimated 1.5 million Iraqis, seven hundred thousand of them children under the age of five.[27] By comparison, during the long decades of apartheid rule the U.S. and Britain never allowed a mandatory trade embargo or naval blockade to be imposed on the South African fascist regime. While South Africa was suspended for a time, it was never expelled from the United Nations.

The popular justification for imposing such extremely punitive measures was that Yugoslavia supported the Bosnian Serbs, who were accused of human rights violations in Bosnia's civil war. An incident on May 27, 1992, three days before the UN vote, in the embattled Bosnian capital of Sarajevo served to galvanize international public opinion for sanctions.

An explosion, said at the time to have been a mortar shell fired from Serbian positions, killed fourteen people waiting in a food line and wounded over one hundred. Extensive media coverage of this atrocity raised worldwide anger against "the Serbs" to a fever pitch. It was only several weeks later that an investigation showed the impossibility of a mortar shell causing such an explosion, and raised serious questions about what the real cause had been.[28] By then, Yugoslavia, whose connection to the May 27 Sarajevo explosion had never been more than guilt by association, was under embargo.

IMPACT OF SANCTIONS

If sanctions were really intended as a cure for human rights abuses, the treatment was to prove more deadly than the disease. The impact of UN Resolution 757 did not take long to be felt. The Yugoslav economy was already reeling from privatization, austerity, and the earlier EC and U.S. sanctions.

On June 26, 1992, less than a month after Resolution 757 was passed, the *New York Times* reported in a front-page story that a 5,000-dinar (Yugoslav currency) note had dropped in value from $550 U.S. to $2.70. Shortages of nearly all goods drove prices up and the value of the dinar down on a daily basis.[29] Inflation was soon 10 percent per day. A year later, according to the *Economist* magazine, inflation in Yugoslavia was 363 quadrillion (363,000,000,000,000,000 percent) annually.[30]

By August 1992, most of the big factories had to shut down due to lack of raw materials and fuel. Hundreds of thousands of workers were sent home with reduced or no wages. One such factory was the Kluz textile plant in Belgrade, which employed six thousand workers. It completely shut down. Dragoslav Kojic, the factory's senior manager, described the impact: "I don't like the embargo because it's affecting my people, who are poor. We're talking about six thousand women, about half of them without husbands, who are raising more than eleven thousand kids. Their lives have become very difficult, and I hate to think what might happen if this keeps on much longer."[31]

This was after just three months. The harshest sanctions were to last three more years, and the downward spiral continued. The *Economist* magazine reported on Feb. 12, 1994, that by then at least 60 percent of the workers were unemployed, industry was running at 20-30 percent of capacity, and 40 percent of all activity was taking place in the illegal, underground economy.[32]

HEALTH CARE

The Yugoslav health care system, once considered the best in southern Europe, was quickly decimated.[33] While food and medicine were supposedly exempt from the sanctions, all purchases had to be licensed by the Security Council, a long, bureaucratic, and often unsuccessful process. In any case, the government could no longer afford to buy medicines and medical supplies on the world market because of the economic blockade. Antibiotics, anti-cancer medicines, anesthesia, and painkillers were soon unavailable through the state health care system. X-ray machines stopped working. There were no spare parts for equipment. Only emergency surgery could be performed. Vaccines for measles, polio, and other contagious diseases ran out. By the spring of 1993, the sanctions-induced health care crisis deepened. Ninety percent of the country's domestic drug production had come to a halt due to lack of raw materials. The incidence of diseases like hepatitis and tuberculosis rose sharply.[34]

On April 25-26, 1993, the UN and the U.S. further tightened sanctions against Yugoslavia. An InterPress Service (IPS) report dated May 19, 1993, described the situation of parents whose six-year-old son was diagnosed with leukemia. To save his life, they had to buy medicines formerly available free or at a nominal cost. Due to the sanctions, these medicines were no longer available from the state health service. The first of eight necessary treatments cost $812, more than twice their combined monthly salaries, due to the runaway inflation.[35] Similar stories were repeated thousands of times. Chronically ill patients and those with easily treatable diseases died for lack of simple medicines. Hospitals were forced to give unscreened blood transfusions and perform surgery with insufficient disinfectants and antibiotics, causing a rise in fatal post-operative infections. Tranquilizers and other medications for psychiatric patients ran out, leading to sharp increases in self-inflicted violence and attacks on others in mental institutions. Doctors reported being "compelled to resort to nineteenth-century methods, so the patients are being tied to beds and locked up" to prevent violent behavior.[36]

In the summer of 1993, it was reported that "people are dying from the most benign diseases and epidemics have appeared—measles, for example. Mortality from easily curable diseases increased five times due to a shortage of medicine."[37] By October 1993, the average daily intake of calories had fallen by 28 percent compared to 1990, while the number of infectious disease fatalities rose 37 percent. Fifteen percent of the population—1.5 million people—was classified as undernourished. The death rate in the capital, Belgrade, increased from 790 to 977 per 100,000 in the same period.

AIM OF SANCTIONS

When confronted about the devastating effects of the sanctions on the Yugoslav health care system, Hannu Vuroi, head of the UN World Health Organization office in Belgrade, responded that "sanctions are designed to hurt."[38] No truer words could be spoken. Economic sanctions are intended to cause maximum suffering among a country's people. At the same time, sanctions of the broad and inclusive type imposed on Yugoslavia and Iraq are designed to choke the target country's economy until its government surrenders or is overthrown.

When sanctions are used, civilian casualties are not "collateral damage," the deceptive phrase used by the Pentagon in the Gulf War. Civilians and the civilian economy are the primary target of sanctions. Under international law, deliberately targeting civilians and destroying a country's means of subsistence are crimes against humanity. So, too, is collective punishment a violation of international law. If, as Yugoslav Assistant Health Minister Ljiljana Stojanovic pointed out, some Serbs committed war crimes in Bosnia, that would not justify punishing all Serbian people.[39]

The "collateral damage" from sanctions is the economic punishment inflicted on the target country's neighbors. In May 1995, seven countries—Greece, Macedonia, Albania, Moldava,

Bulgaria, Ukraine, and Romania—petitioned the UN Security Council for compensation. The seven stated that they had suffered billions of dollars in losses to their economies as a result of the blockade of Yugoslavia.[40] But the rich and powerful countries that rule the Security Council and imposed the sanctions have refused to compensate the poorer nations suffering this "collateral damage." Nor do they have to. Article 50, Chapter VII of the UN Charter stipulates:

> If preventive or enforcement measures against any state are taken by the Security Council, any other state ... which finds itself confronted with special economic problems arising from the carrying out of those measures, shall have the right to consult the Security Council with regard to a solution to those problems.

All countries are compelled, under the UN Charter, to implement sanctions and obey the boycott of a targeted state. But, if it is a poor or developing country which is suffering the economic damage (as is almost always the case), they have only "the right to consult" when it comes to compensation for their losses. (A similar situation, with similar results, followed the Gulf War, when twenty-one developing nations that had suffered major losses due to the sanctions against Iraq sought compensation.)

A senior U.S. official who chose to remain anonymous bragged to *Newsweek* magazine in December 1993: "From an economic perspective, the Serbian sanctions have been the most successful in history." At that time, more than 60 percent of the country's work force was unemployed, the average monthly income had dropped from $500 to $15, and inflation had reached 25,000 percent per month.[41]

In September 1994, the UN blockade was extended to cover that part—and only that part—of Bosnia under Bosnian Serb control. Throughout the civil war there was often fighting between Bosnian Croat and Bosnian Muslim forces. In the winter of 1993-94, the Bosnian city of Mostar was shelled, by

Croatian forces, far more heavily than the capital, Sarajevo. In the Bihac region, anti-Izetbegovic Bosnian Muslims were allied with Serb forces, and fought both the Izetbegovic-led Muslims and right-wing Croatian militias. The war in Bosnia was complex, multi-sided, and filled with horrors on all sides. Most wars are. But economic sanctions were reserved for only one side.[42]

SANCTIONS PART OF INTEGRATED WAR STRATEGY

As devastating as the sanctions were, they were not sufficient by themselves to achieve the objectives of the U.S. and other "great powers." First, to be fully effective, sanctions as all-encompassing as those imposed on Yugoslavia require military enforcement, as did the sanctions on Iraq. Beginning with the NATO (really U.S.) naval blockade in November 1992, all ships sailing toward Yugoslavia in the Adriatic Sea and on the Danube River were halted—74,000 altogether.[43] A "no-fly zone" was declared over Bosnia. The ships and planes that enforced the blockade and "no-fly zone" came from the U.S. Sixth Fleet and bases in Italy. The next month, President Bush threatened Yugoslavia that the U.S. would use military force if the Yugoslav civil war were extended to Serbia's Kosovo province.[44] This was blatant interference in Serbia's internal affairs.

In 1993, "retired" U.S. military officers began retraining the Croatian army, which also began receiving Pentagon-supplied arms.[45] In return, the U.S. was given bases on Croatian islands in the Adriatic. This relationship developed into a "strategic partnership."[46] The U.S. was displacing Germany as the leading outside power in Croatia.

The U.S. was, and is, the main supporter, military and otherwise, of the Izetbegovic government in Bosnia, whose foreign minister, Mohammed Sacirbey, is a U.S. citizen. In 1993-95, the U.S., through NATO, increasingly used air power against Bosnian and Croatian Serbs as well as against anti-Izetbegovic Muslim forces (usually referred to as "renegade

Muslims" in the U.S. media).[47] The Pentagon sent in special forces to train the Bosnian military.

In 1994, the U.S. forced a shaky alliance between Croatian and Izetbegovic forces in Bosnia.[48] Both, despite their mutual antagonism and fierce fighting in the civil war, were becoming increasingly dependent on the U.S.

The newly retrained and re-armed Croatian military, operating under U.S. direction, launched a massive offensive in the summer of 1995 against the Krajina region of Croatia. The Krajina had been a predominantly Serbian area for hundreds of years. Now, more than two hundred thousand Krajina Serbs were driven out in a matter of weeks. This was "ethnic cleansing" on a scale unprecedented in the four-year civil war, and unseen in Europe since World War II.

Allegations of "ethnic cleansing" had served to justify imposing sanctions against Serbia. But no cries for sanctions against Croatia now emanated from the White House or Congress. On the contrary, there were many expressions of satisfaction and self-congratulation in Washington in response to the massive uprooting of the Krajina Serbs.[49]

In August and September 1995, NATO launched a massive air war against positions of the Bosnian Serbs, who, for the first time in the war, suffered major defeats and territorial losses.

The combination of economic blockade and massive military intervention led to the Dayton Accords of 1995. The U.S. made the Yugoslav government a proverbial "offer it could not refuse." The U.S. proposal was basically this: accept our terms, and bring pressure on the Bosnian Serbs to accept them, or face continued economic strangulation and an expanded war. If the Milosevic government agreed, it was told, the economic blockade would be lifted.

The Dayton Accords resulted in a "peace" which remains precarious and unstable. But its principal objective, the establishment of U.S. domination in much of the former Yugoslavia, was achieved. As part of the agreement, sixty thousand

NATO troops, twenty thousand of them U.S. soldiers, were sent into Bosnia under U.S. command.

A giant new NATO base was established in Hungary (since approved for membership in the U.S.-controlled military alliance) to facilitate the troop deployment in Bosnia. The U.S. has also established important new bases in Macedonia and northern Albania.[50] The Pentagon also undertook a major upgrading of the Bosnian military, which is ongoing.

SANCTIONS AFTER THE DAYTON ACCORDS

The promise of a return to prosperity along with peace was not fulfilled for Yugoslavia. In December 1995, the UN blockade was ended and Yugoslavia was once again allowed to engage in trade with other countries. Nearly bankrupted and with its economy in ruins, however, it had little to sell and no money to buy on the world market. Moreover, Yugoslavia's path to recovery faced a major obstacle: An "outer wall" of sanctions remained in place, preventing the country from gaining international credit, loans, and aid with which to restart its severely damaged economy. It could not even recover much of its seized overseas assets, which remained frozen.

On December 28, Presidential Determination 96-7 was signed by President Clinton, suspending the sanctions earlier enacted by the U.S. However, Yugoslav assets "previously blocked remain blocked." The "national emergency" declared in Executive Order 12808 and expanded in Executive Order 12934, it said, "shall continue in effect."[51] An attached memorandum of justification emphasized that this was only a suspension and stated that "sanctions may again go into effect against the Serbs. Accordingly we plan to leave the Sanctions Assistance Mission infrastructure and monitors in place." And the U.S. announced its intention to prevent the lifting of the "outer wall" of financial sanctions by international bodies where it had very strong influence or veto power.

Despite the fact that with the Dayton Accords Yugoslavia had met the conditions for ending the sanctions, the Clinton administration now began coming up with new demands, as in the case of Iraq. For example, Yugoslavia was not allowed to rejoin the United Nations. Then-U.S. Ambassador to the UN Madeleine Albright said that Yugoslavia would not be re-admitted until it solved internal problems in Kosovo province and cooperated fully with The Hague war crimes tribunal.[52] The reinstatement of full sanctions does not require action by the UN Security Council. This power has been turned over to the U.S. officer commanding NATO forces in Bosnia.[53]

Rather than moving toward the lifting of the remaining sanctions, the U.S. has threatened several times since December 1995 to reimpose the entire blockade. In February 1996, U.S. Secretary of State Warren Christopher threatened Serbian President Milosevic with the renewal of trade sanctions unless there was cooperation with the prosecution of "Serbian war criminals."[54] In June 1996 Christopher again threatened re-sumption of a trade and oil embargo.[55] In December 1996, the U.S. threatened to reimpose the sanctions if the government suppressed demonstrations then taking place. The main cause of discontent, it was widely agreed, was the continued depressed state of the economy. A year after the "lifting" of sanctions, the Red Cross reported that nearly 30 percent of the population of Serbia and Montenegro was living in poverty.[56]

The U.S. was now using the continuation of sanctions as a means of creating popular discontent and the threat of even harsher sanctions as a way to control the government's re-sponses. Washington's objective was, and is, to achieve eco-nomic and political domination in what remains of the Yugoslav federation. To do this, the sanctions are being used in an at-tempt to finish off the state sector of the economy.

What Yugoslavia particularly needed after the Dayton Accords were credits and loans to restart its big, state-run in-dustries, like auto and textiles, which had either been shut down or had drastically cut back production. The revival of core in-dustry was a necessary step to revive the economy as a whole while helping to pay for the import of medicines, oil, and other raw materials.

A prime example was the Yugo automobile. Production at the big Zastava plant had fallen from two hundred thousand to 3,500 cars per year from 1990 to 1995. Obtaining large-scale credit to restore production required that Yugoslavia be read-mitted to institutions like the International Monetary Fund.[57]

The IMF said that to be readmitted, Yugoslavia would have to repay its presanctions debt—a relatively small $100 million. More importantly, it would also have to adopt a program of economic reforms that the IMF approved. The IMF, dominated by U.S. banks, has forced governments all over the world to privatize and deregulate their economies as a condition for getting international loans and credit.[58] Thus far, the Yugoslav leadership has refused to accept the U.S. demands to "open" the economy, privatize state industry, and liquidate the state sector. Mirjana Markovic, leader of the largest political organization in the country, the Yugoslav United Left, has declared that privatization violates the socialist constitution.[59]

And so, the U.S. keeps sanctions against Yugoslavia in place.

SANCTIONS AND THE ANTI-WAR MOVEMENT

It is an unfortunate reality that too many anti-war and progressive activists have viewed sanctions as a supportable alternative to war. In fact, sanctions, embargoes, and blockades are forms of war, particularly in a world which is ever more economically interdependent. Cutting off an entire country from trade and other economic relations can be, if maintained over long periods, devastating in the extreme. Nor are sanctions an alternative to war. Blockade-type sanctions are inevitably enforced by military means.

The countries subjected to sanctions and blockades of the type inflicted on Yugoslavia are exclusively developing nations—Iraq, Cuba, Iran, Libya, North Korea, Panama, Nicaragua, Vietnam and others—countries which have attempted to take an independent road.

During the Gulf War, one wing of the anti-war movement opposed military action, but appealed instead to "let the sanctions work." Perhaps this was the result of not understanding what it meant for sanctions to "work." But today, the consequences are clear: Those who suffer most from this type of warfare are the most vulnerable members of any society—the very young, the very old, and those who are ill.

As the International Appeal to End Sanctions, initiated by the International Action Center, states: "Economic sanctions and blockades are weapons of mass destruction directed at a whole people." They must be opposed.

---

[1] *Financial Times*, 9 September 1991.

[2] *Facts on File*, 27 January 1989, p. 57.

[3] Misha Glenny, "The Massacre of Yugoslavia," *New York Review of Books*, 30 January 1992.

[4] *Facts on File*, 31 December 1990.

[5] "Yugoslav Premier Seeks U.S. Aid," *New York Times*, 14 October 1989.

[6] See Appendix of this book.

[7] *New York Times*, 28 November 1990.

[8] *Facts on File*, 4 July 1991.

[9] *New York Times*, 9 November 1991.

[10] Sean Gervasi, "Germany, U.S. and the Yugoslav Crisis," *Covert Action*, Winter 1992-93.

[11] Gervasi, *op. cit.*

[12] *Workers World*, 18 January 1996.

[13] *New York Times*, 31 August 1996.

[14] David Owen, *Balkan Odyssey* (New York: Harcourt, Brace & Co., 1995), pp. 73-74. Owen is a member of the British House of Lords and co-author, with former U.S. Secretary of State Cyrus Vance, of the failed Vance-Owen peace plan. Owen's statements are particularly interesting given his imperial credentials and strongly anti-Serbian stance.

[15] *New York Times*, 9 November 1991.

[16] *New York Times*, 10 November 1991.

[17] Alija Izetbegovic, *The Islamic Declaration*, translated excerpts available from the Balkan Research Centre in "A briefing paper produced for members for the 1992/3 session of the British Parliament," 21 December 1992,

on line; originally printed privately 1970, reprinted Sarajevo, 1990
(http://suc.suc.org/~kosta/tar/bosna/).

[18] Owen, *op. cit.*, p. 82.

[19] Sam Marcy, et al., *Imperialist Intrigue and the Breakup of Yugoslavia*
(New York: World View, 1992), p. 22.

[20] Owen, *op. cit.*, pp. 32-33.

[21] *Facts on File*, April 1992, p. 252.

[22] *Workers World*, 7 December 1995.

[23] Owen, *op. cit.*, p. 46.

[24] *New York Times*, 31 May 1992.

[25] Ibid.

[26] *Facts on File*, September 1992, p. 716.

[27] *The Children Are Dying: Impact of U.S./UN Sanctions on Iraq* (New
York: International Action Center, 1996).

[28] *Cyprus Mail*, 1 August 1993.

[29] *New York Times*, 26 June 1992.

[30] "363 quadrillion percent inflation," *Economist*, 9 October 1993.

[31] *New York Times*, 31 August 1992.

[32] "The sanctions alternative," *Economist*, 12 February 1994.

[33] *Facts on File*, 19 November 1992.

[34] Suzanne Nelson, InterPress Service, 19 May 1993.

[35] Ibid.

[36] *Baltimore Sun*, 20 October 1993.

[37] Timoslav Kresovic, *UN Embargo: Serbia and Sanctions—Chronicle of a
Punishment*, http://www.yugoslavia.com/Society_and_Law/Sanctions/,
Belgrade, 1993.

[38] *Neues Deutschland*, 5 October 1993.

[39] Nelson, *op. cit.*

[40] Ibid.

[41] "A price no one can justify," *Newsweek*, 6 December 1993.

[42] "Mostar: a glimpse of hell frozen over," *Newsweek*, 6 December 1993.

[43] *Los Angeles Times*, 3 October 1996.

[44] *New York Times*, 28 December 1992.

[45] Ken Silverstein, "Privatizing War," *The Nation*, 28 July-4 August 1997.

[46] *San Francisco Chronicle*, 12 September 1995.

[47] U.S. Department of State, "Chronology of Balkan Conflict," 6 December
1995.

[48] Ibid.

[49] U.S. Department of State, "Bosnia Fact Sheet: Economic Sanctions
Against Serbia and Montenegro." Published during the Dayton negotiations, the fact sheet concludes: "Sanctions have contributed to a significant
decline in the FRY (Yugoslavia). Industrial production and real incomes

are down at least 50 percent since 1991. As a result, obtaining sanctions relief has become a priority for the FRY government."

[50] *San Francisco Chronicle*, 12 September 1995.

[51] *Workers World*, 18 January 1996.

[52] *San Francisco Chronicle*, 26 November 1996.

[53] *New York Times*, 17 July 1996.

[54] *Facts on File*, 22 February 1996.

[55] Reuters, 3 June 1996.

[56] Vesna Peric-Zinomjic, InterPress Service, 27 December 1996.

[57] *New York Times*, 9 July 1996.

[58] *San Francisco Chronicle*, 26 November 1996.

[59] *New York Times*, 31 August 1996.

7 The invasion of Serbian Krajina

GREGORY ELICH

In early August 1995, the Croatian invasion of Serbian Krajina precipitated the worst refugee crisis of the Yugoslav civil war. Within days, more than two hundred thousand Serbs, virtually the entire population of Krajina, fled their homes, and 14,000 Serbian civilians lost their lives. According to a UN official, "Almost the only people remaining were the dead and the dying." The Clinton administration's support for the invasion was an important factor in creating this nightmare.

The previous month, Secretary of State Warren Christopher and German Foreign Minister Klaus Kinkel met with Croatian diplomat Miomir Zuzul in London. During this meeting, Christopher gave his approval for Croatian military action against Serbs in Bosnia and Krajina. Two days later, the U.S. ambassador to Croatia, Peter Galbraith, also approved Croatia's invasion plan. Stipe Mesic, a prominent Croatian politician, stated that Croatian President Franjo Tudjman "received the go-ahead from the United States. Tudjman can do only what the Americans allow him to do. Krajina is the reward for having accepted, under Washington's pressure, the federation between Croats and Muslims in Bosnia." Croatian assembly deputy Mate Mestrovic also claimed that the "United States gave us the green light to do whatever had to be done."[1]

As Croatian troops launched their assault on August 4, U.S. NATO aircraft destroyed Serbian radar and anti-aircraft defenses. American EA-6B electronic warfare aircraft patrolled the air in support of the invasion. Krajina foreign affairs advisor Slobodan Jarcevic stated that NATO "completely led and coordinated the entire Croat offensive by first destroying radar and anti-aircraft batteries. What NATO did most for the Croatian Army was to jam communications between [Serb] military commands. . . ."[2]

Following the elimination of Serbian anti-aircraft defenses, Croatian planes carried out extensive attacks on Serbian towns and positions. The roads were clogged with refugees, and Croatian aircraft bombed and strafed refugee columns. Serbian refugees passing through the town of Sisak were met by a mob of Croatian extremists, who hurled rocks and concrete at them. A UN spokesman said, "The windows of almost every vehicle were smashed and almost every person was bleeding from being hit by some object." Serbian refugees were pulled from their vehicles and beaten. As fleeing Serbian civilians poured into Bosnia, a Red Cross representative in Banja Luka said, "I've never seen anything like it. People are arriving at a terrifying rate." Bosnian Muslim troops crossed the border and cut off Serbian escape routes. Trapped refugees were massacred as they were pounded by Croatian and Muslim artillery. Nearly 1,700 refugees simply vanished. While Croatian and Muslim troops burned Serbian villages, President Clinton expressed his understanding for the invasion, and Christopher said events "could work to our advantage."[3]

The Croatian rampage through the region left a trail of devastation. Croatian special police units, operating under the Ministry of Internal Affairs, systematically looted abandoned Serbian villages. Everything of value—cars, stereos, televisions, furniture, farm animals—was plundered, and homes set afire.[4] A confidential European Union report stated that 73 percent of Serbian homes were destroyed.[5] Troops of the Croatian army also took part, and pro-Nazi graffiti could be seen on the walls of several burnt-out Serb buildings.[6]

Massacres continued for several weeks after the fall of Krajina, and UN patrols discovered numerous fresh unmarked graves and bodies of murdered civilians.[7] The European Union report states, "Evidence of atrocities, an average of six corpses per day, continues to emerge. The corpses, some fresh, some decomposed, are mainly of old men. Many have been shot in the back of the head or had throats slit, others have been mutilated. . . . Serb lands continue to be torched and looted."[8]

Following a visit in the region, a member of the Zagreb Helsinki Committee reported, "Virtually all Serb villages had been destroyed. . . . In a village near Knin, eleven bodies were found; some of them were massacred in such a way that it was not easy to see whether the body was male or female."[9]

UN spokesman Chris Gunness noted that UN personnel continued to discover bodies, many of whom had been decapitated.[10] British journalist Robert Fisk reported the murder of elderly Serbs, many of whom were burned alive in their homes. He adds, "At Golubic, UN officers have found the decomposing remains of five people . . . the head of one of the victims was found 150 feet from his body. Another UN team, meanwhile, is investigating the killing of a man and a woman in the same area after villagers described how the man's ears and nose had been mutilated."[11]

After the fall of Krajina, Croatian chief of staff General Zvonimir Cervenko characterized Serbs as "medieval shepherds, troglodytes, destroyers of anything the culture of man has created." During a triumphalist train journey through Croatia and Krajina, Tudjman spoke at each railway station. To great applause, he announced, "There can be no return to the past, to the times when [Serbs] were spreading cancer in the heart of Croatia, a cancer that was destroying the Croatian national being." He then went on to speak of the "ignominious disappearance" of the Serbs from Krajina "so it is as if they have never lived here. . . . They didn't even have time to take with them their filthy money or their filthy underwear!" American ambassador Peter Galbraith dismissed claims that Croatia had engaged in "ethnic cleansing," since he defined this term as something Serbs do.[12]

U.S. representatives blocked Russian attempts to pass a UN Security Council resolution condemning the invasion. According to Croatian Foreign Minister Mate Granic, American officials gave advice on the conduct of the operation, and European and military experts and humanitarian aid workers reported shipments of U.S. weapons to Croatia over the two months preceding the invasion. A French mercenary also witnessed the arrival of American and German weapons at a Croatian port, adding, "The best of the Croats' armaments were German- and American-made." The U.S., "directly or indirectly," says French intelligence analyst Pierre Hassner, "rearmed the Croats." Analysts at Jane's Information Group say that Croatian troops were seen wearing American uniforms and carrying U.S. communications equipment.[13]

The invasion of Krajina was preceded by a thorough CIA and DIA analysis of the region.[14] According to Balkan specialist Ivo Banac, this "tactical and intelligence support" was furnished to the Croatian Army at the beginning of its offensive.[15]

In November 1994, the United States and Croatia signed a military agreement. Immediately afterward, U.S. intelligence agents set up an operations center on the Adriatic island of Brac, from which reconnaissance aircraft were launched. Two months earlier, the Pentagon contracted Military Professional Resources, Inc. (MPRI) to train the Croatian military.[16] According to a Croatian officer, MPRI advisors "lecture us on tactics and big war operations on the level of brigades, which is why we needed them for Operation Storm when we took the Krajina." Croatian sources claim that U.S. satellite intelligence was furnished to the Croatian military.[17] Following the invasion of Krajina, the U.S. rewarded Croatia with an agreement "broadening existing cooperation" between MPRI and the Croatian military.[18] U.S. advisors assisted in the reorganization of the Croatian Army. Referring to this reorganization in an interview with the newspaper *Vecernji List*, Croatian General Tihomir Blaskic said, "We are building the foundations of our organization on the traditions of the Croatian home guard"—pro-Nazi troops in World War II.[19]

It is worth examining the nature of what one UN official terms "America's newest ally." During World War II, Croatia was a Nazi puppet state in which the Croatian fascist Ustashe murdered as many as one million Serbs, Jews, and Romani (Gypsies). Disturbing signs emerged with the election of Franjo Tudjman to the Croatian presidency in 1990. Tudjman said, "I am glad my wife is neither Serb nor Jew," and wrote that accounts of the Holocaust were "exaggerated" and "one-sided."[20]

Much of Tudjman's financial backing was provided by Ustasha émigrés and several Ustasha war criminals were invited to attend the first convention of Tudjman's political party, the Croatian Democratic Union.[21]

Tudjman presented a medal to a former Ustasha commander living in Argentina, Ivo Rojnica. After Rojnica was quoted as saying, "Everything I did in 1941 I would do again," international pressure prevented Tudjman from appointing him to the post of ambassador to Argentina. When former Ustasha official Vinko Nikolic returned to Croatia, Tudjman appointed him to a seat in parliament. Upon former Ustasha officer Mate Sarlija's return to Croatia, he was personally welcomed at the airport by Defense Minister Gojko Susak, and subsequently given the post of general in the Croatian Army.[22] On November 4, 1996, thirteen former Ustasha officers were presented with medals and ranks in the Croatian Army.[23]

Croatia adopted a new currency in 1994, the kuna, the same name as that used by the Ustasha state, and the new Croatian flag is a near-duplicate of the Ustasha flag. Streets and buildings have been renamed for Ustasha official Mile Budak, who signed the regime's anti-Semitic laws, and more than three thousand anti-fascist monuments have been demolished. In an open letter, the Croatian Jewish community protested the re-habilitation of the Ustasha state. In April 1994, the Croatian government demanded the removal of all "nonwhite" UN troops from its territory, claiming that "only first-world troops" under-stood Croatia's "problems."[24]

On Croatian television in April 1996, Tudjman called for the return of the remains of Ante Pavelic, the leader of the Croatian pro-Nazi puppet state. "After all, both reconciliation and recognition should be granted to those who deserve it," Tudjman said, adding, "We should recognize that Pavelic's ideas about the Croatian state were positive," but that Pavelic's only mistake was the murder of a few of his colleagues and na-tionalist allies.[25] Three months later, Tudjman said of the Serbs driven from Croatia: "The fact that 90 percent of them left is their own problem. . . . Naturally we are not going to allow them all to return." During the same speech, Tudjman referred to the pro-Nazi state as "a positive thing."[26]

During its violent secession from Yugoslavia in 1991, Croatia expelled more than three hundred thousand Serbs, and Serbs were eliminated from ten towns and 183 villages.[27] In 1993, Helsinki Watch reported: "Since 1991, the Croatian authorities have blown up or razed ten thousand houses, mostly of Serbs, but also houses of Croats. In some cases, they dyna-mited homes with the families inside." Thousands of Serbs have been evicted from their homes. Croatian human-rights activist Ivan Zvonimir Cicak says beatings, plundering, and arrests were the usual eviction methods.[28]

Tomislav Mercep, until recently the advisor to the Inte-rior minister and a member of Parliament, is a death-squad leader. Mercep's death squad murdered 2,500 Serbs in western Slavonia in 1991 and 1992, actions Mercep defends as "heroic deeds."[29] Death squad officer Miro Bajramovic's spectacular confession revealed details: "Nights were worst for [our prison-ers] . . . burning prisoners with a flame, pouring vinegar over their wounds, mostly on genitalia and on the eyes. Then there is that little inductor, field phone, you plug a Serb onto that. . . .

The most painful is to stick little pins under the nails and to connect to the three phase current; nothing remains of a man but ashes. . . . After all, we knew they would all be killed, so it did not matter if we hurt him more today or tomorrow."

"Mercep knew everything," Bajramovic claimed. "He told us several times: 'Tonight you have to clean all these shits.' By this he meant all the prisoners should be executed."[30]

Sadly, the Clinton administration's embrace of Croatia follows a history of support for fascists when it suits American geopolitical interests: Chile's Augusto Pinochet, Indonesia's Suharto, Paraguay's Alfredo Stroessner, and a host of others. The consequences of this policy for the people affected have been devastating.

---

[1] "Weekly: U.S. Gave Zagreb 'Green Light,' " *Tanjug* (Belgrade), 26 July 1995. "In Croatia, U.S. Took Calculated Risk," Stephen Engelberg, *New York Times News Service*, 12 August 1995. "Cleansing the West's Dirty War," Joan Phillips, *Living Marxism* (London), September 1995. "Who Has Given the Go-Ahead?," interview with Stipe Mesic, *Panorama* (Milan), 8 August 1995. "The United States Gave Us the Green Light," interview with Mate Mestrovic, by Chantal de Rudder, *Le Nouvel Observateur* (Paris), 10 August 1995.

[2] "International Inaction in Croatia Will Complicate Bosnian War," George Jahn, *Associated Press*, 7 August 1995. "NATO Destroyed Krajina Missile Systems," *Bosnian Serb News Agency (SRNA)* (Belgrade), 6 August 1995. "Abandoned People Must Flee," interview with Slobodan Jarcevic by Cvijeta Arsenic, *Oslobodjenje* (Sarajevo—Bosnian Serb), 23 August 1995. "Cleansing the West's Dirty War," Joan Phillips, *op. cit.*

[3] "Huge Refugee Exodus Runs Into Shelling, Shooting, Air Attacks," George Jahn, *Associated Press*, 8 August 1995. "Croat Planes Shell Refugees," *Tanjug*, 8 August 1995. "SRNA Review of Daily News," *SRNA*, 8 August 1995. "Cleansing the West's Dirty War," Joan Phillips, *op. cit.* "Refugees Trapped by Croat Shelling," Robert Fox and Tim Judah, *Electronic Telegraph* (London) (Online), 8 August 1995. "Croat Mob Attacks Nuns in Fleeing Convoy," Patrick Bishop, *Electronic Telegraph*, 11 August 1995. "Over 1,000 Serbs Missing in Krajina," *Tanjug*, 28 January 1997. "Croat Grip Is Tightened as 100,000 Flee," Tim Butcher, *Electronic Telegraph*, 7 August 1995.

[4] "UN Says Croatians Loot, Use Peacekeepers as Shields," *Associated Press*, 6 August 1995. "Helsinki Committee Reports on Krajina Opera-

tions," Hartmut Fiedler, *Oesterreich Eins Radio Network*, 21 August 1995.
"EU Observers Accuse Croatia of Breaches of Law," *Tanjug*, 27 October
1995. "UN: Croatians Systematically Burned Serb Homes," *Tanjug*, 14
August 1995. "Croats Slaughter Elderly by the Dozen," Robert Fisk, *The
Independent* (London), 10 September 1995. "Croats Plunder Their Way
through Krajina," Mon Vanderostyne, *De Standard* (Groot Bijgaarden, The
Netherlands), 9 August 1995. "UN Says Croats Loot Serb Villages in Kra-
jina," *Agence France-Presse*, 17 August 1995. "EU Report Accuses Croa-
tia of Atrocities Against Rebel Serbs," Julian Borger, *The Guardian*
(Manchester), 30 September 1995. "Krajina 'Torched State,' " *SRNA*, 21
August 1995. "What Was Once Home to 300 Families Is Now a Grave-
yard," Sarah Helm, *The Independent*, 24 August 1995. "Helsinki Committee Chronicles Human Rights Abuses," *Tanjug*, 28 August 1995.
"Memorandum on the Ethnic Cleansing of and Genocide Against the Serb
People of Croatia and Krajina," *Yugoslav Survey*, third quarter, 1995.
[5] "Krajina Bears Signs of Croat Ethnic Cleansing," Randolph Ryan, *Boston
Globe*, 8 October 1995. "UN Official Confirms Croatian Crimes in Kra-
jina," *Tanjug*, 13 October 1995.
[6] "Krajina Bears Signs of Croat Ethnic Cleansing," Randolph Ryan, *op. cit.*
[7] "Croats Burn and Kill with a Vengeance," Robert Fisk, *The Independent*,
4 September 1995. "Croats Leave Bloody Trail of Serbian Dead," Tracy
Wilkinson, *Los Angeles Times*, 9 October 1995. "Reports Say Croatia Uses
Killing, Arson," John Pomfret, *Washington Post*, 30 September 1995. "UN
Asks for Inquiry into Krajina Killings," *Reuters*, 18 August 1995. "EU
Observers Accuse Croatia of Breaches of Law," *op. cit.* "UN Finds Evi-
dence of Mass Killings in Croatia," *Reuters*, 2 October 1995. "Croats
Slaughter Elderly by the Dozen," Robert Fisk, *op. cit.* "EU Report Accuses
Croatia of Atrocities Against Rebel Serbs," Julian Borger, *op. cit.* "UN:
Executions, Possible Mass Graves in Krajina," *Agence France-Presse*, 18
August 1995. "Helsinki Committee Chronicles Human Rights Abuses," *op.
cit.* "Evidence Emerging of Crimes Against Krajina Serbs," *Tanjug*, 30
August 1995. "Croats Accused of Atrocities," *Associated Press*, 29 September 1995.
[8] "Croats Burn and Kill With a Vengeance," Robert Fisk, *op. cit.* "EU Report Accuses Croatia of Atrocities Against Rebel Serbs," Julian Borger, *op.
cit.* "Television Report," *RTBF-1 Television Network* (Brussels), 20 August
1995. "Memorandum on the Ethnic Cleansing of and Genocide Against the
Serb People of Croatia and Krajina," *Yugoslav Survey*, third quarter, 1995.
[9] "Krajina Operation: Helsinki Committee Member Describes Atrocities in
Krajina," *BBC Summary of World Broadcasts*, 25 August 1995.

[10] "UN Asks for Inquiry Into Krajina Killings," *op. cit.* "UN Finds Evidence of Mass Killings in Croatia," *op. cit.* "UN: Executions, Possible Mass Graves in Krajina," *op. cit.*

[11] "Croats Slaughter Elderly by the Dozen," Robert Fisk, *op. cit.*

[12] "Croats Ready for a Fresh Offense Against Serbs," Patrick Bishop, *Electronic Telegraph*, 16 August 1995. "Tudjman's speeches," *Radio Croatia Network*, 26 August 1995. "U.S. Says Croatia Is Not Guilty of 'Ethnic Cleansing,' " Patrick Moore, *Open Media Research Institute,* 10 August 1995.

[13] "Croatian Minister Says U.S. Gave Advice on Offensive," Jasmina Kuzmanovic, *Associated Press*, 5 August 1995. "Croatia Takes Effective Control of What's Left of Bosnia," *San Francisco Chronicle*, 11 August 1995.

[14] "NATO in Dubrovnik," Vladimir Jovanovic, *Monitor* (Pogorica, Yugoslavia), 23 June 1995.

[15] "AP Report on U.S. Peace Strategy," *Associated Press*, 13 November 1995.

[16] "AP Report on U.S. Peace Strategy," *Associated Press, op. cit.* "U.S. Troops Operate in Croatia," *Associated Press*, 3 February 1995.

[17] "Invisible U.S. Army Defeats Serbs," Charlotte Eagar, *The Observer* (London), 5 November 1995.

[18] "Military Cooperation Agreement Signed with U.S.," *HTV Television* (Zagreb), 13 October 1995.

[19] "We Can Prevent Any Serbian Maneuver," Interview with Tihomir Blaskic by Jozo Pavkovic, *Vecernji List* (Zagreb), 11 March 1995.

[20] "Croatian Leader's Invitation to Holocaust Museum Sparks Anger and Shock," Diana Jean Schemo, *New York Times News Service,* 21 April 1993.

[21] "Croatia, at a Key Strategic Crossroad, Builds Militarily and Geographically," *Defense and Foreign Affairs Strategic Policy* (London), 31 January 1993. "Who is Franjo Tudjman?," *Narodna Armija* (Belgrade), 1 March 1990.

[22] "Criticism of Tudjman Award to Ustasha," *Foreign Broadcast Information Service Media Note* (Media summary), 27 January 1995. "Nationalism Turns Sour in Croatia," *New York Times News Service*, 13 November 1993. "Plan to Honour Ustashe Killers Outrages Minorities in Croatia," Ian Traynor, *The Guardian*, 18 October 1993. "Trpimir for an Executioner and a Victim," Mirko Mirkovic, *Feral Tribune* (Split, Croatia), 20 February 1995. "Croatian General Former Ustasha," *Tanjug*, 26 February 1995.

[23] "Croatia Grants Awards to Nazi-Era War Veterans," *Reuters*, 7 November 1996.

[24] "New Croatian Money Anathema to Serbs," John Pomfret, *Washington Post*, 31 May 1994. "Plan to Honour Ustashe Killers Outrages Minorities

in Croatia," Ian Traynor, *op. cit.* "Pro-Nazi Legacy Lingers for Croatia," Stephen Kinzer, *New York Times News Service*, 30 October 1993. "Monument to Anti-Fascism Desecrated in Croatia," *Tanjug*, 4 February 1995. "Another Anti-Fascist Monument Blown Up in Croatia," *Tanjug*, 11 April 1995. "Croatia, Symbols of Crimes," Miodrag Dundjerovic, *Tanjug*, 1 June 1994. "Croatia Adopts New Currency Recalling Fascist Era," Reuters, 9 May 1994. "Hiding Genocide," Gregory Copley, *Defense and Foreign Affairs Strategic Policy*, 31 December 1992. "Croatia Is Rehabilitating Ustashism and the Independent State of Croatia," *Politika* (Belgrade), 12 February 1993. "Tudjman Calls for All-White Peace Force in Croatia," Eve Ann Prentice, *The Times* (London), 11 April 1995. "Croatia to Seek Expulsion of Non-White U.N Troops," *Tanjug*, 10 April 1995.

[25] Interview with Franjo Tudjman, *HTV Television*, 22 April 1996.

[26] Address by Franjo Tudjman to the Croatian World Congress in Brioni, *Radio Croatia Network* (Zagreb) 6 July 1996.

[27] "Croatian Towns, Villages Cleansed of Serbs," *Tanjug*, 26 January 1993. "Savovic: Croatia Expelled 300,000 Serbs," *Tanjug*, 5 November 1993. "Serb Party Official: 350,000 Serbs Driven Out," *Tanjug*, 26 August 1994.

[28] "Croatian Police Tactics Cited," *Associated Press*, 3 October 1994. "Helsinki Committee Chair: Collective Vendetta Against Croatia's Serbs," *Tanjug*, 7 May 1994. "Protests Prevent Latest Wave of Croatian Apartment Evictions," *Radio Free Europe*, 12 July 1994. "Croatian Human Rights Activist: Zagreb Backs Human Rights Violations," *Tanjug*, 28 September 1994. "Rights Groups Report Abuses by Croatia," David Binder, *New York Times News Service*, 7 December 1993.

[29] "Interior Minister Aide Accused of War Crimes," *ZDF Television Network* (Mainz), 17 May 1994. "Slovene Daily Says Croatian Leaders Keep Quiet About Massacre of Serbs," *Tanjug*, 14 January 1994. "Croatian Paper Calls Mass Killings of Serbs a National Disgrace," *Tanjug*, 12 July 1994. "Zagreb Knows about Mass Killings of Serbs," *Tanjug*, 23 July 1994. "Dossier: Pakracka Poljana," *Feral Tribune*, 1 September 1997. "Death Camps and Mass Graves in Western Slavonia: Marino Selo and Pakracka Poljana," dossier prepared by Serbian Council, Belgrade, *American Srbobran*, 22 September 1997.

[30] "Miro Bajranovic's Confession," *Feral Tribune*, 1 September 1997. "Croatian's Confession Describes Torture and Killing on Vast Scale," Chris Hedges, *The New York Times*, 5 September 1997.

8 The Dayton Accords reshape Europe

U.S. troops in Bosnia have not brought peace to the peoples of the Balkans. There is at most a suppression of hostilities. The Muslims, Croats, Serbs, and all the other peoples of the region have suffered greatly. But to find a solution that can really end the conflict in the Balkans, it is necessary to understand the problem.

The U.S.-NATO military occupation of Bosnia was forced on that country by the Clinton administration during talks in Dayton, Ohio, in the autumn of 1995. At that meeting, a gun was put to the heads of the Bosnian peoples as Washington threatened a bombing campaign like the one the Pentagon waged against Baghdad, Iraq, during the Gulf War. They were given no choice in the matter. *Newsweek* magazine saw great glory in the U.S.-imposed agreement. Its report declared: "Hail Pax Americana! Salute the return of the superpower!"[1]

The dividing up of the former Yugoslavia dictated by the Dayton agreement was in some ways reminiscent of the first division of the Balkan peninsula at the Congress of Berlin in 1878. It was not done by the people of the Balkans. It was not decided on the basis of self-determination for each nationality—Serb, Croat, Slovene, Macedonian, Montenegrin, Albanian, Romani. Nor was it based on religion—Muslim, Serbian Ortho-dox, Jewish, Roman Catholic.

The Congress of Berlin was one of the first great meetings of the emerging imperialist powers to divide up the world among the robber-baron capitalists for their own profit. History books refer to this as the classic period of imperialism. The CD-ROM version of *Grolier's Encyclopedia*, which is used in schools across the country, says, "The term imperialism is most commonly identified with 19th-century colonialism and the carving of the globe into 'spheres of influence' by the European powers." The Congress of Berlin divided the collapsing Ottoman Empire, with the bulk of the spoils going to the British and Austro-Hungarian imperialists. The Balkans were divided into petty states that had no independent economic viability.

Is this only history? Lawrence Eagleburger, who had been secretary of state during the Bush administration, said in 1994 that what was needed was "a modern-day Congress of Berlin" run by the U.S., "the Germans and the French and the Italians," that would draw a new map dividing the Balkans. Yugoslavs should be told, Eagleburger said, "If you don't do this, we're collectively going to kick the shit out of you."[2]

The Dayton accord was just that event. The U.S. drew the map and dictated its terms. And an occupation army was imposed to make sure there would be no resistance. For the peoples of the region, living under an occupation army of any kind is unacceptable. And while the overwhelming U.S.-NATO force has blunted the civil war that gripped the Balkans, it has not brought real peace. In fact, it is impossible to impose such a peace. There is not only opposition in the Balkans to the occupation. There is opposition across the United States to having U.S. troops in the Balkans. The popular sentiment remains, "Bring the troops home." And if the facts were to become known and understood, there would be a movement demanding the withdrawal of U.S. troops much like the movement of the 1960s that demanded an end to the U.S. war against Vietnam.

Because of this, what can only be described as a propaganda war has been launched in the major media intended to make the U.S. military occupation seem reasonable. The media, run by and for big business, reflect the bias of those who are ultimately in control. Most media reports on events in the Balkans are sensationalized and filled with quotes from State Department, CIA, or Pentagon sources. When this happens in other countries, they call it propaganda. When it happens here, they pretend it's just "objective journalism."

If you were to ask a half-dozen U.S. citizens, picked randomly, who are the most aggressive people in the world, at least one would answer "the Serbs." Everyone has heard reports about Serbian war criminals reportedly running rampant in Bosnia. But would anyone point to Washington? And yet the United States has more military bases around the world—in one hundred countries at last count—than any other power in history. Almost three hundred thousand U.S. troops are stationed at major bases abroad. In addition, thousands are deployed in hundreds of other locations worldwide.[3] According to the Center for Defense Information, the United States government is spending more than $6 billion a week on military operations.

The U.S. government is unquestionably the most aggressive in the world today. Yet few seem to realize this. That's how powerful the propaganda is. The difficulty is that the propaganda has clouded people's thinking. For most people in the United States—except those with relatives in the Balkans region—the civil war in the former Yugoslavia seems distant and obscure. Many have to confess they're not even sure where it is. But working-class youth in the United States may find they'll have to learn about the Balkans—not as tourists or students in a geography class. They may learn about it as soldiers.

Here are some questions and answers that may help explain what this struggle is all about.

You say this is like the Vietnam War? Please explain.

Both the Vietnam War and the Balkans occupation involve the world's strongest superpower trying to impose its demands on a much smaller country.

When President Bill Clinton sent troops into Bosnia he promised they would be out in one year—by December 1996. A year later he said it would be two more years. Vietnam-era presidents kept promising there would be a quick end to that war and troops would be out soon. But U.S. involvement kept expanding. U.S. troops were there for more than a decade.

Bosnia is like Vietnam in another way, too. What Washington says is not what it really means. Official statements cite humanitarian concerns for why the U.S. military is in the Balkans region. But that was never the reason. There have been bloodier battles around the world and the Pentagon hasn't gone in. So there must be other goals. The driving force behind the breakup of Yugoslavia and behind the ethnic divisions that emerged there has been obscured. The roots lie in the Cold War drive of the United States and Western Europe to destroy socialism in Eastern Europe and the Soviet Union. The occupation of the Balkans by U.S. NATO forces is intimately tied to the expansion of NATO into all the former socialist countries.

Doesn't the U.S. plan to pull its troops out of Bosnia soon?

The 1990s have become the era of a new colonialism. And the occupation of the Balkans is really part of that. Not only are as many as twenty thousand U.S. troops in Bosnia, but U.S. troops are now based in Albania, Macedonia, Croatia, and Hungary. The *Defense News* says the Bosnia operation actually involves up to eighty thousand U.S. troops and a quarter-million NATO troops altogether.[4]

Retired U.S. Army Gen. William E. Odom is a long-time Pentagon insider. He was the head of the U.S. government's biggest spy agency—the ultra-secret National Security Agency —during the Reagan administration. In an opinion-page piece in the *New York Times*, Odom indicated that the occupation of Bosnia is part of a plan for U.S. military and political domination of Europe and the former Soviet Union through NATO.[5] NATO is the arm of U.S. policy in Europe. It is so completely dominated by the United States that French President Charles

DeGaulle once called it the United States' colonial army in Europe. Odom advocates a long-term military occupation of the Balkans. "Having forty thousand [NATO] troops stationed in Bosnia for a generation is a good thing," says Odom, "even if it requires twenty thousand American troops to keep them there."

You call this a civil war. Why is that? The major newspapers and TV reports never say that.

Part of the reason Washington and the media refuse to call it a civil war is that they can't really explain why the peoples of Slovenia, Croatia, Bosnia-Herzegovina, Serbia, Macedonia, Montenegro, and Kosovo lived together peacefully for about forty-five years. They want to bolster their claim that this is an ethnic war of one people against another. In truth, it is a civil war involving the breakup of Yugoslavia. And civil wars can be bloody, with many casualties. The whole population suffers. It is not unlike the U.S. Civil War in that respect. The deaths and destruction are consistent with a civil war, not the genocide of a people by an oppressor power.

The legal definition of genocide is "the systematic and planned extermination of an entire national, racial, political, or ethnic group." That is what the fascists did to the Jews. And to the Serbs, as well as the Romani (Gypsies), gay people, communists, and socialists. Detention camps are not the same as Nazi death camps. And yet detention camps in Bosnia have been described as centers of genocide.

I've frequently heard the Serb leaders being compared to the Nazis. You say they're not the same. Why not?

The U.S. media and politicians often portray the Serbian army in Bosnia as being like the Nazi army. This is propaganda. There is no basis in fact. That's why sometimes the reports are just absurd. Consider remarks made by National Public Radio commentator Daniel Schorr.

President Clinton had said in a speech that the Serb army in Bosnia was like the Nazi army of the 1930s and 1940s.

Schorr, in talking about Clinton's speech, added that in fact the Serbs were *worse* than the Nazis. "At least the Nazis never raped Jewish women," he said.[6] Schorr was later forced to issue a correction to this incredible lie. But it is a sign of how crazy the media have become in their drive to convince the people of this country that there is a "just" reason for U.S. occupation of the Balkans.

There is no similarity between the Serb army and the Nazi army. In this century, Germany has been one of the biggest and most modern capitalist economies in the world. In the 1930s, it had the world's second-largest economy. It was a great power with the industrial and military capability to challenge its rivals. The fascist Nazi party grew from a small group of right-wing fanatics into a force able to take over the German government because rich industrialists like the Krupps recognized them as the ruthless, extra-legal force they needed to crush the strong workers' movement. It was during the Great Depression, when capitalism was in chaos and even politicians from the bankrupt middle class were talking of revolution. Hitler won the financial and political backing of capitalists like Krupp, who weren't worried about his "national socialist" demagogy. In fact, the Nazi policy of genocide was part of their plan to crush the communist and socialist movements, which had the allegiance of the great majority of the workers.[7] Once that was accomplished, they quickly built a huge army whose mission was to dominate Europe and take over the colonial possessions of Britain, France, The Netherlands, and Belgium.

The Serbian army in Bosnia is completely different. There is no great military or industrial power behind the Serbs. There is only a small industrial base. The Serbs in Bosnia are mostly peasant farmers.

So why are there NATO troops in the Balkans?

In 1990, the United States government put into place plans for a military occupation of Eastern Europe and possibly the former Soviet Union. That plan includes the one hundred thousand-strong Allied Command Europe Rapid Reaction Corps, the NATO unit in charge of the Bosnia operation.

At the end of November 1995, Reuters reported that:

> The Allied Command Europe Rapid Reaction Corps (ARRC), based at Rheindahlen in western Germany, has worked relatively unnoticed since 1992 to put into practice NATO's new emphasis.

> [It has] NATO's full array of firepower [and] a tailor-made fighting force of up to one hundred thousand soldiers able to deploy quickly. As ARRC commander, British Lt.-Gen. Michael Walker is in charge of running the multinational ground force to be stationed in and around Bosnia for NATO's first ground deployment outside its own area. The corps, with headquarters in Sarajevo, is taking three divisions into Bosnia. Two of them, the U.S. First Armored Division and the British Third Mechanized Division, are permanently assigned to it. The third division is French.[8]

The United States is using the Bosnian occupation as a wedge for the expansion of NATO into Eastern Europe. This is part of U.S. political and economic expansion into the region. A plan for a U.S.-NATO occupation of the Balkans was revealed in an opinion piece appearing in the *New York Times*. Writing in the style of a Pentagon briefing, George Kenney of the Carnegie Endowment for International Peace and Michael J. Dugan, a retired Air Force general and former Air Force chief of staff, outlined a blueprint for what they called "Operation Balkan Storm."

The goal of the plan? Kenney and Dugan concluded: "A win in the Balkans would establish U.S. leadership in the post-Cold War world in a way that Operation Desert Storm [the war against Iraq] never could."[9]

Warren Zimmerman, the U.S. ambassador to Yugoslavia during the Reagan and Bush administrations and a consultant with the Pentagon-funded Rand Corporation, said that a NATO domination of Bosnia is essential. At stake, he said, is NATO's capability of "expanding" into Eastern Europe. If a NATO occupation of Bosnia fails, Zimmerman said, "not only will NATO's expansion look ludicrous, but serious roles for NATO anywhere else will be hard to imagine."[10]

You say that this war is just a part of the expansion of NATO into Eastern Europe and the former Soviet Union. Didn't it start because of internal conflicts in Yugoslavia?

The hidden hand of the big powers behind the civil war that ripped Yugoslavia apart remains mostly unknown to the public. One of the few reports in the major media appeared in the British daily newspaper *The Guardian*. It was titled "Bosnia: The Secret War."

The report concluded, "Despite official denials, the CIA and other American 'secret services,' including the CIA's Pentagon cousin the DIA, have been engaged deep within Bosnia's war since its inception."[11]

Another report providing some details was made by T.W. "Bill" Carr of the London-based *Defense & Foreign Affairs* magazine. In a speech on Bonn's and Washington's role in breaking up Yugoslavia and arming counter-revolutionary nationalist forces—particularly those led by Franjo Tudjman in Croatia and Alija Izetbegovic in Bosnia—Carr said:

> Reliable intelligence sources claimed in 1990 that in 1988 Mr. Tudjman paid a secret visit to the Federal Republic of Germany and met with Chancellor Kohl and other senior government ministers. It was said that the aim of the visit was to formulate a joint policy to break up Yugoslavia, leading to the recreation of a new independent State of Croatia with international borders in the form originally set up by the German chancellor, Adolf Hitler, in 1941.

> At a secret meeting in Bonn, the German government pledged its political, financial, and covert military

support for Croatia's secession from the Federal Republic of Yugoslavia.[12]

This, Carr says, "fitted neatly into Germany's strategic objectives in respect to the Balkans." Those included bringing "Croatia and Slovenia within the German economic zone [and] gaining direct access to the Adriatic and Mediterranean."

Carr said that in order to finance the secessionist forces under Tudjman, Germany arranged an interest-free $2-billion loan. Tudjman was the president of the Croatian republic that, at the time, was still part of Yugoslavia. The loan was never reported to the central Yugoslav government, as required by law.

Carr also gave details on the maneuvering of the U.S. government. He said the most notable feature of U.S. secret policy in the beginning was to make military threats against the Yugoslav Army unless it completely surrendered to U.S. demands. But it often didn't work. Carr offered a description of one memorable interaction between U.S. military officers and the Yugoslav Army's top staff.

> A senior U.S. officer was introduced as having wide experience in the Vietnam War and that his armored units in the Gulf War had destroyed seven Iraqi armored divisions. The threat was made to send him to the Balkans to do a similar destruction job on the JNA [Yugoslav National Army]. [But] despite having been told not to argue by [Yugoslav] Gen. Panic, the [Yugoslav] Chief of Military Intelligence could not resist saying that the U.S. officer had lost in Vietnam and he would find the mountains of Bosnia and Serbia much tougher than a flat desert.[13]

Carr showed how the U.S. government created a joint Croatian and Bosnian military command. "At the same time, the U.S. government dispatched to Croatia, Bosnia, Albania, and the former Yugoslav Republic of Macedonia, a number of 'recently retired' U.S. Army officers as 'advisors.' " These advisors developed a coordinated military strategy to defeat the Serbs and trained the Croatian and Bosnian officer corps. Carr said, "While this training was in progress, intelligence sources claim the advisors brought in U.S. Special Forces. Though initially denied, the deployment of the U.S. Special Forces was later admitted by a U.S. government spokesman." In 1995, the Bosnian Army was headed by a U.S. Army general, Carr said—Gen. John Galvin, a former NATO commander and recently the head of West Point—who "planned and executed" a Bosnian Army offensive that year. It should be remembered that there was no civil war in Yugoslavia until Slovenia and Croatia seceded.

Who is Franjo Tudjman?

Croatian President Franjo Tudjman has received considerable backing from the German government as well as the U.S. Pentagon and State Department. His backing by Washington is so great that he was invited to be a guest of honor at the opening of the Holocaust museum. This is the man who once declared, "Thank God my wife is neither a Serb nor a Jew." Tudjman is a Croatian nationalist who gained support from Germany and the United States on the basis of his rabid anti-communism. When Croatia broke off from Yugoslavia, Tudjman's government adopted the flag and currency that had been used by the fascist Ustashe regime during World War II.

His book *Wastelands: Historical Truths* asserts that "only" nine hundred thousand Jews died in the Holocaust, not six million. He also asserts that no more than seventy thousand Serbs were killed in the Ustashe death camps.

Scholars specializing in World War II, however, estimate that the number of Serbs killed in these camps ranged between six hundred thousand and a million plus.

Tudjman wrote, "Genocide is a natural phenomenon in keeping with human social and mythological divine nature. It is not only allowed, but even recommended."[14] Tudjman has never been indicted by the war crimes tribunal in The Hague for his advocacy of genocide.

Although the U.S. has brokered a Croatian-Bosnian federation between Tudjman and Alija Izetbegovic, it is a shaky
alliance at best. Tudjman is violently anti-Muslim, to the point
of even denying Muslim legitimacy. In an interview published in
the French daily *Le Figaro*, Tudjman said that the Muslims are
really Croatians who should eventually be incorporated into
Croatia. He sees his task in the Croatian-Bosnian federation as
"Europeanizing" the Muslims, "bringing them into European
civilization."[15] Tudjman is a raving racist.

According to a *New York Times* profile of Tudjman, he
came to power "helped by financing from anti-communist
Croatian émigrés in the United States and Canada."[16] What the
Times doesn't mention is that these groups are ultimately financed by the CIA.

What about Alija Izetbegovic?

When Bosnia-Herzegovina broke off from Yugoslavia,
the most popular Muslim leader was not Alija Izetbegovic. By
popular vote, Fikret Abdic was the most widely supported
Muslim leader. But he was against the breakup of Yugoslavia
and not in the pocket of Washington. He supported Muslim-
Serbian-Croatian cooperation. With U.S. support, a narrow
grouping around Izetbegovic forced Abdic out of the Bosnian
government, where he was part of the collective presidency. He
then led an army that allied with the Bosnian Serbs and opposed
the Izetbegovic forces. In the spring of 1995 he was captured by
the Croatian Army and forced into exile.[17]

The regime of Alija Izetbegovic is completely dependent
on the United States for its existence. In fact, its first foreign
minister was a U.S. citizen.

Izetbegovic is another long-time anti-communist fanatic.
He's typical of the anti-communists supported by the U.S. government throughout the Cold War. During World War II, he
belonged to a group that collaborated with the Nazi occupiers.
In 1949, Izetbegovic was one of the leaders of a revolt against
the Tito government. He and several others were sent to prison.

After he got out, Izetbegovic continued his counter-revolutionary activities. He maintained close contact with U.S.-backed exile groups.

In 1970, he published his *Islamic Declaration* that said "there can be neither peace nor coexistence between the Islamic faith and non-Islamic social and political institutions."[18] In 1983, he and twelve others were convicted for counter-revolutionary acts, including advocating an "ethnically pure Bosnia-Herzegovina."[19]

What about the ethnic genocide that's been reported in Bosnia? And the war crimes tribunal in The Hague?

The war crimes tribunal sitting in The Hague is not really about law. In fact, it doesn't even follow recognized international law and procedure.[20] The tribunal is staffed mostly by appointees from Washington and serves as an extension of U.S. political policy in Europe.[21]

In 1992, U.S. Secretary of State Lawrence Eagleburger declared Yugoslavia's leaders to be war criminals and practically dictated the agenda for the tribunal.[22] The judges for the tribunal were hand-picked by the very powers that now occupy the former Yugoslavia. It has not been given authority to look into war crimes committed anywhere else.

Of the seventy-six people publicly indicted by the tribunal, almost sixty are Serbs. Although the U.S. media have convinced many that everyone publicly indicted by The Hague tribunal—and the untold numbers secretly indicted—are guilty, there is little evidence for this that could stand up in a real court of law. Serb leaders like Radovan Karadzic and Ratko Mladic are not presumed innocent until proven guilty. They are being told they must prove they are not guilty.

The charge of genocide in Bosnia has been made so often that many believe it has already been proven. But George Kenney, one of the framers of U.S. policy in the Balkans under the Bush administration, says: "The U.S. government doesn't have proof of any genocide. And anyone reading the press critically can see that paucity of evidence, despite interminably re-peated claims and bloodcurdling speculation."[23]

In the first trial before The Hague tribunal, charges were quietly dropped because the man charged had been living in Germany the whole time that his alleged crimes were commit-ted. The second trial, that of Dusko Tadic, ended May 7, 1997. He was sentenced July 14, 1997. By the court's own admission, Tadic was not a major military figure. And the court was unable to come up with evidence that he had committed any specific murders. All the widely publicized charges of genocide against him were also dropped for lack of evidence. In the end, he was convicted of beating prisoners and being responsible for the deaths of two Bosnian police officers.

A revealing side to the trial of Tadic is that it started on May 2, 1996, just after the Israeli military, using U.S.-provided technology and weapons, bombed a refugee camp in Lebanon, killing over a hundred people. Wasn't this a war crime? But no Israeli or U.S. military and civilian officials were ever charged for this. And no indictment was brought when it was revealed that German soldiers training for their military mission into the former Yugoslavia had staged mock executions and rapes of civilians during a break. The *Bild am Sonntag* newspaper printed pictures from a videotape that showed German soldiers in battle fatigues pretending to rape Yugoslav women and a uniformed soldier putting his gun into the mouth of another soldier. Other photos show enactments of "civilians" being tor-tured and hanging from trees.[24]

To put the indictments and arrest warrants in perspec-tive, consider some well-known war crimes since 1945, when the first war-crimes tribunal was held that put the German Nazi regime in the dock. U.S. President Harry Truman was never indicted for ordering the incineration of hundreds of thousands of Japanese civilians in the atomic attacks on Hiroshima and Nagasaki. Winston Churchill was never indicted for murdering some 135,000 civilians when he ordered the firebombing of Dresden. An International War Crimes Tribunal, sponsored by

Bertrand Russell, amply documented U.S. violations of international law in the war against Vietnam. It had enormous moral and political authority, but no executive arm to issue warrants. No "international force" ever roamed the streets of the United States arresting war criminals.

French war crimes in Algeria during that country's liberation struggle are also well documented—including systematic torture to obtain information. Apartheid South Africa committed heinous atrocities in its suppression of the Black majority at home, in its invasion of Angola, and in its sponsorship of a right-wing guerrilla force in Mozambique. Britain has a long history of war crimes in northern Ireland. And yet no indictments have been issued for these or any other war crimes.

More recently, no U.S. general or member of the Bush administration faced indictment for war crimes in the 1991 Gulf War, even though civilian shelters in Baghdad were targeted and bombed—a crime under international law. No Russian general or member of Boris Yeltsin's regime has been indicted for the crimes committed in Chechnya.

The Hague tribunal is pursuing a limited political agenda defined primarily by U.S. interests.

Are you saying there weren't crimes in the Balkans war?

There have been terrible, bloody events in the Yugoslav civil war. No one can deny that. And the media reports have been about some of these events. But what has been emphasized has been very selective. For example, a mass slaughter of Serbs occurred in the Krajina area of Croatia in the summer of 1995. According to investigators for the United Nations, "Croatian army and police units allegedly burned 60 percent of the houses" in the Krajina region.[25] Unlike almost every other report of genocide in the civil war, these reports were "unusual in their first-hand detail."

An open letter written at that time from the Serbian-Jewish Friendship Society based in Belgrade to the American Jewish Committee said that "anti-Serbian propaganda" is "a twin sister of anti-Semitism." The letter stated that Croatia had instituted a policy of eliminating the Serbs. This policy was so thorough that "in Croatia there are [now] no more Serbs than there are Jews in Germany or Poland." The letter was signed by the chief rabbi of Yugoslavia as well as by many other prominent Jews of Yugoslavia.

The Croatian Army that carried out this massacre was being directed by U.S. military officers. A report in *The Nation* magazine on "Privatizing War" describes the activities of Military Professional Resources Inc., based in Arlington, Va., which trained both the Croatian and Bosnian armies. MPRI, run by "retired" U.S. military officers, has been described as having more four-star generals than the Pentagon. *The Nation* reports:

> Just months after MPRI went into Croatia, that nation's army—until then bumbling and inept— launched a series of bloody offensives against Serbian forces. Most important was Operation Lightning Storm, the assault on the Krajina region during which Serbian villages were sacked and burned, hundreds of civilians were killed and some 170,000 people were driven from their homes."[26]

The Nation report says that MPRI "played an important role in the Krajina campaign." The war crimes tribunal in The Hague has never indicted any U.S. military officer—or anyone else, for that matter—for the Krajina massacre.

The Bosnian Army is also being "helped" by U.S. military advisors, including Gen. John Sewall and Gen. John Galvin, the former NATO supreme commander. The entire Bosnian Army wears U.S. military uniforms provided by U.S. military contractors. Gen. Charles Boyd, the deputy commander in chief of the U.S. European Command from November 1992 to July 1995, says that the much-publicized arms embargo in the region is almost nonexistent. He says that the U.S. insures a regular flow of arms to the Bosnian Army.[27]

U.S. media reports on the Krajina massacre were filled with references to "rebel Serbs" and talked of the Krajina as a region "conquered" by the Serbs. The implication was that the Croatian Army was simply retaking something that had been stolen. But the truth is exactly the opposite. The following exchange shows the propaganda view of the major media and gives a response. On a broadcast of National Public Radio's "All Things Considered," news reader Noah Adams interviewed author Misha Glenny:

> *Adams:* Why did Serbia take the Krajina four years ago, if it is indefensible?
>
> *Glenny:* We've got to set one or two things straight here, Noah, about Serbia taking the Krajina. The Krajina came into being at the same time as the Croatian republic became independent when Yugoslavia was collapsing. The Croats wanted to leave Yugoslavia and the Serbs who lived in the Krajina wanted to stay in Yugoslavia. So we simply can't use terms like "Serbia occupying the Krajina" or something like that. These people had been, until five days ago, living and farming this territory for over three hundred years.[28]

So who supports the NATO occupation of Bosnia?

U.S. arms merchants are some of the most ardent supporters of this occupation. Arms manufacturers are making big bucks on the $6.5 billion that the U.S. government is conservatively estimated to have spent on the occupation of Bosnia.[29] The U.S. military is driven to continually expand and use its arms. And the U.S. military-industrial complex must continually make sales or shut down for lack of profit. As one Pentagon official said, "It's an ugly little story, but there's a lot of money and perceived prestige at stake" in having weapons deployed in any military operation.[30] The payoff goes to giants of the military-industrial complex like General Dynamics, General Electric, General Motors, Lockheed Martin, McDonnell Douglas, Raytheon, and United Technologies. U.S. military expenditures continue to grow. According to the Center for Defense Information web site, U.S. military spending between 1948 and 1991 averaged $291 billion a year. And the military plans endorsed in 1996 by the supposedly budget-conscious Congress and White House will add up to more than $1.6 trillion over the next six years.

In the first decades of this century, huge military expenditures bought military victories. The big powers of Europe, the United States, and Japan "won" sources of raw materials and markets by outright seizures of territory. The competition between these big capitalist powers for control of markets and resources led to two world wars. But things have changed since the end of World War II. Military expenditures are increasing, even at a time of budget reductions, but there are no corresponding victories. From a strictly economic point of view—and leaving out for the moment the interests of different classes—the building of an aircraft carrier or a cruise missile system used to pay for itself if it seized new markets to exploit or grabbed material resources like oil, or if it took control of sales territories that had been controlled by competing rivals.

But beginning with the Korean War, U.S. military expansion has not brought back the returns in superprofits necessary to support military expansion. Under capitalism, an enterprise must generate a profit. And by this measure, the military has not been a profitable venture. Even the so-called victory over Iraq failed to seize much of that country's vast oil wealth, though it did manage to remove some key oil fields from Iraqi control.

Consider the cost of one aircraft carrier—$3.4 billion. But these enormous projects have no economic value to the U.S. government unless they can bring back a profit for U.S. big business. More and more, militarism is being paid for by cutting social programs.

Are only the arms merchants behind this?

No. U.S. banks and big business see the former Yugoslavia as a place for expansion, much as pirates see a conquered galleon as a source of loot. The death of U.S. Commerce Secretary Ron Brown and thirty-four others in a plane crash on April 3, 1996, while on a mission to Croatia and Bosnia, was revealing. Brown was leading a delegation of U.S. business and banking executives. On the plane were twelve chief executives and fourteen U.S. government employees, one identified by the State Department only as a CIA employee. The executives included the chair and chief executive of Riggs International Bank in Washington, the U.S. executive director of the European Bank for Reconstruction and Development, and a vice president of AT&T's Submarine Systems division. There was also the president of Bechtel's operations in Europe, Africa, the Middle East, and Southwest Asia. The San Francisco-based Bechtel engineering company is one of the biggest Pentagon contractors in the United States. In addition, the chair and chief executive of Parsons Corporation of Pasadena, California, was on board. Parsons is one of the world's biggest engineering and construction corporations. Another passenger was the *New York Times* bureau chief in Frankfurt, Germany.

This was a high-level operation. The *New York Times* reported that a great many unanswered questions surrounded the crash of Brown's plane in Dubrovnik, Croatia.[31] The crash reflected the breakneck pace of the competition to exploit new markets opening in the former socialist countries. The *Times* even suggested there were "profit motives, unspoken pressures" involved in the crash.

During the "classic" period of imperialism, trade—that is, the export of goods—was dominant. That was before the emergence of giant monopolies. Now trade is secondary to the export of capital. This includes government loans or loans through giant financial institutions dominated by the U.S., like the International Monetary Fund and the World Bank, or the European Bank for Reconstruction and Development. Such loans are usually made to finance projects like office buildings, factories, or military bases where the work is contracted to companies based in the country where the loan originated.

Companies like Bechtel, for example, whose representative was on Secretary Brown's plane. The loans might also be to build or redevelop highways, railroads, ports, and so on. Parsons Corporation specializes in just such projects.

Capital exports have for a century created a way to utilize the "surplus" capital of the dominant countries. But most of the world market is already carved up and under the control of one or another cartel. There are only a limited number of "new" projects that finance capital can undertake. There is fierce competition among similar corporations in each of the big powers—primarily the U.S., Germany, Britain, France, and Japan—for these markets. The takeover of the socialist countries and industries in Eastern Europe and the Soviet Union has generated a new capitalist frenzy to control these new markets.

You refer to Socialist Yugoslavia. Was that any better?

Yugoslavia was different from most other countries in the world in its ethnic diversity. It had no majority nationality. It was a nation of minorities. Socialist Yugoslavia had gone a long way toward uniting the nationalities while recognizing the rights of self-determination for the different peoples of the region. Although there were certainly problems and mistakes were made during that time, without a doubt it was better than what is happening now.

The history of the Yugoslav socialist revolution is instructive for those looking for another way out of the Balkans war. Here's a description from the *Encyclopaedia Britannica*:

> Armed resistance to the [Nazi] occupation began in Bosnia, and there the Croatian Fascists began a massacre of Serbs which, in the whole annals of World War II, was surpassed for savagery only by the mass extermination of Polish Jews. The Serbs took to the hills and forests to defend themselves. In Serbia itself a force led by the regular army colonel, Dragomir (Draza) Mihajlovic, fought Germans in the early summer. After Hitler attacked Russia, the Yugoslav Communists, who had already made military prepa-

rations, took the field in Serbia and Montenegro. By September a large part of both these lands was liberated by these two forces, which at first helped each other but then came to blows. In November the Germans drove all resistance forces out of Serbia and massacred thousands of people in reprisal.

In the following three years the Communist forces grew, while the forces of Mihajlovic lost ground. One reason was that Mihajlovic came to depend on the support of various Serbian armed units in Italian-occupied territory which fought under Italian command against the Communist partisans. Another was that the partisans attracted thousands to their ranks by their slogan of unity of all Yugoslav nations against the invaders and traitors. This slogan provided the only alternative to the fratricidal massacres, first of Serbs by Pavelic's Croatian Fascists and then of Croats and Moslems by Serbian nationalist Chetniks owing allegiance to Mihajlovic. In their liberated territory the Communists, led by Josip Broz, known as Tito, a Croat, built not only an army but a crude civil administration. . . .[32]

A new government emerged in 1946 after the defeat of the fascists. "Its main feature," the *Encyclopaedia Britannica* said, "was the creation of six constituent republics: Serbia, Croatia, Slovenia, Bosnia-Herzegovina, Montenegro, and Macedonia. Vojvodina and the Albanian-inhabited Kosovo-Metohija district were autonomous provinces within the Serbian republic." The entry adds, "Of the six republics, the one that gained most was certainly Macedonia, whose people were for the first time allowed to use their language in public and to call themselves Macedonians."

---

[1] David H. Hackworth, "Learning about war the hard way," *Newsweek*, 4 December 1995, p. 30.

[2] Michael Kelly, "Surrender and blame," *The New Yorker*, 19 December 1994.

[3] Center for Defense Information web site (www.cdi.org), 1995 figures.

[4] *Defense News*, 25 November 1995.

[5] *New York Times*, 5 December 1995.

[6] National Public Radio, "Saturday Edition," 17 April 1993.

[7] See Daniel Guerin, *Fascism and Big Business* (New York: Pioneer Publishers, 1939).

[8] Reuters, 30 November 1995.

[9] *New York Times*, 9 November 1992.

[10] *New York Times*, 23 June 1995.

[11] *The Guardian*, 29 January 1996.

[12] Transcript of a speech by T.W. ("Bill") Carr, associate publisher, Defense & Foreign Affairs Publications, London, delivered at a symposium on the Balkan War, "Yugoslavia: Past and Present," Chicago, 31 August-1 September 1995.

[13] *Op. cit.*

[14] Moira Martingale, *Cannibal Killers: The History of Impossible Murderers* (New York: St. Martin's Press, 1995), pp. 199-200.

[15] *Le Figaro*, 25 September 1995.

[16] *New York Times*, 19 August 1995.

[17] "In Bosnia, an ethnic exception," *Washington Post*, 13 June 1997.

[18] Alija Izetbegovic, *The Islamic Declaration*, translated excerpts available from the Balkan Research Centre in "A briefing paper produced for members for the 1992/3 session of the British Parliament," 21 December 1992, on line; originally printed privately 1970, reprinted Sarajevo, 1990 (http://suc.suc.org/~kosta/tar/bosna/).

[19] A private letter from Dr. Milan Bulajic, director of the Museum of Genocide Victims in Belgrade, Yugoslavia, written 7 November 1995, says: "The present leader of the Bosnian Muslims, Alija Izetbegovic, joined the organization 'Young Muslims' in Sarajevo on March 5, 1943. As a member of this organization he took active part in establishment of the notorious 'SS Hanjjar Division' and collaborated with Hitler's intelligence services (Abver and Gertago). . . . Alija Izetbegovic because of his fascist activities was sentenced in the year 1946 to three years of prison and two years of deprivation of civil rights. These documents (verdict and facsimile of the documents) were presented at the trial in 1983."

[20] "Critical jurists have pointed out that in its structure the tribunal had little to do with genuine legal principles or practices," pointed out former *New York Times* bureau chief David Binder in "Thoughts on United States policy towards Yugoslavia," *The South Slav Journal*, vol. 16, no. 61-62, Autumn-Winter 1995.

[21] United Nations Document A/C.5/49/42 dated 5 December 1994 says that the personnel in the Office of the Prosecutor are: twenty-two United States; four The Netherlands; two Germany; two Denmark; two Norway; two

Sweden; two Zimbabwe; one Great Britain. The war crimes tribunal is paid for by voluntary contributions. The United States paid $3 million of its $7-million budget.

[22] *New York Times*, 16 December 1992.

[23] "Steering Clear of Balkan Shoals," *The Nation*, 8/15 January 1996, p. 21.

[24] *Bild am Sonntag*, 6 July 1997.

[25] *Washington Post*, 30 September 1995.

[26] Ken Silverstein, "Privatizing War," *The Nation*, 28 July/4 August 1997, p. 11.

[27] General Charles G. Boyd, "Making Peace with the Guilty: The Truth About Bosnia," *Foreign Affairs*, September/October 1995, p. 22.

[28] National Public Radio, "All Things Considered," 11 August 1995.

[29] *New York Times*, 5 October 1997.

[30] *Washington Post*, 12 September 1996.

[31] *New York Times*, 6 April 1996.

[32] *Encyclopaedia Britannica* (Encyclopaedia Britannica, Inc., Chicago, 1957), vol. 23, p. 920.

PART THREE

THE WAR
AND
THE MEDIA

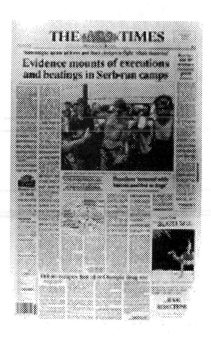

British tabloids front-paged the picture that fooled the world.

9 The picture that fooled the world

THOMAS DEICHMANN[*]

The picture that appeared in several tabloids reproduced on the facing page is of Fikret Alic, a Bosnian Muslim. Emaciated and stripped to the waist, he is apparently imprisoned behind a barbed-wire fence in a Bosnian Serb camp at Trnopolje. The picture was taken from a videotape shot on August 5, 1992, by an award-winning British television team led by Penny Marshall of ITN. Marshall was accompanied by her cameraman Jeremy Irvin, Ian Williams of Channel 4, and reporter Ed Vulliamy from *The Guardian* newspaper.

For many, this picture has become a symbol of the horrors of the Bosnian war—"Belsen '92," as one British newspaper headline captioned the photograph.[1] But that image is misleading. The fact is that Fikret Alic and his fellow Bosnian Muslims were not imprisoned behind a barbed-wire fence. There was no barbed-wire fence surrounding Trnopolje camp. It was

[*] This chapter is an edited translation of an article that appeared in the German magazine *Novo*, January/February 1997 issue. It was then published in English in the British magazine *LM*, Issue 97, February 1997. The British television station ITN sued to prevent *LM* from publishing the story, demanding that its editor withdraw the issue and pulp every copy. *LM* now faces a costly legal battle for insisting on its right to publish the truth.

not a prison, and certainly not a "concentration camp," but a collection center for refugees, many of whom went there seeking safety and could leave again if they wished.

The barbed wire in the picture is not around the Bosnian Muslims; it is around the cameraman and the journalists. It formed part of a broken-down barbed-wire fence encircling a small compound that was next to Trnopolje camp. The British news team filmed from inside this compound, shooting pictures of the refugees and the camp through the compound fence. In the eyes of many who saw them, the resulting pictures left the false impression that the Bosnian Muslims were caged behind barbed wire.

Whatever the British news team's intentions may have been, their pictures were seen around the world as the first hard evidence of concentration camps in Bosnia. "The proof: behind the barbed wire, the brutal truth about the suffering in Bosnia," announced the *Daily Mail* alongside a front-page reproduction of the picture from Trnopolje: "They are the sort of scenes that flicker in black and white images from fifty-year-old films of Nazi concentration camps."[2] On the first anniversary of the pictures being taken, an article in the *Independent* could still use the barbed wire to make the Nazi link: "The camera slowly pans up the bony torso of the prisoner. It is the picture of famine, but then we see the barbed wire against his chest and it is the picture of the Holocaust and concentration camps."[3]

Penny Marshall, Ian Williams, and Ed Vulliamy have never called Trnopolje a concentration camp. They have criticized the way that others tried to use their reports and pictures as "proof" of a Nazi-style Holocaust in Bosnia. Yet over the past four and a half years, none of them has told the full story about that barbed-wire fence which made such an impact on world opinion.

It was through my role as an expert witness to the War Crimes Tribunal that I first realized that something was wrong with the famous pictures from Trnopolje. As a journalist with a track record of reporting on Bosnia, I was asked to present the tribunal with a report on German media coverage of Dusko Tadic, a Bosnian Serb accused of war crimes. Reviewing press articles and videotapes that had been shown on German TV, I became aware of the major importance of the Trnopolje pictures. The picture of Fikret Alic behind the barbed wire, taken by Penny Marshall's team, could be seen again and again.

One night, while I was going through the pictures again at home, my wife pointed out an odd little detail. If Fikret Alic and the other Bosnian Muslims were imprisoned inside a barbed-wire fence, why was this wire fixed to poles on the side of the fence where they were standing? As any gardener knows, fences are, as a rule, fixed to the poles from outside, so that the area to be enclosed is fenced-in. It occurred to me then that perhaps it was not the people in the camp who were fenced-in behind the barbed wire, but the team of British journalists.

My suspicions were heightened by a conversation I had with Professor Mischa Wladimiroff, Dusko Tadic's Dutch defense advocate at the War Crimes Tribunal in The Hague. The main witness against Tadic, Dragan Opacic (later exposed as a trained liar), had told the court about the barbed-wire fence surrounding the camp at Trnopolje and had even made a drawing of where it was. But when Professor Wladimiroff went to Bosnia to investigate for the defense, it became clear to him that Opacic had lied in the witness box; he could find no evidence of a barbed-wire fence surrounding Trnopolje camp.

I decided to go back to Bosnia, and to review the British news team's coverage of Trnopolje, in order to unravel the real story of how those pictures had come about.

The British news team's trip to Bosnia in the summer of 1992 took place against a background of mounting hysteria, as the first reports claiming that the Bosnian Serbs were running brutal internment camps were published in the West. On July 19, 1992, the American journalist Roy Gutman wrote in *Newsday* about the camp at Manjaca, and Andre Kaiser's pictures of prisoners with shaven heads at Manjaca were shown around the world. On July 29 in the *Guardian*, Maggie O'Kane quoted eyewitnesses who claimed that Muslims had been crammed into cattle cars and shipped off from Trnopolje station. On August 2 Roy Gutman published another article in which he called the Bosnian Serb camp at Omarska a "death camp." Gutman's and O'Kane's articles drew heavily on hearsay and unconfirmed claims. Nevertheless, they caused an international sensation.

When Marshall, Williams, and Vulliamy arrived in Bosnia at the end of July 1992, they were under intense pressure to get the story of the camps. Roy Gutman's article about the "death camp" Omarska, published while the British team was in Bosnia, had further raised expectations in the London editorial offices. After her return, Penny Marshall told how she and Williams had received orders from the managing editors of ITN and Channel 4 to do nothing else before they had the camps story in the bag: "They had set Ian Williams and myself loose with an open-ended brief to find and visit the detention camps, and with orders to file nothing until we had come up with the story."[4]

As the end of their trip approached, however, the British news team had been unable to find the camps story they were after. Their final stop was to be the refugee camp at Trnopolje, next to the village of Kozarac which had been overrun by Bosnian Serb units a few months earlier in May 1992. This was to be their last chance to get the story their editors wanted.

The pictures they shot at Trnopolje camp on August 5 were edited in Budapest the next day, then sent to London and broadcast the same night. The broadcast centered on shots of the journalists talking to Fikret Alic and the group of Bosnian Muslims through the barbed wire. These were the pictures that were widely interpreted as evidence that the Muslims were penned behind a barbed-wire fence, and that the international media seized upon to make a symbolic link to the Nazi camps. But how did the British team get them?

I have looked through the rest of the team's film from Trnopolje, at the pictures that were not broadcast. They reveal a lot more about the story.

The camp at Trnopolje consisted of buildings that had previously been a school, and a community center that housed a medical center and a public hall, alongside a large open area that had been a sports ground. The only fences around parts of the camp were little more than a meter high, of the kind you might find around any school or public building. The British news team was able to enter all areas of the refugee camp. They shot some pictures in the buildings. Their attention, however, focused on a group of Muslims who had just been brought from the camps in Keraterm close to Prijedor. They were waiting in the open air to be registered and given food and somewhere to sleep.

To film these refugees, Marshall and her cameraman Irvin entered a compound next to the camp area. Inside this small compound were a kind of garage shed, an electricity transformer station, and a brick barn. Before the war, horticultural products could be bought there and tractors and construction machinery had been housed in the barn. To protect all this from thieves, the compound area of approximately five hundred square meters had been fenced in with barbed wire a couple of years before. The erection of the barbed-wire fence had nothing to do with the refugees, the camp, or the war. The poles to which this barbed wire was attached are still standing today, and traces of the wire can be found on the west side of the compound.

When Marshall, Williams, and Vulliamy entered the compound next to the camp, the barbed wire was already torn in several places. They did not use the open gate, but entered from the south through a gap in the fence. They approached the fence on the north side, where curious refugees quickly gathered inside the camp, but on the outside of the area fenced in by barbed wire. It was through the barbed-wire fence at this point that the famous shots of Fikret Alic were taken.

The unused footage shows how cameraman Irvin zoomed through the compound's barbed-wire fence from various angles, apparently searching for the most dramatic shot.

Most of the refugees in the camp were marked by their experience of the war, but few looked as emaciated as Fikret Alic. Yet he captured the camera's attention.

On her return, Penny Marshall wrote in the *Sunday Times* that "Jeremy Irvin, our cameraman, knew he had come away with powerful images from Prijedor, but only when we screened them in our Budapest editing suite did we begin to sense their impact." Ed Vulliamy summarized this impact in his book, *Seasons in Hell*: "With his rib cage behind the barbed wire of Trnopolje, Fikret Alic had become the symbolic figure of the war, on every magazine cover and television screen in the world."[5] Mike Jeremy, ITN foreign editor, later called the picture "one of the key images of the war in former Yugoslavia."[6]

Yet an important element of that "key image" had been produced by camera angles and editing. The other pictures, which were not broadcast, show clearly that the large area on which the refugees were standing was not fenced in with barbed wire. You can see that the people are free to move on the road and on the open area, and have already erected a few protective tents. Within the compound next door that is surrounded with barbed wire, you can see about fifteen people, including women and children, sitting under the shade of a tree. Penny Marshall's team were able to walk in and out of this compound to get their film, and the refugees could do the same as they searched for some shelter from the August sun.

Another unpublished sequence on the tape shows Fikret Alic and the other refugees who had just arrived from a different angle. The cameraman is no longer inside the barbed-wire area, but about twenty meters to the west of it. From here it is obvious that the refugees are not caged behind barbed wire. While they wait to be registered and told where to go, they are standing behind an ordinary wire-mesh fence that is little more than a meter high, adjacent to the barbed wire. But these pictures did not make it on to the world's TV screens and front pages.

When I visited Trnopolje in December I asked local people about the camp and the barbed wire. Dragan Baltic, seventeen, went to school in Trnopolje until the spring of 1992. He is certain that, apart from the one around the small compound, "there has been no other barbed-wire fence." His nineteen-year-old sister, Dragana, now works in a refugee center in the school. Dragana confirms her brother's account. She adds that there was a metal fence about one meter high in front of and around the school building, to prevent the children from running on to the road. That fence can be seen on the ITN tapes. Refugees lean on it, others jump over it to enter the camp area. Dragana also remembers a small wire-mesh fence about 1.2 meters high, "as is used for keeping hens," running from the road up to the community center and adjacent to the barbed-wire fence. This wire-mesh fence, which stood before the war, can also be clearly seen on the ITN pictures.

I met Pero Curguz in his office in Prijedor. He manages the regional Red Cross, and was stationed in Trnopolje during the operation of the refugee center. He was interviewed by the British journalists in August 1992. He says he told them that the people had come to the camp of their own free will for protection. He told me that during the entire time of the operation of the camp, no fence had been erected. On the contrary: when the other camps in Keraterm and Omarska were closed, and Trnopolje became overcrowded with up to 7,500 people, the refugees had pulled down fences and taken all other available materials to build shelters. Curguz stressed that this was no internment or prisoner camp; it was a collecting camp for exiled Muslims. Everybody I spoke to confirmed that the refugees could leave the camp area at almost any time.

When I showed the picture of Fikret Alic behind the barbed wire to people in Trnopolje, I saw always the same reaction: anger and disappointment. They had expected fair treatment from the Western journalists and had welcomed them. Veljko Grmusa and his family were exiled from Bosanska Bojna near Velika Kladusa and were assigned the house of an exiled Muslim in Trnopolje. In the middle of August 1992 he worked as a guard in the refugee center for a couple of days, before he was sent to the front. He was glad when I told him that Fikret Alic had survived the war, but angry about this image. His wife, Milica, told me that she assisted in the camp by order of the local authorities during the war: "We wanted to help the journalists at that time, we had no idea how the Western newspapers work. Later we received orders not to talk any more with reporters who could not produce a special authorization."

Misa Radulovic, sixty-eight, was a teacher in Kozarac and Trnopolje. Now he walks with a stick and is nearly blind. But like all other men considered able-bodied, he was enlisted in the army during the war and stationed as a camp guard in Trnopolje for three days. "We protected the Muslims from Serbian extremists who wanted to take revenge," he said. "The people could leave the camp without papers, but this was dangerous. A barbed-wire fence existed only at this corner around the barn, this little shop for rural products and the electricity station."

Without doubt most of the refugees in Trnopolje were undernourished. Civilians were harassed in the camp, and there were reports of some rapes and murders. Yet the irony is that, if this collection center for refugees had not existed under the supervision of Bosnian Serb soldiers, a far greater number of Muslim civilians might have lost their lives.

The collection center was spontaneously created by refugees when the civil war escalated in the Prijedor region. In May 1992 Bosnian Serb forces took the town of Kozarac and drove its Bosnian Muslim occupants out, just as Serb and Croat civilians had been driven out of their homes elsewhere in the war zone. Many of the fleeing Muslims sought refuge on the school grounds at Trnopolje. They congregated there in the hope of avoiding being picked off by Bosnian Serb militia or press-ganged into the war by Bosnian Muslim forces. Many of the Bosnian Serb guards sent to the camp were local civilians, mobilized a few days before, who knew the refugees. And there was a permanent Red Cross presence under Pero Curguz, who told me that he, too, had met many old acquaintances in the camp.

For all that, in the middle of a bloody war zone, the camp could never be completely safe. But many refugees preferred to stay there rather than risk their lives outside. There are reports of refugees who left the camp briefly to visit their fields and homes, hoping to find food and belongings, and were never seen again.

Paddy Ashdown, the British Liberal Democrat leader, visited the camps in Manjaca and Trnopolje a few days after Penny Marshall's team. Ashdown is no ally of the Bosnian Serbs, and had been a loud advocate of British military intervention in the conflict. Yet his impressions of Trnopolje, described in the *Independent* on August 13, 1992, struck a more sober note at a time of widespread hysteria about the camp: "They have gathered here because they have to go somewhere. Their houses have been burnt and their lives threatened. Muslim extremists pressurize the men to join up with the guerrillas, so they have come here for safety. But on most recent nights the unprotected camp has been raided by Serbian extremists who beat them, rob them of what little they have left and, it is claimed, rape the women. Things are better now."

In the eyes of the world, however, the dramatic pictures of Fikret Alic apparently imprisoned behind barbed wire in Trnopolje had left the impression that the Bosnian Serbs were running Nazi-style camps. This set the tone for the coverage that followed. Misa Radulovic told me that, after the British team visited Trnopolje, other Western journalists came to the camp: "Every one of them wanted to see only the front part of the camp area and take pictures of the most emaciated bodies. I had a dispute with a journalist and requested him to take his pictures somewhere else, for example in the school building. But he did not want to enter it."

Ed Vulliamy's first article on Trnopolje was published in the *Guardian* on August 7, 1992, the morning after the ITN pictures had been broadcast for the first time. Vulliamy had probably not seen the edited ITN broadcast when he wrote it. This article did not mention the barbed-wire fence, and stated that Trnopolje should not be called a concentration camp. Vulliamy presented quite a balanced view of the situation in the camp, quoting Muslim refugees who reported that no force had been used against them, that the place offered them a certain security, and that they would not know where to go otherwise.

However, by the time Vulliamy came to describe his impressions of Trnopolje in his 1994 book, *Seasons in Hell*, the *Guardian* reporter's tone had changed. The barbed wire that he had not considered worth mentioning in his first article had now become the focus of attention. In his book, Vulliamy described his first impressions of Trnopolje in these terms: "More dirt tracks, more burned villages, and finally what was formerly a school in its own grounds, and another startling, calamitous sight: a teeming, multitudinous compound surrounded by barbed-wire fencing."[7]

The tone of some of Vulliamy's discussions with local people also seemed to have changed between his original report and his later writings on Trnopolje. For instance, Inar Gnoric, a Bosnian Muslim, told Vulliamy that she had come to Trnopolje of her own will, seeking safety. In the *Guardian* article of August 1992, Vulliamy quoted her as saying that "The conditions are very hard here, but there was terrible fighting and we had no food at all. It is safer here, but we don't know what kind of status we have. We are refugees, but there are guards and the wire fence." What fence she was talking about is not clear. In Vulliamy's book, however, Gnoric clearly talks of a barbed-wire fence around the camp.

Penny Marshall did mention the barbed-wire fence in the first report she wrote after returning from Trnopolje, published in the *Sunday Times*.[8] About her first visit to the camp she simply wrote that "Outside was barbed wire." Describing her second visit to the camp in the same article, she noted that "Outside, the camp had changed in the week since our original report. The barbed-wire fence had been removed and the Serbians had left building materials for the prisoners to make shelters."

This was true; the barbed-wire fence (and the ordinary wire-mesh fences) that Marshall's cameraman had shot during the first visit had indeed been removed before her return. But Penny Marshall had left open the question of precisely whereabouts "outside" the barbed-wire fence had been located. She thus failed to correct the false interpretation that so many people had placed upon the pictures. Similarly, Ed Vulliamy wrote in his book that "Four days after our visit to Trnopolje, the fence came down."[9] This left untouched the impression that had settled in the public mind—that the camp had been fenced in with barbed wire.

A year after the ITN pictures were first broadcast, Penny Marshall reacted to the suggestion that her report might have been sensationalist: "I bent over backwards, I showed guards—Bosnian Serb guards—feeding the prisoners. I showed a small Muslim child who had come of his own volition. I didn't call them death camps. I was incredibly careful, but again and again we see that image being used."[10] Despite her plea of objectivity, however, she did not explain how "that image" of Fikret Alic behind barbed wire had been produced by her team.

In a German television program, "Kozarac—Ethnically Cleansed," broadcast on October 11, 1993, Marshall told German movie producer Monika Gras about the impact of the Trnopolje picture: "That picture of that barbed wire and these emaciated men made alarm bells ring across the whole of Europe. I believe that the report would not have caused such a reaction had it been transmitted without that picture, although the facts would have been the same." Marshall said that the Bosnian Serbs did not know how to deal with the Western press: "It was a PR mistake in the Bosnian Serbs' terms." She did not mention her team making any mistakes in their presentation of the Trnopolje story.

The notion that there was a barbed-wire fence around Trnopolje camp, and the comparison with Nazi concentration camps, have been widely accepted as matters of fact. "When the first journalists had arrived there a few days earlier, barbed wire surrounded the place and there was no welcoming banner," Peter Maass wrote in *Love Thy Neighbor: A Story of War*, about his visit to Trnopolje in the late summer of 1992.[11] "I walked through the gates and couldn't quite believe what I saw. There, right in front of me, were men who looked like survivors of Auschwitz." Marshall, Williams, and Vulliamy have not used such language themselves. But neither have they corrected the false interpretation of the picture of Fikret Alic apparently imprisoned behind the barbed wire.

When the ITN pictures of Trnopolje were broadcast around the world, they sparked widespread calls for the Bosnian Serbs to close the camps. Sir John Thomson, head of a Conference on Security and Cooperation in Europe investigation committee in Bosnia, warned the West against leaping to premature conclusions: "If some camps were just opened, I have the impression some of the prisoners would not get very far— there would be nearby graves."[12] But the international pressure on the Bosnian Serbs had already had its effect.

Omarska camp, which the ITN team had also filmed, was shut down in August 1992, and most of the refugees from there along with other Muslims from Keraterm and Manjaca were taken to Trnopolje, which was transformed from a refugee camp into a transition camp in a couple of days. The International Committee of the Red Cross complained that, thanks to the global excitement caused by the ITN reports, every chance had been lost to attain a solution which would allow the Muslims to remain in the region. On October 1, 1992, the first big Red Cross convoy set off from Trnopolje to ship 1,560 refugees over the border into Croatia. In a sense, the exile of thousands of Muslims from their home in Bosnia-Herzegovina was thus inadvertently facilitated by the international reaction to the ITN reports from Trnopolje.

Roused by the pictures, British Prime Minister John Major summoned cabinet colleagues back from holiday for an

emergency meeting. Shortly afterwards, his government announced that British troops would be sent into Bosnia. In the
U.S., where the 1992 presidential election campaign was in full
swing, Democratic Party candidate Bill Clinton and running
mate Al Gore used the ITN pictures to demand that President
George Bush take military action against the Bosnian Serbs. In
Brussels, meanwhile, NATO staff responded by planning a
military intervention in the Balkans.

The pictures of Fikret Alic in Trnopolje were also to
influence the work of the War Crimes Tribunal in The Hague,
set up by the UN Security Council to prosecute those accused
of atrocities in the former Yugoslavia. The tribunal has relied
heavily on the report of an expert commission, led by Frits
Karlshoven, who was later replaced by Cherif Bassiouni. The
report, published in the summer of 1994, mentions the barbed-
wire fence in Trnopolje in several places. Although the report is
full of contradictions, it does state clearly in Annex V, "The
Prijedor Report," that "The camp was surrounded by barbed
wire, and a number of camp guards watched the detainees." The
same chapter describes Trnopolje as a Serbian concentration
camp: "Albeit Logor Trnopolje was not a death camp like
Logor Omarska or Logor Keraterm, the label 'concentration
camp' is nonetheless justified for Logor Trnopolje due to the
regime prevailing in the camp." As a source for this chapter, Ed
Vulliamy's book *Seasons in Hell* is referenced several times.

The story of the barbed-wire fence played a prominent
part in the trial of the Bosnian Serb Dusko Tadic, the first case
heard before the War Crimes Tribunal. Tadic was accused by
witness "L," later revealed as Dragan Opacic, of committing
atrocities at Trnopolje. On August 15, 1996, Opacic made a
drawing in the courtroom to show how the barbed wire fenced
in the camp area. Questioned by the British defense attorney
Stephen Kay, he insisted that the barbed-wire fence had enclosed the entire camp.

By the end of October 1996, however, the accusations
against Tadic with regard to Trnopolje had been dropped; the

prosecution's main witness, Opacic, had been exposed as a liar trained to make false statements by the Bosnian authorities. Opacic finally broke down and admitted his deceit when confronted by his father, whom he earlier claimed had been killed in the war. Tadic's Dutch defense advocate, Professor Wladimiroff, told me that he interviewed Dragan Opacic the day after he was exposed as a liar. Opacic said that the police in Sarajevo had schooled him for the witness box by repeatedly showing him videotapes of Dusko Tadic and of Trnopolje, which he scarcely knew. Prominent among these tapes were the pictures from ITN which were supposed to show Muslims imprisoned behind the barbed-wire fence.

Ed Vulliamy himself was also invited by the prosecution to give evidence in the trial of Dusko Tadic. In June 1996, Vulliamy gave the War Crimes Tribunal his impressions of Trnopolje, which he described as a refugee and transition camp. Much of his evidence was accompanied by the ITN videotapes. But when Vulliamy came to the point where the barbed wire and Fikret Alic were shown on screen, he asked the judges to switch the tape off while he described the news team's meeting with the refugees: "I am going to describe who was behind the wire with the video off because I can do it better if I am not trying to accompany the picture." Why did Vulliamy not want the court to see this impressive sequence?

[1] *Daily Mirror*, 7 August 1992.
[2] *Daily Mail*, 7 August 1992.
[3] *Independent*, 5 August 1993.
[4] *Sunday Times*, 16 August 1992.
[5] Ed Vulliamy, *Seasons in Hell: Understanding Bosnia's war* (New York: St. Martin's Press, Thomas Dunne Books, 1994), p. 202.
[6] *Independent*, 5 August 1993.
[7] Vulliamy, 106.
[8] *Sunday Times*, 16 August 1992.
[9] Vulliamy, p. 113.
[10] *Independent*, 5 August 1993.
[11] *Love Thy Neighbor: A Story of War* (New York: Alfred A. Knopf, 1996), p. 41.
[12] *Guardian*, 5 September 1992.

10 Media complicity in a scripted Balkan tragedy

LENORA FOERSTEL

"If the media can influence public opinion and determine political decisions of the international community on key foreign policy issues, then the same media which belongs to certain nations and warring sides—by way of fabricated reports on actual or alleged actions—can become the most efficient instruments in achieving certain military and political goals."[1]

By fallaciously attributing the breakup of Yugoslavia to "aggressive nationalism," the inevitable result of deep-seated ethnic and religious tensions rooted in history, the Western media served as a "Second Front" for German and U.S. involvement in the Balkans. The U.S. and Germany view Albania, Macedonia, Bulgaria, Romania, Moldava, and the Ukraine as areas for future economic control. Germany has once more embraced its World War II goal of carving up Europe, this time using an economic strategy. With the fall of the Berlin Wall, Chancellor Helmut Kohl gained the opportunity to reunite the two parts of Germany and to formulate policy which would make Germany the dominant power in Europe.

Under the pretense of ensuring peace in the Balkans, the U.S. has used NATO troops to establish a wall of containment around Yugoslavia, forging military bonds with every country that borders Yugoslavia. Hungary, Romania, Macedonia and Albania are all participants in NATO's Partnership for Peace, the U.S.-designed program for joint training and military ties. The U.S. provides Croatia and the Bosnian Muslims with military advisors, arms and training.

Germany and the U.S. are supporting a project "to build a new Balkan highway atop an ancient Roman road, the Via Egnatia, from the port city of Durres in Albania to Istanbul."[2] This will open up better access to the Adriatic, Aegean and Black seas, and according to U.S. analysis, will break Serbia's monopoly on transportation links to the Middle East.

Despite clear evidence that Serbia has been devastated by the American-led military action and economic boycott, the media continue to characterize Serbia as a powerful military threat to other Balkan countries. This has become the rationale for U.S. military industries to make huge profits by selling weapons to the Eastern European countries. The U.S. is considering the sale of F-16 fighter aircraft to the Polish government. According to the Stockholm International Peace Research Institute, the U.S. has sold four C-130B Hercules military planes and five AN/F PS-117 surveillance radar units worth $82 million to Romania. "Romania has signed an agreement with Bell Helicopter Textron to begin producing AH-1F Cobra attack helicopters for the Romanian armed forces to be carried out between 1999 and 2005."[3]

NATO's plans to incorporate such nations as Poland, Hungary and the Czech Republic are seen by Russia as a wall of containment similar to the one around Yugoslavia. Russia is well aware that NATO is mainly an instrument of the U.S. Treasury and Defense departments. Instead of guaranteeing peace, NATO's further military expansion to the east, according to Russia's Minister of Defense Igor Rodionov, "would doom arms control treaties with the West and resurrect zones of confrontation in Europe."[4] Rodionov has also suggested that "Moscow might respond by targeting nuclear missiles at East European countries that join the alliance."

Even as these confrontations pose serious threats to world peace, Western soldiers make headlines as peace enforcers in the Balkans. What goes unmentioned is the role played by Western leaders to help bring the Yugoslav economy to its knees and make the Balkans into a safe haven for a market economy. At a news conference in Brussels on January 11, 1997, Assistant Secretary of State John Kornblum announced a U.S. "four point plan." The plan, which is not backed by the European Union, would freeze U.S. trade and official relations with Serbia and harden international pressure on the Milosevic government. The plan would also target "structural obstacles" in the Serbian economy. Although those obstacles were not spelled out, it can be assumed that any loans from the World Bank would be granted under the International Monetary Fund (IMF) Structural Adjustment policies. These policies are a set of "free market" rules imposed primarily on Third World countries as a condition for receiving assistance—with privatization being a categorical imperative.

In an interview with Germany's *Stern* magazine, Kornblum characterized Bulgaria and Serbia as having "nondemocratic command economies"—meaning planned economies. Kornblum added that the U.S. will approve an assistance program that would help "independent" media in Serbia. Earlier, State Department spokesman Nicholas Burns announced that Washington will permit the Voice of America (VOA) to broadcast news programs through the independent Serbian radio station B-29. VOA, the international radio service of the U.S. Information Agency, broadcasts in fifty-two languages and claims eighty-six million listeners per week worldwide.

In Eastern European countries, the first institutions to undergo the transition to privatization seem to be the media, both in ownership and content. Western capital helps to subsidize the media in Poland, Hungary, Romania, the Czech Republic, and Slovakia. The political views which are reported are virtually indistinguishable from those of the U.S. media. *Blitz*, a newspaper funded by German capital, appeared in Serbia on September 16, 1996. The paper, which at nineteen cents is the cheapest in the country, sells raffle tickets and gives away cars. Within a month after its first printing, *Blitz* had a circulation of 100,000.[5] "This process of moving toward a pro-capitalist, pro-imperialist ideological monopoly is described straight-faced by U.S. leaders and media commentators as the 'democratization of Eastern Europe.'"[6]

The highly publicized Yugoslav opposition movement Zajedno (Together) has cooperated openly with Western economic interests. U.S. and German flags can be seen at all of the Together rallies. Vick Drashovic and Zoran Djindjic, the leaders of Zajedno, have close ties to the West. Drashovic has advocated the return of Yugoslavia to a monarchy. Djindjic was characterized by Desimir Tosic, a co-founder of Yugoslavia's Democratic Party, as a "demagogue without scruples."

Since the fall of the Berlin Wall, the demise of the Soviet Union, and the breakup of Yugoslavia, the U.S. has made large investments in the Balkans and Eastern Europe. The Overseas Private Investment Corporation (OPIC), for example, is an independent agency of the U.S. government which advertises itself as promoting economic growth in developing countries. OPIC assists in financing investment through direct loans or loan guarantees and insures these investments against a broad range of political risks. OPIC is operating in Albania, Bosnia-Herzegovina, Bulgaria, Croatia, Czech Republic, Estonia, Hungary, Latvia, Lithuania, Macedonia, Poland, Romania, Slovakia, and Slovenia. In theory, OPIC, like other U.S. agencies, is committed to strengthening U.S. markets overseas and the economies of the countries they invest in. "In practice, however, they are scouts for corporate bonanzas, and vehicles for attracting paybacks to whatever party is in power in Washington."[7]

In 1994, OPIC itself turned a profit of $167 million on repayment of its loans. U.S. agencies and corporations make huge profits, but little of that wealth is felt by the citizens of the assisted countries or by the U.S. citizens whose taxes keep these agencies going.

Like the U.S., Germany is collecting dividends from the new European order. They have expanded their political and economic influence throughout the Balkans and Eastern Europe, becoming the Czech Republic's biggest trading partner and one of its largest sources of direct investments. Thirty percent of all plants in Slovenia and the Czech Republic now belong to German companies. In addition, Germans own the greatest part of the Croatian hotel industry on the Adriatic coast. They have bought from Zagreb many islands and beaches in exchange for arms." [8]

With the demise of Eastern Europe's planned economies we have seen the use of ideologies that promote privatization and a class system that stimulates nationalism, racism, and zenophobia. Right-wing racist violence and marches for racial purity have again appeared in Germany and Croatia. In Hungary, the Hungarian Democratic Forum (MDE) holds an ideological view which is close to fascism. These various extremist parties and organizations trace their origins to the pre-World War II political movements which precipitated the war. The emerging right-wing in the Eastern European countries seeks a limited governmental role for the distribution of resources but favors authoritarian modes of rule. "On the issue of collective decision procedures, the extreme right puts little faith in pluralism and democratic institutions, preferring not only corporate solutions, but veering off into outright state-corporatist modes (a situation where the state actually creates certain interest groups, defining their legal relationship with the state)." [9]

The U.S. and Germany prepared plans for the dismemberment of Yugoslavia in the late 1980s. Both countries have since worked to reconfigure the Balkans into a Croatian-dominated, Germany-dependent group of mini-states, a situation which opened the way to the recolonization of the region. The American press coverage of the civil war in the former Yugoslavia focused on "ethnic cleansing" while ignoring the history of the region and Germany's role in aiding the secession of Croatia and Slovenia from the Yugoslav federation.

Most of the world's people receive their news through Western news networks and sources. The Atlanta-based Cable News Network (CNN) currently reaches over one hundred countries. Reuters TV, Worldwide Television News, and the Associated

Press TV, the world's largest television news companies, are Western corporations which provide television news coverage to stations all over the world. The four largest international news agencies—Associated Press (AP), United Press International (UPI), Agence France-Press (AFP), and Reuters—are Western, with the first two being American.

The homogeneous, Western-oriented presentation of the news prevents real analysis and alternative points of view. As a result, most readers/viewers have little grasp of the wider political context in which to make sense of world events. A more democratic use of the media will require a more balanced flow of information and opinions and a greater diversity of perspectives.

---

[1] Z. Ivanovic, *The Media War Against the Serbs* (Belgrade: Republic of Serbia Ministry of Information, Tanjug News Agency, May 1994), p. 5.

[2] J. Pomfret, *Washington Post*, 19 December 1996, p. A-28.

[3] *Ibid.*

[4] W. Drozdiak, *Washington Post*, 19 December 1996, p. A-29.

[5] J. Pomfret, *Washington Post*, 27 November 1996, p. A-25.

[6] M.P. Parenti, "Free Market Media in Eastern Europe," *Lies of Our Times*, September 1990, p. 112.

[7] J. Feffer, "The Browning of Russia," *Covert Action Quarterly*, Spring 1996, #56, p. 43.

[8] E.H. Solano, "German Fingers in the Yugoslav Crisis" in *The Media War Against the Serbs*, *op. cit.*, p. 64.

[9] T.S. Szayna, *The Rise of the Extreme Right in Post-Communist Central Europe*, Document No. DRU-153 RC (Santa Monica, CA: Rand Publications, January 1993), p. 7.

11   New and old disorder

NADJA TESICH[*]

Ultimately I am talking about fascism of a different sort, but I cannot write about fascism in a few pages. It would take at least a book. For the purpose of this essay I'll limit myself to the propaganda against the Serbs these past four years. And my own experience—not just as a writer, filmmaker, professor of film, but as a person who observed events, people, the war itself, often risking my life.

When the civil war started in 1991, I went back. I had decided that if what I saw in the papers about Serbia was true, then I'd never go back again. I was born there, but I have lived in the United States most of my life.

What I saw was a drastically different image from the one in the U.S. press: people crying about the breakup of Yugoslavia, the wounded, the refugees from Slavonia, and the first very mutilated kids in the hospitals. I speak the language, I could move in and out, listen unobserved. These were not the people described as barbarians in the *Times*. The *Times* reporter, Chuck Sudetic, would set the tone, a man whose background was Croatian. The essential thing is that prior to this, he had a top security job in Washington. I didn't know this at the time, I just knew something was wrong about his reporting.

---

[*] The first part of this article was delivered as a speech in October 1995 to a New York teach-in on Bosnia sponsored by the International Action Center.

Back in New York, I attempted to correct this information—what was true, what was lies—but largely I tried to add the missing parts of the picture. Always with names and events that could be checked. Without attacking any other group, I tried to talk about the suffering on the Serb side. The embargo that turns the country into an economic concentration camp, factories shut, hospitals without spare parts, doctors without plastic gloves, operations with no anesthesia, lack of medicine, kids dying because of the embargo, along with old people and those not so old. When I reported these things, I was called a nationalist.

I contacted most of the papers, most of the women's magazines, television stations including PBS, Nightline, *Time*, *Newsweek*, *Vanity Fair*, the *Times* magazine section, *Mother Jones*, *Harper's*, the *New Yorker*, etc. Nobody wanted to hear about doctors, or ordinary people, or about a woman called Azra from a Muslim background who goes to Belgrade every year from Florida. Nobody wanted to hear about Croatians living in Belgrade or the real story of how three women, me included—Muslim, Croat, and Serb—traveled together to a funeral in a village in western Serbia. This was too peaceful for them, not exciting enough. They wanted to hear about rapes. (Got any rape stories, we want to hear about rapes.) But the moment I mentioned Serb women raped, they were not interested.

My letter against the embargo of any of the ethnic groups in Yugoslavia appeared in the *Times* badly mutilated. All the references to Germany and the U.S. were cut, as well as references to Cuba, and to U.S. weapons sales. It was the only letter published even though I wrote many. An essay of mine appeared in *The Nation* because it was about theater in Belgrade. Every detail in it was checked for accuracy.

My brother Steve Tesich was the author of many plays and screenplays—*Four Friends, Eyewitness, The World According to Garp*, and *Breaking Away*, which received an Oscar. Yet his essays on Yugoslavia were not published here, nor were thousands of letters written by Americans—historians, anthropologists who knew the Serbs and Serbia.

Films about Serbia were not shown, not those made by Americans nor those made by documentary filmmakers in Belgrade. Footage done by an American woman from Channel 2—Amy Bodden—about refugees and badly scared kids, done without a single cut, with her present in every shot, with my simultaneous translation, nobody wanted to see. Nobody wanted to see a half-hour interview with Karadzic, even though I offered to do the same half-hour films with the same questions with Mr. Izetbegovic and with the Croatian leader in Bosnia. When I spoke on the radio about U.S. advisors and the CIA in Bosnia, I was called a communist.

My only pleasure was that they knew I was there watching. I would find my words used by some of them in the interviews on TV. If I push hard, if I annoy them, I get letters back. Sometimes they get angry, then lose control when I call and give me very valuable information. I try to enjoy even that tiny bit—I made them angry. Still, on a given day it's a lonely struggle. You grow desperate. I would tell them then, for the hell of it, what their reporter is doing, where and who he sleeps with. I suggested a piece for the *Village Voice* called, "How to spot Serbs on the subway."

I could talk about American journalists in Belgrade who often didn't even know where they were. They wanted someone to tell them fast, fast in fifteen minutes about history and the people, but they didn't really need anything since they knew from day one what they would write. It was easy. Many carried a sheet from Ruder Finn that told them who is the good and who the bad guy.

In this war, journalists abdicated—or let's say they wanted to keep their jobs. The honest ones were barred from their papers. I learned much about journalism, what gets printed, what not, and much about propaganda and American culture at this moment. I lived as if in wartime, gathering information from short-wave radios and from all sorts of people—in Texas, France, Sweden.

My telephone bills were huge. And as in wartime, things happened. My family united vis à vis the U.S. bombs. We stopped arguing about politics. And as in wartime, some friends left me, others I divorced. All sorts of middle-class liberals of Manhattan's Upper West Side who didn't want to hear a single detail after my many trips but would ask instead, "Do you think Belgrade should be bombed?" I realized I was confronting something unprecedented in my experience, a new type of dictatorship, deadly because invisible, subtle, like a virus. It's a part of the air and culture you breathe. It's there even when you sleep. I call it the dictatorship of the new world order.

In order for the Pentagon and NATO to accomplish their aim, they had to, together with Germany, destabilize the country, put Yugoslavia under embargo, bomb the Bosnian Serbs with clean bombs, killing nobody. Right. Eliminate the entire community of Serbs in Krajina who have lived there for centuries—but first they had to create an enemy in the American mind so it would look like a fight of good against evil, the West fighting savages, barbarians, and everyone would cheer, feel good and hate collectively as a replacement for suppressed hatreds here in America's own civil wars.

The image was done in ten days. Good Christian, God-loving Slovenes, or Croats, in a family setting or church, and the Serbs looking like fascists and with a gun. Later, Muslims in Bosnia were added as good and Western, too, people who are just like you and me, and they play the piano. A Serb was a male, without women, children, or church. Later his face almost disappeared and he remained as an evil presence, except when shown as a rapist or criminal.

"We had a job to do and we did it. We are not paid to moralize," said James Harff, director of Ruder Finn Global Public Affairs, a Washington, DC, public relations firm that was paid to turn Serbs into monsters, fascists, and beasts. "Speed is vital," he said, "it is the first assertion that counts. All denials are entirely ineffective." Any means were good. Remember, this could happen again to any other group.

As in advertising or audience research for a movie, you know your target, your aim, you know this country's obsessions and fears (sex and violence), and you keep it going either as psycho-drama or a soap opera. Everyone looks the same in Yugoslavia so you can use dead or massacred Serbs and claim they are others. Images of dead Serbs are called Muslims or Croats by the time they reach New York, although they were something else in some European papers and in the original photos. But the essential thing is how long you show the image. An entire community of Krajina Serbs disappears in four days, while Sarajevo goes on for three years. Croatia takes over one third of the territory in one day and it's over. A few protesting letters appear. It only proves how democratic the U.S. is. Meanwhile, entire villages disappear and nobody here knows.

It helps that Americans don't know the country or the history, so that too can be rewritten. Serbs who fought against fascism, who saw so many die, exterminated in the camp at Jasenovac, are now lying about it, we are told. President Clinton invites Mr. Tudjman to the inaugural of the museum for Holocaust victims but not a single Serb survivor is permitted to be there, even though the present state of Croatia borders on fascism and Mr. Tudjman says the Holocaust never happened and that Jews really killed those Serbs in the Jasenovac camp because the Jews wanted their money. And here are Tudjman and Clinton looking happy together. America always was comfortable with fascism.

It helps that Americans have short memories. The *New York Times* prints that Bosnian Serbs owned 64 percent of the land. Then a few months later you are told that they conquered 75 percent. It doesn't add up but nobody pays any attention. Everything gets erased and chewed up, no past or future, just profit now. Whole landscapes disappear, and cultures, and nobody pays much attention, nobody remembers that America killed millions of Vietnamese and then recently said it's time for us to forgive them. Nobody remembers Chile, Panama, Guatemala, El Salvador, etc., etc. And they won't remember Yugoslavia either, after they helped destroy it. This is a nation run by psychopaths. We are in the new world order.

From a PR agency hired by Croatia, then by Muslim Bosnia, with huge budgets that include funding from outside, secret bank accounts (America, Germany and even the Vatican), with the help of Washington, the image machine goes to the main newspapers. By the time it reaches TV, the words "presumed guilty" are dropped. Instead it says, "The *New York Times* reports. . . ." That makes it legitimate.

The headlines are against the Serbs even when the article is supposed to be about their suffering.

In all this, the other side is not permitted to speak. It looks like a jury for a Black man who has no lawyer, his mouth is taped shut, the jury is all white, and some are members of the Klan.

Experts and false witnesses appear. Gelb, Lewis, and Eagleburger, all three at once on PBS. Bomb Belgrade, Gelb wrote one day, and then became an expert on TV. Eagleburger said, I want to wipe the smile off the face of all Serbs. He became an expert, too.

The CIA becomes a reliable informer on TV and in the press. They are there whenever it's needed. They have pictures taken from planes of the Bosnian Muslim graves—but not a single picture of Serbs from Krajina walking on foot in the terrible heat and bombed in addition from planes. Of course not. The CIA is part of the cleanup.

American witnesses appear, like the CIA, for credibility. Fake stories in women's magazines, fake documentaries. Like the one narrated by an American nurse on Channel 7. We don't know where she is or who she is. It's enough that she is American. She talks about rapes and she cries.

An American journalist narrates in a montage of a few shots how he has discovered mass graves. We don't see his face, at all. Bianca Jagger becomes an expert on Bosnia. She cries too.

Slavenka Drakulic, a journalist from Zagreb and a small-time opportunist, uses the *Times* for a piece about thousands upon thousands of rapes which she could not have witnessed. Besides, her dialogue is bad. A ten-year-old girl does not talk like a fifty-year-old woman. I used to teach dialogue and screenplays.

By the time the correction is done, by an independent group of doctors, this is only a few lines in the *Times* that nobody sees. The figure of twenty thousand victims was based on actual interviews with only four people.

On the radio, new specialists—all Americans—talk about how the Ottoman Empire was wonderful to everyone.

The staged massacres in Sarajevo get a splash, but not the investigation of them, nor the result. It occurs to me that maybe it was the CIA who did the job. It wouldn't be the first time, after all.

The massacres appeared always before an important step the U.S. would take against Serbia and the Serbs. The last massacre becomes the reason why NATO or the U.S. must bomb Bosnian Serbs in an unprecedented orgy of missions, yet NATO decided on it two days before the massacre. They lie on and on, but nobody really pays attention because we are in the new world order.

Words like genocide, ethnic cleansing, camps are there to produce an emotional response, yet they actually whitewash the real genocides done to Serbs and Jews in the Second World War. In fact, the first ethnic cleansing was done to Serbs in Western Slavonia at the beginning of the current war, and the biggest cleansing was the U.S.-CIA-Croatia united effort against Serbs in Krajina. Two hundred thousand people. Hundreds dying in the heat. And what do you call thousands of missions against Bosnian Serbs, the largest military operation in Europe since World War II? What do we know about the number of dead? Zero. It's called "low collateral damage" by the Pentagon.

The word "Western" appears all the time in the U.S. media. The good is Western. Western is honest and clean. What is the other? I ask *New York Times* correspondent Steven Kinzer, from whom I took pictures as we ran to interview Bosnian Serb refugees from Sarajevo who looked like the dead dug up. Why is it, I ask him, that Croatia—which he says borders on fascism—is called a democracy and Belgrade is called a dictatorship? Belgrade at that time—in 1992—looked like anarchy: hundreds of opinions, twenty different parties. He said, Americans think of them as Western and you not.

What is Western? NATO is. Germany is, and so is the U.S. The East is sly, they lie and they cheat. Serbs lie all the time, according to the U.S. media. In Nazi propaganda, Jews lied and raped Christian virgins, too, but there is more to this. German fascism and American racism unite at some point. *Vanity Fair* gives me a clue in an essay on how Serbs make love. They do it with savagery, the entire hotel shakes and he, the writer, just suffers from jealousy and horror listening to their screams. Those savages are interrupting his sleep. So, a Serb is a male with no mother or father, no wife or kids, he has no culture, plays no piano, and rapes thousands. Does this remind you of anything? Who is the rapist in the American racist mind? The answer is given to me. People I have known for many years and those I have not known asked me where I was from in Yugoslavia. Serbia, I said.

You don't look like them, they would say, stepping back, looking scared or embarrassed. None of these people had ever been to Yugoslavia. Why, I asked finally. You are nice, they say. You mean civilized, I ask. Well yes, and you are so fair, you could be a German or a Swede.

It occurred to me then that Serbs, who look the same as the other groups in Yugoslavia, were actually dark in the American mind. I can't decide if this darkness was internal or some other or both at the same time.

While all this went on, Croatians thanked Germany and America now, Bosnian Muslims kept crying oh America come help, please help, we are really Western just like you, while the Serbs kept moaning oh America why don't you love us, we fought fascism together. In spite of all the misery that the embargo has done to present Yugoslavia, I think they are ahead now because they know America does not love them. Ultimately America loves nobody, not even their own children. Or there would be money for schools without rats, no leaking roofs, money for hospitals, money for life instead of prisons here and death with those billion dollars worth of perfect clean killing machines in Bosnia.

I am glad the Serbs' and my mother's romance with the American dream is over. It never really existed or it was a Hollywood production that the country dumps like its garbage all over the world. You can destroy with it, you can kill entire cultures, but that's a whole other story.

* * * * *

January 1997[*]

In Belgrade, anti-government demonstrations have continued into the fourth week. Nothing in the *New York Times* or on television presents a coherent picture—but that's no different from the rest of the reporting on the civil war these last years.

I want to approach this subject from the point of view of being a writer, filmmaker, media specialist, and a "U.S. watcher" for many years. My views are different from most Americans and most Yugoslavs because I know more, and am not easily disturbed by superficial elements or easy words. My background helps—I was born in Serbia and have returned there every year, and I have

---

[*] This piece emerged out of an interview conducted by Samori Marksman of New York radio station WBAI-FM in December 1996 and a discussion a few weeks later at the International Action Center among three Yugoslavs from Serbia and five Americans attempting to figure out what was going on in Belgrade.

also lived in France and in New York City most of my adult life. And most of my adult life, as a participant and an observer, I have opposed U.S. aggressions, murders, embargoes, wars. Some hidden, others less so.

U.S. politics are presented to the American people as melodramas in a close-up. A TV series of sorts. Sex scandals—who our president slept with, when, courtroom dramas à la O.J. Simpson for months—instead of who holds the economic power, why do we have more than a million prisoners, why millions of Americans do not have health care, why infant mortality in certain ghettos is the same as in India.

As in melodramas, we have good and bad guys. We fight wars to save babies in incubators in Kuwait or to save women from rapes in Bosnia. We kill half a million kids with the Iraqi embargo, millions of Vietnamese, we poison people and plants with uranium and other experimental weapons. And it's all done with certain catch words—democracy, open society, freedom, freedom fighters, free market economy, Western. The context is missing, the larger picture, the long shot that would permit a person to judge what is going on. We never see the forest, we focus on a few trees. This is not an accident. It's a culture where children and adults are moronized and brainwashed systematically in order to think, talk, and wish for more and more new things.

Still, if you watch carefully, you notice that after years of muddiness on why we are in Bosnia, the rapes and other reasons were suddenly dropped around September 1995 after the removal of all the Serbs from Krajina and after the systematic, every few minutes, daily, around-the-clock bombing of the Bosnian Serbs.

A new, clearer image appears. "U.S. interests" is introduced. Timidly at first. Here and there, then more. To get you used to it. Nobody asks on PBS or elsewhere, "What interests?" A State Department spokesperson's job is to inform us which new country the U.S. is attacking or putting under embargo. Most Americans, too busy and too worried with their own problems and confused by many new words—downsizing, collateral damage, aggressive pacification, etc.—are bullied into submission in a culture of each person struggling alone.

In January 1997 there was a further development. Defense Secretary William Perry left office, smiling, looking like a loving father to contradict with sweetness his statement that the U.S. can decide which country, no matter where on this planet, must be dominated because of U.S. security interests. One timid question: "Are we being attacked?" "No," he says, "but since we are the *only* superpower in the world, *every* country is in our national interest." No questions, no objections on PBS.

The events in Belgrade, presumably triggered by disputed local elections held in November 1996, as well as other events elsewhere, have to be seen in this perspective, along with the Dayton peace plan, the so-called "world tribunal" in The Hague, human rights, U.S. observers, words like freedom, democracy, free market, and so on. We in Yugoslavia are only minor players in this world drama, where a single country acts as jailer, judge, and executioner. And a definer of words.

If The Hague tribunal were actually a world court it would mean that any country could also bring charges against the U.S. For crimes against humanity. The problem is there would be too many countries, and how far back do you start? They might fight for who will go first.

Where are the outside Human Rights Watches watching for the abuses in this country, snooping around schools, hospitals, prisons, to see how the homeless live, how poor women live, what they die from, how soon. Imagine this: A Cuban delegation appears, to watch over U.S. hospitals and schools in the ghettoes. The Yugoslav delegation flies in to watch for violations of freedom of the press and life on the Indian reservations.

Dream on.

Another term, often used: free market economy. The U.S. government wants the whole world to have it and demonstrators in Belgrade are dying to get it, too, without knowing quite what it means. The word "free" makes it sound good. Free like birds, like clouds—who is ever opposed to freedom? The question nobody asks is, free for whom? Free for multinational billion-dollar corporations to plunder Eastern Europe, to rob the former Soviet Union of its national resources? And NATO is there making sure the slaves don't rise up. Certain comparisons could be made with prisons here in the U.S.

Who can buy state-owned factories in Yugoslavia except someone from the outside? The country becomes dependent, no longer capable of taking care of itself so that such basic needs as medicines might have to be bought elsewhere at a higher price. It means losing control. The free-market economy is a new attempt at colonization, sneakily done, turning all of Eastern Europe into countries of the Third World. And NATO is nothing more than a police force. Mr. Perry bragged that day, leaving office, how NATO was dead when he came in and now it has been resurrected. Nobody asked him: Why is NATO spreading? What is its role? He hinted that it's needed for the usual reasons—to protect our freedom so Americans can sleep in peace.

I watched the demonstrations in Belgrade—the so-called "opposition, pro-democracy" forces—with many years' knowledge of which demonstrations are shown, for how long, which not, some not at all. I thought of Chile and 1973. Even though the circumstances are different in Belgrade, there was something similar about the ominous carnival atmosphere. At that time, the media said nothing about the CIA—which staged, pushed, and paid for the events in Chile—though it was obvious to some of us. And we know what happened. My friends died in that stadium. Those who could, escaped into exile as the bloody dictatorship took over.

A major setback for Chile and a victory for the U.S. A whole generation of progressive thinkers and leaders destroyed. Years later, an admission, a regret that yes, the CIA was involved. A paragraph in the *Times*.

The third day of demonstrations in Belgrade, the Voice of America and Radio Free Europe clarified the picture for me. Not that it was ever unclear. But now I had proof of what was going on. I was so grateful to the Voice of America for helping me in this search that I called them up to tell them how much they meant to me. By then it was obvious that opposition protests for freedom and democracy are led by the USA to create a state of chaos in a country already chaotic and weak from six years of embargo.

In whose interest is the chaos? Not the Serbian people. Just as in Chile, the blame for the economy is put entirely on the government. There is no mention of the economic sanctions, what the U.S. did, is doing now. As one doctor said to me last November in Belgrade, "The U.S. prevents us from functioning, kills our kids, and then it wants to send us charitable funds."

Health care was good and free for everyone in Yugoslavia. It was a country full of healthy people. Even now, crippled with shortages, badly needing spare parts for diagnostic procedures, they manage, inventing new ways to save the population from epidemics. Can you imagine what would have happened had the main factory producing most of the antibiotics and pain killers belonged to a foreign country which could for profit reasons sell it, move it, or turn it into, let's say, a perfume factory?

Each country, especially one small and poor, needs to protect itself, its resources. It has a right to decide what's to be done, what not, to guarantee its survival.

The Voice of America, paid for by the CIA and Co., began its aggressive campaign early in the morning when most people get ready for work in Belgrade. This constitutes meddling in the internal affairs of a country—an act that should have been condemned in the United Nations. As far as I know, Chinese radio is not urging us in New York City to rise up. Can you imagine what would happen if it did?

There was no Voice of America urging people in Zagreb, Croatia, to rise up last spring—in spite of there being thousands in the streets protesting an illegal voting situation. However, since President Tudjman was a "partner" and a "good guy" while the demonstrators were left of center, no Voice of America was needed at that time.

In Belgrade, members of the U.S. Congress led the anti-government demonstrations. For freedom, democracy, market economy, and bliss. Rep. Bruce Vento of Minnesota spoke at the rally in Belgrade on January 10. He denounced the Milosevic government and declared U.S. support for the opposition.

In New York, there were weeks of coverage—all TV channels, newspapers, editorials, front page, pictures. Compare this with other countries where demonstrations are ignored or barely covered. The fraudulent, U.S.-backed elections in Nicaragua. The major strikes in South Korea.

And remember this: in August 1995 two hundred thousand Serbs vanished from the Krajina in Croatia, where they had lived for centuries. This unbelievable exodus—old people dying in the terrible heat, nursing mothers, women giving birth on the side of the road, hunger, thirst, bombed from the air in addition—all this disappears in a few days from the U.S. media. Of course there is no mention of U.S. advisors, a U.S.-trained Croatian army, U.S. retired generals, U.S. ships in the Adriatic helping clean and clear the path for the Croatian army. The bombing of Bosnian Serbs, the biggest bombing in Europe since World War II, also vanishes from our TV screens. There are no after-effects on civilians. There is no mention of chemical warfare, a spectrum of new poisons from uranium to psychogenic weapons to "break their will to resist."

Remembering this, I also remember that these anti-government, opposition democratic forces did not demonstrate over Krajina nor the bombing in Bosnia. They are not opposed to The Hague nor the U.S. takeover. It's obvious that they and the U.S. work together and the U.S. government supports, encourages, and pays for these events on the streets of Belgrade.

Why?

For the usual reason—it's in their interest. It has nothing to do with freedom and so-called democracy.

I remember how certain words were used as a camouflage from the beginning of the civil war in Yugoslavia. In 1991 Croatia was called "Western and democratic." A *New York Times* journalist can't explain to me why this is so, since Croatia is close to fascism and Serbia resembles anarchy of sorts. Serbia was called a dictatorship then, and again now in 1997.

Izetbegovic's government is also called "Western" and "democratic." Bianca Jagger and Susan Sontag tell us so. Everybody is good and freedom-loving, except the Serbs.

Demonstrators in Belgrade who carry an American and a German flag become *suddenly* good too. Do you wonder why? They, too, are called Western and democratic.

Laura Silver in an op-ed article in the *New York Times*, originally written for the *Financial Times* from Belgrade, tells us as much. The opposition is Western. And democratic. These are good guys. Could *I* get an op-ed piece in the *Times*? No way. Even though I know the culture, I speak the language, I could not. I don't write for the *Financial Times*, that's why. Such is my freedom in the U.S. Of course, I could shout and scream or talk to myself on the street, but my freedom is zero in effectiveness.

The charade continues. All the usual "good guys"—L. Zimmerman, known for his hatred of the Serbs; Bogdan Denitch, who advocated bombing Belgrade on Channel 5; various State Department officials—all these gray characters and spooks sing now in unison the same song—"the opposition is good"—with the Voice of America as background music.

The present government in Belgrade is called the last dictatorship which has to be eliminated. On U.S. TV there are even discussions on how this should be done—murder or exile. No matter what we think about Milosevic, he was freely elected by his people. If I suggested on television a similar approach for Mr. Clinton, I would be locked up. For security reasons.

It's silly to call Belgrade a dictatorship. You can only sell this to someone who doesn't know. There are hundreds of different opinions on the street. All the newspapers belong to the opposition except two. Compare this with the U.S. Where are our daily opposition papers? Where is our alternate news?

As a writer I can say that Belgrade is much more interesting than New York and, yes, I feel freer there. My work—an essay, a novel or a play—would get done if it had literary merit. Regardless of my views. The market approach to literature still has not eroded the mind. Consequently there is a richness of voices, discussions about life and art, while here we writers discuss money and contracts and will it sell or not. All thinking has been reduced to one dimension—profit only.

No, Belgrade is not a dictatorship. If anything, it has permitted through naiveté or ignorance or absence of a clear ideology a very chaotic situation conducive to destabilization from the outside. Suspicious foundations paid by the U.S. or Germany, new would-be "feminist" groups without addresses, new mystical religions and cures, courses on levitation, how to be happy in three days courtesy of EST look-alikes from California.

Here's something to consider. Months of demonstrations like those in Belgrade couldn't happen in the U.S. There would have been thousands of dead and thousands locked up. For a small two-hour demonstration in New York City you need permits, are squeezed into a restricted area, and there are as many cops as demonstrators. And the cops have motorcycles, guns, and horses.

With the dead on my mind, I have another flashback: Greece, 1967. The military junta, backed by the U.S., jails, tortures, executes—including a friend of mine. U.S. ships are in the harbor. The *New York Times* reports how "the sun is shining, people laugh and dance. What is this talk about dictatorship?" Sulzberger writes, "Life is wonderful in Greece."

I am also reminded of Sean Gervasi and the conversations we had starting in 1992 and continuing up to his death in Belgrade in June 1996. He predicted that the U.S., which helped destroy Yugoslavia and produced unnecessary bloodshed in Bosnia, would go even further: divide the Bosnian Serbs among themselves and against Serbia, divide Montenegro from Serbia, and create a situation where Serbs in Serbia will kill each other. In whose interest is this?

Sean specialized in analyzing the economic side of destabilization while I focus on the political and cultural. The great majority of students don't even know what they are demonstrating about. Some vague ideas of democracy and living well. Refugees, chased from their homes in Krajina, unable to strike the real enemy, turn their anger toward their own. Various middle-class people who lived well under socialism and traveled to Paris, Rome, London believe that once they have America on their side, they'll live as well as before. Funny how deluded they are. Most imagine they'll have what they already have—free health care, schools, prenatal care, a year of paid maternity leave with guaranteed return to the job—and will also get everything in the U.S. movies—turquoise-blue swimming pools, fancy cars, wardrobes from U.S. sitcoms.

All these people on the street with the carnival atmosphere in the air are too caught up in their own family and national dramas to pay attention to the larger picture. None of the parties, including the present government, understands the U.S. government. They perceive it as a sweet, friendly father you have to please. They badly need education on U.S. foreign wars and the wars this country wages against its own people.

In Yugoslavia, many still have not digested who they are dealing with. The U.S. government sells 70 percent of the world's weapons, often to both sides in a conflict. It encourages ethnic conflicts, supports temporarily various heads of state and then dumps them when necessary, leaving wastelands behind. It spends a trillion dollars on the military, not schools, not hospitals, not the American people. Everything the U.S. does elsewhere—chaos and destabilization—it does equally at home. There is one aim: to weaken any ties to collective identity unless they are market defined (you and I have much in common because we wear the same sneakers or go scuba diving together or ski). But there is more: to create units of one, lonely, separate from others, anxious and in fear, buying and spending for relief. As a substitute for everything else.

The way I see it, there is no government or leadership. There is just money and markets. It's an amoral, mechanical monster whose heart is the beat of Wall Street. Up and down it goes. More and more it needs and it's never enough. All the phrases like "family values," Christmas spirit (imagine NATO troops giving Barbie dolls to bombed kids in Bosnia), freedom, democracy—it's all camouflage, fluff, a sugar coating to cover up the real thing. Murder and destruction to create new markets, to oppose whoever stands in its path. It's the opposite of freedom; it does not tolerate independent countries or any degree of self-determination.

Still, it can be resisted. I remain optimistic. Machines break, after all. Here in New York, where the liberals have become the same as the Republicans, the subways are full of people so poor it looks like a country of the Third World. Nobody objects when I talk about Yugoslavia. They agree with me. This population which is not market defined and has nothing to lose is greater every day. And they seem to be informed.

My optimism grows. I even get cheered up by Mr. Perry who, when leaving office, said that the U.S. could afford maybe three wars at the same time. Mind you, he is not talking about real fighters but paid soldiers with technology, that's all. And suddenly, reminded of Ernesto Che Guevara, killed by U.S.-trained Rangers, I can't help but wonder: What if there are five or ten or twenty wars, what then? All at the same time. In our lifetime.

12 Media deception and the Yugoslav civil war

BARRY LITUCHY*

It is said that the first casualty of war is the truth. Of course, today with the appalling spectacle of the civil war in Yugoslavia filling our TV screens and newspapers, this old axiom has taken on an uglier, more sinister meaning. If four years ago we could say that the American public was totally *uninformed* about the conflict ready to unfold, today we can say with equal justification that Americans are doubly or triply *misinformed*, and dangerously so, about this tragic and completely unnecessary war.

And there's a very good reason why. A malicious campaign of war propaganda, anti-Serb hatred, and just plain lies has flooded the American media. It has been financed and run through public relations firms, non-governmental organizations and human rights groups with the patronage of various governments, all with the single purpose of mobilizing public opinion on the side of the Bosnian Muslims and Croats, and against those "horrible people," the Serbs. The truth, the lives of innocent people, and the real dangers of a wider war are all forsaken; the main thing is to twist or to invent the facts so that they fit in with America's foreign policy ob-

---

* This article was originally published in the February 1995 issue of *The College Voice*, College of Staten Island, City University of New York.

jectives in Bosnia. Every step of the way, the media has acted as a co-belligerent, with the aim of whipping up anti-Serbian sentiment and support for military intervention on the side of the Muslim and Croat forces.

Many of the stories on the Bosnian conflict that we read about and see on TV are actually fed to the media by public relations firms. Jim Harff, President of Ruder Finn Global Public Affairs, the public relations firm that handles the accounts of Bosnia, Croatia, and the Albanian opposition in Kosovo, argues that modern wars cannot be fought and won today without good public relations work. "In terms of persuading and convincing the UN to take proper measures," says Harff, "it's even more important." According to U.S. Justice Department records, Bosnia and Croatia pay Ruder Finn more than $10,000 a month plus expenses "to present a positive image to members of Congress, administration officials, and the news media."[1]

The amount of covered "expenses" is many times greater than the disclosed fee. Harff is himself an insider in Washington, where he has worked for three different Representatives over the past decade. Because of international economic sanctions imposed on the Serbs by the UN—largely due to false stories in the media—the Serbs, ironically, are barred from hiring a public relations firm.

The use of public relations firms to manufacture "the news" and shape public opinion is a dangerous phenomenon that threatens the lives and freedom of people around the world. But it is not entirely new. It was used to devastating effect during the Gulf War. John R. MacArthur, publisher of *Harper's* magazine and author of *Second Front*, an exposé of media disinformation during the Gulf War, has compared media coverage of the Bosnian conflict to that of the Gulf War.

In one of the most hideous examples of disinformation ever used to launch a war, the public relations firm of Hill and Knowlton produced a fifteen-year-old girl named Nariyah who testified before a congressional committee that she had seen Iraqi soldiers tearing Kuwaiti babies from hospital incubators. After the war was over and 100,000 Iraqis had been killed, the story was revealed to be a fraud, and the girl to be the daughter of Kuwait's ambassador to the U.S.

Hill and Knowlton was employed by the government of Kuwait. But at the time, the media ran the story uncritically, as did most of the leading human rights organizations, such as Amnesty International and Human Rights Watch, which widely publicized these faked atrocities. MacArthur says that "human rights hawks have become less interested in the objective investigation of atrocities than they are in their own arguments for armed intervention, whether genuine or merely alleged."[2]

In the case of the Yugoslav civil war, the sheer scope of the propaganda campaign hurled at the Serbs far exceeds anything used against Iraq. Stories depicting the Serbian side in the conflict as subhuman have been a constant feature in the media. Serbs have been accused of everything from systematic rape to ethnic cleansing to bombings of civilians to genocide. But facts are stubborn things. None of these extraordinary charges has stood up to close scrutiny.

A regular feature of nearly every article in the *New York Times* or *Newsweek* has been an accompanying photograph of Muslim women and children fleeing from war. We never see Serbian women and children maimed or killed by the war. Nor are we told that gunfire coming from Serb positions in Sarajevo is return fire aimed at Muslim snipers in the city's tall buildings. Occasionally, in the desperate search for pictures to "document" Serbian atrocities, the media uses photos of dead Serbs and labels them "Muslim victims," as was the case with the January 4, 1993, issue of *Newsweek*.[3] The August 7, 1993, issue of the *New York Times* contained a photo purporting to be that of Croats grieving over Serbian atrocities when in fact the murders had been committed by Bosnian Muslims.[4]

In August 1992 British television helped publicize the supposed existence of concentration camps allegedly used by the Serbs to exterminate Muslims and Croats. To prove that what they had discovered was not a prison but rather a Nazi-type death camp, ITN and others broadcast pictures around the world, focusing on two emaciated men, both presumably Muslim. However, one of them was eventually identified as Slobodan Konjevic, a Serb suffering from tuberculosis for ten years, arrested for looting. The concentration/death camp story, having served its purpose, was dropped. But by then the story already had been seen by millions of people. The fact that everyone else in the photos of these "death camps" was well fed just somehow escaped reporters' attention.[5]

At about the same time as the death camp fabrication was the "ethnic cleansing" story. While it is true that some Bosnian Serb forces had evicted Muslims from their homes in Serb-held areas, what was not said was that Muslim and Croat forces were carrying out the exact same policy. But the media still presented it as a purely Serbian crime, peculiar to Serbian policy and thinking.

Thus, it would surprise most people to learn that six hundred thousand Muslim and Croatian refugees had been given refuge in Serb-dominated Yugoslavia. That's never mentioned. Nor was it reported that after Croatia declared independence in 1991, Serbs in Croatia were asked to take a loyalty oath. Forty thousand who refused to do so were forced out of their homes. Nor did the media cover the Muslim government's bloody campaign in August 1994 that ethnically cleansed northern Bosnia of Serbs, and then forced sixty thousand Muslims in Bihac, who support the Serbs and hate the criminal government in Sarajevo, to flee from their homes. The media just didn't think the story was worth reporting.

In the fall of 1992 came the story of Serb rapes of Croat and Muslim women. The *New York Times* reported on December 13, 1992, that fifty thousand Muslim and Croatian women had been raped and that it was official Serb policy to do so.

Anyone with the least bit of common sense should have said: "Hey, what is this?!" But not the media nor the human rights groups; they ate it up and, believing their own lies, sent teams of reporters to Bosnia to interview the victims. One embarrassed French journalist, Jerome Bony, explained it this way: "When I got to fifty kilometers from Tuzla, I was told, 'Go to Tuzla high school. There are four thousand raped women.' When I got twenty kilometers from Tuzla, the figure dropped to four hundred. At ten kilometers only forty were left. Once at the site I found only four women willing to testify."[6]

Poor Peter Jennings from ABC. Having organized an entire special program on Serb atrocities, he was forced to air the statement of a representative from Helsinki Watch that the story of massive Serbian rapes had originated with the Bosnian and Croatian governments and had no credible evidence. What she didn't say was that Ruder Finn was mainly responsible for disseminating the story in the first place.

The rape story has not gone away despite the fact that no proof exists anywhere of more rapes by Serb soldiers than by Muslims or Croats. But that hasn't stopped the media's yellow journalists. *New York Times* columnist Anthony Lewis declared that the Serbs were "at the level of beasts."[7] The message is clear: these people are no good. But imagine if *your* entire ethnic background were described that way? Of course, if you are African-American, you don't have to imagine it; you've been there. When the American ruling class wants to destroy a particular ethnic group, they will invent racial stereotypes to degrade and vilify the entire people. The Serbs have been so marked.

Incredibly, there are even worse examples. On February 5, 1994, there was the infamous Sarajevo market massacre where sixty-eight people were killed. The Serbs were blamed for it, until the story leaked out on French TV that the UN knew that the Muslims had bombed their own people in order to induce UN and NATO military involvement.

The disgusting ploy worked. NATO bombed Serb positions several days later. But the truth will out eventually, and the UN has revealed other instances of Muslim government forces bombing their own and selling it as a Serb atrocity.

Similarly in April 1994 there was the battle for Gorazde. The media reported that the Serbs had intentionally bombed Gorazde hospital, killing many civilians. It turned out that the hospital was never hit. Then there was the battle for Bihac in December 1994 when the media claimed that the Serbs were poised to commit horrible atrocities against the civilian population. As it turned out, the Muslim government forces committed the atrocities, occupying civilian homes and putting thousands of Muslim civilians in peril by using them as human shields. The so-called "safe havens" have served as a treasure trove of "atrocity" stories because they are defended by the UN and used by the Muslim government as staging areas for military offensives.

The media have disseminated even crazier stories designed to keep anti-Serbian feeling at a high pitch. But what may be worse are all the stories swept under the rug. Croatia today is ruled by a neo-fascist leader who has denied that the Holocaust ever happened and who claims that Croatian fascists during World War II were just doing their jobs. Soldiers in the Croatian military, the HOS, salute with the same straight-armed gesture used by Nazis half a century ago. Neo-Nazis from around the world have flocked to Croatia to fight in the HOS. The HOS has been the source of real, unreported atrocities.

Just as Croatia is a client of Germany, the Bosnian Muslims are bankrolled by Saudi Arabia, Kuwait, Iran, Pakistan, and Turkey. The government is led by a man who for twenty-five years has called for an Islamic fundamentalist state and society that leaves no room for non-Islamic cultures. The presence of CIA and U.S. military advisors on the ground—building airstrips, providing intelligence and training—is reported in the European press, but not in the United States.

Forty-seven years ago George Orwell gave us a cautionary prediction of where the modern media was headed in his novel *1984*. People today concerned with issues of peace and social justice have plenty of reason to be disturbed by the precedents set in the media's propaganda war against the Serbs, and not just because the propaganda war is the prelude to a real war. Clinton has already promised twenty thousand American troops for Bosnia if the UN requests them. But will Americans know what they are fighting and perhaps dying for? Not if the media, human-rights groups, and P.R. firms "do their job." Then Ruder Finn can proudly proclaim, "*1984* 'R Us."

[1] Harff is quoted here by Mike Trickey in *The Spectator* (Hamilton, ON), 12 February 1993. All public relations firms working for foreign governments must register with the Justice Department. I found in documents obtained from the Justice Department that while Croatia was contracted to pay Ruder Finn $16,000 a month and Bosnia was to pay $12,000 in 1992, payments in some later months were as high as $200,000, and total payments per year were ultimately in the millions of dollars. Moreover, Ruder Finn was not the only P.R. firm employed in Bosnia. Hill and Knowlton was also contracted early in the war. Waterman & Associates was employed by Croatia. Financial backing came from countries such as Saudi Arabia, which alone funneled nearly $1 billion to the Sarajevo regime from 1993 to 1996, according to the *Washington Post*, 2 February 1996. Ruder Finn was also contracted by the non-existent "Republic of Kosovo" for $5,000 a month, according to a Justice Department document dated 1 November 1992.

[2] "Letters," *The Nation*, 18 July 1994.

[3] The infamous photograph of a Serb killed by Croats in Vukovar in November 1991 has been used over and over again by CNN, "60 Minutes," and others as an example of Serbian "genocide" and "ethnic cleansing," most recently by Christiane Amanpour on CNN on 1 June 1997.

[4] The *New York Times* printed a retraction the following week.

[5] *Newsweek*, 17 August 1992. The photo of Konjevic in *Newsweek* should not be confused with the photo of Fikret Alic, also from ITN footage, and displayed on the cover of *Time*, 17 August 1992. A clarification about the two men was made by Peter Brock in *Foreign Policy*, Spring 1994, p. 165.

[6] *Le Point*, 13 March 1993.

[7] *New York Times*, 27 June 1994. A few other examples of overt racism include Senator Joseph Biden's comments on CNN on 1 August 1993, calling Serbs "illiterates, degenerates, baby killers, and cowards." Political cartoons in the *Chicago Tribune* of 1 January 1993, and the *New York Times* of 18 April 1993, depicted Serbs as pigs and vultures, respectively. Morton Kondrake pronounced Serbs to be "bastards" on an April 1994 airing of the PBS program "The McLaughlin Group."

13 War propaganda aimed at Jewish opinion

HEATHER COTTIN
& ALVIN DORFMAN

There is at present widespread support in American public opinion for the policies of the U.S. government in the Balkans. It is a striking and dark paradox that Jewish opinion has played an important role in helping to mobilize that support.

U.S. policy in the Balkans has now carried the United States into direct intervention in two civil wars—one between Croatian Serbs and the new proto-fascist state of Croatia, and the other between the Bosnian Serbs and a Bosnian Muslim government that has become increasingly fundamentalist.

In the first case, the United States helped the new Croatia to plan, organize, and carry out the invasion of the Krajina region in Croatia, which led to the uprooting of more than a quarter of a million Serbs and the slaughter of thousands who tried to remain in their ancestral homes there.

In the second case, the U.S. used NATO, against the advice of many of its allies, to destroy the military infrastructure of the Bosnian Serb army and to shift the balance of power in favor of a minority Muslim government in Bosnia-Herzegovina. This, too, has led to the flight of well over one hundred thousand Bosnian Serbs.

In intervening in this manner, the United States has not just taken sides in an internal European war, it has allied itself with the most reactionary elements in Europe, including a newly expansionist, racist, and increasingly militaristic German government. Worse still, the United States, in order to create a more favorable atmosphere for the re-election of President Clinton, sought to impose an unworkable overall peace "settlement" in Yugoslavia and to enforce it with a NATO task force of sixty thousand, including some twenty-five thousand U.S. troops. Even Richard Holbrooke, the Assistant Secretary of State for European Affairs, admits that this could well lead to another Vietnam.

To anyone who lived through World War II and who still understands the meaning of Nazism—and this applies especially to Jews—all this should be not just astonishing but repulsive. The United States in alliance with the German government is now pursuing policies very similar to those pursued by the Nazis in the Balkans. It was the Nazis who wished to splinter the Balkans in order to dominate the area. It was the Nazis who unleashed clerical fascism in Yugoslavia during World War II. And it was the Nazis who displayed a pathological hatred of the Serbs, as well as of Jews and Romani (Gypsies).

It is difficult to understand how U.S. policy toward the Balkans could have taken such a turn in any reasonably democratic country.

Unfortunately, a large part of the explanation is that public opinion in this matter has been driven into something like a frenzy by what seems to be an officially inspired and large-scale campaign of propaganda. No foreign policy can succeed without public support. And U.S. policy in the Balkans is clear testimony to that fact. Although as recently as four years ago, the American public did not even know the location of the regions known as Serbia, Bosnia-Herzegovina, Croatia, the Krajina, and Montenegro—and perhaps many Americans still don't—key individuals and groups in this country were targeted for a propaganda barrage designed to demonize the Serbs, to hide the reality of Croatian fascism, and to canonize the Bosnian Muslims.

Several groups received special treatment by the government and the media in the course of this propaganda campaign. Since they, like many other Americans, were for the most part ignorant of the history of the region, they were relatively easy to convince. The groups singled out were liberals, women, and Jews. Government spokesmen and the media have been hammering at them for years now.

To take but one example, in Washington the public relations firm of Ruder Finn mounted a campaign to get American Jews to associate the civil war in Bosnia-Herzegovina with the Holocaust. This campaign, according to Justice Department documents, was paid for by the governments of Croatia and Bosnia-Herzegovina, although the head of Ruder Finn later explained these governments had not paid for all the costs of the campaign. What other governments were passing money to Ruder Finn? Was the CIA helping to subsidize the campaign through traditional means, the usual kinds of "front" companies, or "proprietaries," as insiders like to call them?

Every effort was made by Ruder Finn to reach the leading Jewish organizations in the United States at an early stage. Facts were distorted. Lies were reiterated so many times that they became "facts." In April 1993 Jacques Merlino, associate director of French TV 2, interviewed James Harff, director of Ruder Finn Global Public Affairs. Harff boasted that the achievement he was most proud of was "to have put Jewish opinion on our side."

Harff said, "We outwitted three big Jewish organizations—the B'nai Brith Anti-Defamation League, the American Jewish Committee and the American Jewish Congress. . . ." Getting these organizations to publish a pro-Bosnian Muslim ad in the *New York Times* and to organize demonstrations outside the United Nations, Harff said, was "a tremendous coup." He crowed, "By a single move we were able to present a simple story of good guys and bad guys which would hereafter play itself. We won," said Harff, "by targeting the Jewish audience. . . ." He explained, "Our work is not to verify information . . . our work is to accelerate the circulation of information favorable to us," adding that "We are not paid to moralize."[1]

It should be remembered that Jews have also been singled out as targets of official propaganda in the not-too-distant past. When the Reagan administration was secretly trying to overthrow the Sandinista government in Nicaragua, it used the same techniques that Ruder Finn used in demonizing the Serbs. And some Jewish leaders allowed themselves to be used to discredit the Nicaraguan government. They helped promote the idea that the Sandinistas were anti-Semitic. There was not a grain of truth to the claim. But some Jewish leaders signed a full-page ad in the *New York Times*, the *Washington Post*, and the *Los Angeles Times* which referred to the Contras as the moral equivalent of American revolutionaries and as "freedom fighters." Today American Jewish organizations have been used in a similar way.

It is important to contrast what has happened in America with what has happened in Israel. The Israeli public has proved much harder to deceive than the American public. Jews are people of the Book. And they are very much aware of their place in history. Israelis are, not surprisingly, much more aware of history in general than American Jews, and especially of European history. Israeli Yugoslav Jews were therefore more immune to media manipulation during the world-wide campaign against the Serbs.

American Jews jumped on the anti-Serb bandwagon as it rolled through the American media. In Israel, Yugoslav Jews knew very well that the Serbs had been their strongest allies during the Holocaust, which was carried out in Yugoslavia primarily by Croatian fascists. They remembered that the Croatian Ustashe had murdered hundreds of thousands at the Jasenovac death camp. They remembered that the Croatian President, Franjo Tudjman, had declared that "only" one million Jews had died in the Nazi Holocaust. They knew that Tudjman had proclaimed proudly that his wife was "neither a Serb nor a Jew."

Israel may have recognized Croatia—under pressure. But it is no secret that Israeli arms have ended up in Serb hands. As of late 1995, Israel has still not recognized Bosnia-Herzegovina. It would be a near-suicidal step for any Israeli government to support a Bosnian Muslim regime whose President, Alija Izetbegovic, has written that "There can be no peace or coexistence between the Islamic faith and non-Islamic societies."

In the United States, the process of rehabilitating Croatia has been incredibly successful. Croatian fascists, who still provide the model of ideal nationalism for the Croatian government today, killed sixty thousand Jews in World War II. They recently destroyed Jewish synagogues as well as Serbian churches. If one can ignore such things, it is hardly surprising that there was little international protest in August 1995 when 250,000 Serbs living in the Krajina region of Croatia were driven off the land on which their families had lived for three hundred years. How could such "ethnic cleansing" have been carried out without international opprobrium? The Croatian campaign in the Krajina was the largest and most violent attack on European soil since the end of World War II. And because the Croatian Serb army was quickly shattered, much of it was directed at unarmed civilians.

The international media called the Serbs "rebels" even though this region was recognized as Serb by the Croatian government during World War II. No CNN horror films catalogued the Croatian air force strafing of Serb refugees, the destruction of their churches, the cold-blooded assassination of old people, the burning of more than sixteen thousand homes and other properties. No American refugee organizations concerned themselves with the hundreds of thousands of Serbs, from Croatia and Western Bosnia, streaming into Yugoslavia.

And since, by the summer of 1995, American Jews had been properly brainwashed and made anti-Serb, no Jews spoke out about a horror which should have been chillingly familiar.

Somehow the fact that Croatia expelled more than forty thousand Serbs when it declared its independence in 1991 has been ignored. Somehow the fact that Croatia has denied its population basic human rights such as freedom of speech and freedom of the press and operates a repressive secret police has been hidden. In fear of their lives and livelihoods, some Croatian Jews extol the virtues of the Croatian government. When Croatian fascists commit atrocities, people seem to respond with the familiar refrain, "We didn't know."

Things have not been very different with respect to Bosnia-Herzegovina. In the U.S. media and among senior American officials, Bosnian Muslim spokesmen are taken at their word, while Serbs are not. Jewish leaders have been trotted out to make condemnatory anti-Serb pronouncements. Even when United Nations forces—UNPROFOR—and United Nations spokespersons denied or raised doubts about stories of questionable veracity, the Bosnian Muslim position or claim has been taken as truth.

Feminists in the United States were treated to a propaganda blitz about rapes allegedly carried out by Serbs. It had an electrifying effect. In the end, the radical group Madre, which previously supported Central American women, launched an emotional campaign to save thousands of Bosnian Muslim women allegedly raped by Bosnian Serb soldiers. Gloria Steinem lent the story respectability in *Ms.* magazine. The *New York Times* wrote that twenty thousand to fifty thousand Bosnian women had been raped, despite the fact that there was no substantiation for such numbers, except of course from the Bosnian Muslim "Ministry of Information."

Despite doubts expressed by Helsinki Watch, Human Rights Watch, and respected individuals such as Simone Weil, the President of the European Parliament, the American media relied on the Bosnian War Crimes Commission and the Catholic charity Caritas, which has connections to the Croatian government, for verification of these outrageous claims. The German media promoted the rape hysteria for their own reasons, which

British historian Nora Beloff ascribed to the German need "to Satanize the Serbs in order to cover their own responsibility for pitching Yugoslavia into war."

In the U.S., from the beginning of the conflict, there was never any attempt to see the civil wars in Yugoslavia from a position of neutrality. Croatia and Bosnia-Herzegovina were simply "new states" welcomed into the fellowship of nations, with seats quickly obtained for them at the United Nations. They were never pictured, as any briefing on history and politics would demand, as the fruits of the most extreme, exclusivist nationalism, the kind of nationalism that turned Central Europe upside down in the 1930s and led to World War II. But Yugoslav Jews in Israel, understanding what was really happening in the Balkans, actively opposed any government support of Croatians or Muslims, despite Croatian public relations efforts directed at Israel.

It is distinctly peculiar that so many Americans, and more curious still that so many American Jews, should have taken the side of the Bosnian Muslim government. Of course, the U.S. has backed Muslim fundamentalism before—in Afghanistan, for instance, where it was a useful tool for ending Russian aid to the Afghan government. But these are European Muslim fundamentalists. That is perhaps why the theocratic ideas of Mr. Izetbegovic and his colleagues have received so little attention here.

Jews might wince if they learned that Bosnian President Izetbegovic has said in his book *The Islamic Declaration* that ". . . the struggle for Islamic order and the fundamental reconstruction of Muslim society can be successfully waged only by battle-tested and hardened individuals. . . . The Islamic order should take power as soon as it is morally and numerically strong enough not only to overthrow non-Islamic rule but to develop new Islamic rule."[2] Are these the heroes of the West? It is strange that Americans and American Jews, as a people who believe in multi-cultural diversity and freedom of religion, have embraced the Bosnian Muslims' struggle as their own.

The horror of the last four years was brought upon the Balkans primarily by Germany and the United States for geopolitical reasons. In 1991 or 1992, Yugoslavia might already have begun to break up as a result of internal disagreements. But, in the absence of German and U.S. interventions, it is unlikely that there would have been civil wars there. By the end of 1992, however, Germany, throwing around its weight as an economic power, was able to force the international community to recognize Croatia, Slovenia, and Bosnia-Herzegovina as independent states. It was quietly but effectively assisted by the Bush administration, which, almost immediately after the Yeltsin takeover of 1991 in the Soviet Union, publicly abandoned its support for the territorial integrity of Yugoslavia.

By their joint maneuverings, the two great powers created a situation that reduced the status of the more than two million Serbs outside Serbia and Montenegro to that of "ethnic minorities" in hostile states.

When Croatia denied Serbs all political standing, the Krajina Serbs declared their independence from Croatia—and with as much right as the Croatians had in declaring their independence from Yugoslavia. In Bosnia, where under Izetbegovic Serbs were denied all political and economic rights, the Bosnian Serbs also embarked on a struggle for self-determination. They had no wish to be dominated by a repressive fundamentalist regime.

But Germany and the U.S. were determined to succeed in their efforts to break up Yugoslavia. Germany poured millions of Deutschmarks into the Croatian military, and it trained and armed Bosnian Muslims, with help from Saudi Arabia, Iran, Turkey, and other Islamic governments. Weapons, money, and men poured into Bosnia. And the Muslim government opposed every peace agreement that would have given anything of value to the Bosnian Serbs. The U.S. has provided finances, political support, and covert military assistance to both the Bosnian Muslims and the Croatians.

Thus there had to be a battle to win the hearts and minds of the American people. Their support was needed if these

policies were to succeed. The support of American Jews became a key to moving public opinion. Their major organizations
carried weight, both in terms of resources and in terms of moral
leadership. Jewish support underwrote the morality of the German-American policies in the Balkans.

It also followed that a great deal had to be hidden. Germany's pursuit of divisive and expansionist policies in the Balkans for the third time in the century had to be hidden. The fundamentalist values of government leaders in Bosnia had to be
kept hidden. And the role of Germany and the U.S. in building
up extremist nationalist movements so that Yugoslavia could be
torn apart had to be hidden. Widespread information about any
of these would have made it very difficult to win the prize of
Jewish opinion.

The time has come to question our position on this issue. Progressives in this country, and Jews especially, have been
inundated by a tidal wave of poisonous falsehoods. We must
ask ourselves, "Since when were aggressive, anti-democratic
foreign policies worthy of support?" We need to establish why
Yugoslavia broke up. We need to understand the meaning of
the U.S.-German alliance after the Cold War. And we need to
question why we have deserted the Serbs, our only friends in
Yugoslavia, the only people who stood with us against the Nazis and who died with us at the death camp Jasenovac.

Serbs in Belgrade to whom we have spoken by phone
are appalled at what American Jewish organizations have done.
Jews of Yugoslav origin in Israel are mortified. One has only to
read the Israeli press to realize that. We must see our shame. If
it comes from not knowing, or being misled, we need to atone
for it. By continuing to turn our backs on the Serbian people,
Jews have nothing to gain and can lose everything we morally
stand for.

---

[1] Jacques Merlino, *Les Vérités yugoslaves ne sont pas toutes bonnes à dire*
(*The Truth from Yugoslavia Is Not Easy to Report*) (Paris: Editions Albin
Michel S.A., 1993). Unofficial translation.

[2] Alija Izetbegovic, *The Islamic Declaration*, translated excerpts available from the Balkan Research Centre in "A briefing paper produced for members for the 1992/3 session of the British Parliament," 21 December 1992, on line; originally printed privately 1970, reprinted Sarajevo, 1990 (http://suc.suc.org/~kosta/tar/bosna/).

APPENDIX

The Foreign Operations, Export Financing, and Related Programs Appropriations Act, 1991, Public Law 101-513, appropriated funds for the fiscal year ending September 30, 1991. Below is the paragraph relating to Yugoslavia:

Sec. 599A. Six months after the date of enactment of this Act, (1) none of the funds appropriated or otherwise made available pursuant to this Act shall be obligated or expended to provide any direct assistance to the Federal Republic of Yugoslavia, and (2) the Secretary of the Treasury shall instruct the United States Executive Director of each international financial institution to use the voice and vote of the United States to oppose any assistance of the respective institutions to the Federal Republic of Yugoslavia: *Provided,* That this section shall not apply to assistance intended to support democratic parties or movements, emergency or humanitarian assistance, or the furtherance of human rights: *Provided further,* That this section shall not apply if all six of the individual Republics of the Federal Republic of Yugoslavia have held free and fair multiparty elections and are not engaged in a pattern of systematic gross violations of human rights: *Provided further,* That notwithstanding the failure of the individual Republics of the Socialist Federal Republic of Yugoslavia to have held free and fair multiparty elections within six months of the enactment of this Act, this section shall not apply if the Secretary of State certifies that the Socialist Federal Republic of Yugoslavia is making significant strides toward complying with the obligations of the Helsinki Accords and is encouraging any Republic which has not held free and fair multiparty elections to do so.

INDEX

NATO IN THE BALKANS
Voices of Dissent

Selections from Ramsey Clark, Sean Gervasi, Sara Flounders, Nadja Tesich, Thomas Deichmann and others.
The truth about what NATO is doing in the Balkans is simply not being told in the mass media. Those who have the facts and the courage to voice them have been all but excluded. For an understanding of the secret deals behind the U.S.-imposed Dayton Accords and the implications of a U.S.-controlled War Crimes Tribunal, *NATO in the Balkans* fills in the missing pieces of the picture.
International Action Center, 236 pp., indexed, $15.95

THE CHILDREN ARE DYING
Reports by UN Food & Agriculture Organization
Selections from Ramsey Clark and others.

Over one million people have died in Iraq as a result of the U.S./UN sanctions–over 700,000 of them have been children. Read the book that exposes and documents the truth! Contains the complete report of a UN scientific investigation team, with charts, graphs and a dramatic 22-page photo essay. Contributions by international figures including Ramsey Clark, Margarita Papandreou, Ahmed Ben Bella and Miguel D'Escoto.
International Action Center, 170 pp, $10

Companion video brings the statistics and charts alive through the faces and voices of the victims of the sanctions.
Peoples Video Network, 28 min., VHS $20

METAL OF DISHONOR
Depleted Uranium

How the Pentagon Radiates Soldiers & Civilians with DU Weapons.

Selections by Rosalie Bertell, Helen Caldicott, Ramsey Clark, Jay M. Gould, Michio Kaku, Manuel Pino, Anna Rondon and others.
Scientists, Gulf War veterans, leaders of environmental, anti-nuclear, anti-military and community movements discuss:
• A new generation of radioactive conventional weapons.
• The connection of depleted uranium to Gulf War Syndrome.
• The Pentagon recycling of nuclear waste–a new global threat.
• An international movement to BAN all DU weapons.
International Action Center, 260 pp. with photos & index, $12.95

Companion video, interviews with noted scientists, doctors and community activists explaining the dangers of radioactive DU weapons. Explores the consequences of DU from mining to production, testing, and combat use. Footage from Bikini and the atomic war veterans.
Peoples Video Network, 45 min., VHS $20   PAL $35

WORKFARE WORKERS ORGANIZE

Workfairness and the struggle for jobs, justice and equality

By Larry Holmes, Co-founder of Workfairness, and Shelley Ettinger.
Before the ink had dried on the August 1996 welfare repeal law, workfare workers in New York City began a movement to organize themselves. This book chronicles rallies at City Hall and welfare agencies and the initiation of a city-wide union organizing drive by District Council 37 of AFSCME. The powers that be are indicted for their attempt to create a second-class, slave labor work force–made up predominantly of women with children. Moving interviews with Workfairness leaders Vondora Jordan and William Mason personalize this important struggle. Included are 11 photos and 30 pages of organizing materials.
International Action Center, 100 pp. $11.95

Companion video, *Workfairness*, depicts the heroic 1930's labor upsurge that won vital welfare benefits, decent wages, and labor law protections for all workers. The video traces the development of Workfairness, featuring the images and voices of workfare workers and union leaders as they join forces in a modern-day continuation of those historic struggles.
Peoples Video Network, 28 min., VHS $20

ORDER INFORMATION

All mail orders must be pre-paid. Send check or money order including $4 shipping and handling on first item, $1 each additional item, international $2 each additional item:

International Action Center
39 West 14th St., #206, New York, NY, 10011
Tel: 212-633-6646, Fax: 212-633-2889
e-mail: iacenter@iacenter.org
http://iacenter.org/

To place CREDIT CARD orders for book or video (VISA & MC)
or for bookstore and university invoice orders and discounts
call: 800-247-6553 24-hour service, 7 days a week

Available at discounted bulk rates for educational or fundraising use by community organizations. Pre-paid bulk orders of 20 or more available at 50% off the cover price.